True Stories
THE ELITE FORCES

True Stories of
THE
ELITE FORCES

Edited by
Jon E. Lewis

Robinson Publishing
London

Robinson Publishing Ltd
7 Kensington Church Court
London W8 4SP

First published by Robinson Publishing Ltd 1993

ISBN 1–85487–227–3

Typeset by Hewer Text Composition Services, Edinburgh.

Printed by HarperCollins, Glasgow.

10 9 8 7 6 5 4 3 2

Contents

DESERT SCORPION
Vladimir ("Popski") Peniakoff

Of all the British special forces of the Second World War, none had more romance attached to it than the Army's smallest independent unit – Popski's Private Army. The unit was formed in October 1942 after Major Vladimir Peniakoff ("Popski") of the Long Range Desert Group was persuaded to take an independent command. Stuck for a name for the new force (War Establishment ME WE 866/1), Lieutenant-Colonel Shan Hackett, co-ordinator of special forces in North Africa, jokingly suggested it should be titled "Popski's Private Army". The name stuck, and the War Office even approved it officially. The unit's badge was a silver astrolabe (a type of astronomical measuring instrument), and its brief was to be a highly mobile force gathering intelligence and spreading "alarm and despondency" behind enemy lines in Tunisia and Libya.

Initially, the PPA numbered 23 all ranks, but eventually rose to a total of 195, all volunteers hand-picked by Popski personally. Its raids – by jeep and three-ton truck- were frequently spectacular successes, and included the discovery of a route to outflank the German-held Mareth Line. Popski's account of that mission, from his autobiography Private Army, is set out below.

With the effective end of the war in North Africa in 1943, the PPA was switched to Italy, where the unit operated with the 12th and 27th Lancers until the German surrender. (It was in Italy, in December 1944, that five jeeps of the PPA armed with Browning 0.3 and 0.5 inch machine guns famously engaged two German companies supported by tanks to rescue a group of 27th Lancers trapped in a farmhouse, loosing off 25,000 rounds in the process).

Popski himself was born in Belgium in 1897, the son of intellectual Russian parents. He enrolled at Cambridge University in 1914, but left *after several terms to join the French Army as a gunner (the quickest route to the front). With the end of the First World War, he became an engineer and later a sugar manufacturer in Egypt. It was at this time that Peniakoff learned the desert lore – mostly gained in long, solo expeditions in a Model A Ford he called "The Pisspot" – that made him invaluable to the British in North Africa, and he was commissioned in 1939. Nor was Popski the only "foreigner" in his Private Army, which included, as well as Britons, Frenchmen and Arabs. During the Italian campaign, it even incorporated some Italian anti-fascists and escaped Russian POWs.*

After the war Popski worked as a liaison officer between the Russian and the British in Vienna. He died in London in May 1951. In the introduction to his autobiography Peniakoff writes: "only to the fools amongst the men of my generation will the realization come as a surprise that we liked war." That liking is evident in what follows, which begins with Popski returning to base after the PPAs' first mission, a somewhat mixed success.

W E SLUNK INTO the wadi at Shweref with our tails between our legs to find a kind of general assembly of L.R.D.G.,* which mercifully took little notice of us. Never had I seen so many patrols together in one place, some going out, some coming home to Hon, where Headquarters had moved from Zella.

Prendergast flew his Waco over on the second day. He listened to our reports and commented: "It was rather unfortunate, wasn't it?" – a very strong rebuke from him. We had no time to cry over spilt milk for the war was moving on. Eighth Army was attacking Rommel at Buerat that very day, expected to be in Tripoli a fortnight later, and wanted urgently information about the Mareth Line. Nick Wilder, now on his way back, had signalled that he had found a pass through the Nefusa range suitable for Montgomery's left hook, some forty miles north of Dehibat, and now the ground leading north from Wilder's Gap to the Mareth Line had to be reconnoitred and a route found, not just for an agile L.R.D.G. patrol, but

* Long Range Desert Group

such as could be negotiated by an armoured division. The defences between Matmata and Jebel Tebaqa had also to be investigated: no time could be lost because in a few weeks, with Rommel's forces established in that desolate area, it would be awkward for us to move around.

Dumps of petrol had been established near the Tunisian border and also at Tozeur, an oasis in southern Tunisia, in the hands of the French troops of North Africa, who were now fighting half-heartedly on our side. Jake Easonsmith had flown over to the Headquarters of First Army in Algeria for this purpose, and had brought back a number of incredible tales. One of these, which never failed to raise incredulous laughter, was that the officers in First Army wore *ties*: "Did they also carry swords and were their men armed with crossbows?"

With these dumps at hand we could now reach Tunisia with supplies to spare for operations: on January 18th, P.P.A., complete and all there was of it, set out in company with Lieutenant Tinker's New Zealand patrol. My orders were to proceed with Tinker to Ksar Rhilane, three hundred miles away, in Tunisia, to reconnoitre with him the going leading up to the Mareth Line; then to get information concerning the defences of the line itself between Matmata and El Hamma. When these reconnaissances had been carried out, my intelligence role would come to an end and I should have a free hand to operate in any area *behind* the Mareth Line and do what harm I could to the enemy according to the information I could collect locally. Thinking of eventual contacts with the officers in ties on the other side, I got these orders written down, stamped and signed (a most unusual procedure with us), and went off to consult my old friend, Bill Shaw, L.R.D.G. intelligence officer. Captain Shaw, a civilian like myself, archaeologist in the Palestinian service before the war, was a veteran desert traveller. He had started with camels, then had joined Bagnold in his early motor trips to Oweinat and the Gilf el Kebir. His name appears in many places on the maps of these areas where dotted lines marked "Shaw 1935" are the result of his running surveys. In the L.R.D.G. from the foundation, he knew more about the desert, its topography, its inhabitants (present and past), and its military possibilities

than any man alive, and he could tell what every patrol that
had gone out from the first day had done, where it had been
and who were the men on it. His memory was prodigious, and
though lately he had no opportunities of going out on patrols,
he had a gift of describing a route or the clues to a hidden
dump as if he had just been there himself. His desert lore
was superior even to the Arabs'; it extended to areas where
no Arab had ever been.

I went to him to be briefed about southern Tunisia: of the
topography he couldn't tell me much more than appeared on
the map, for none of us had yet visited this area, but he advised
me not to count on being able to penetrate the Grand Erg,
the sands of which I would find much less accessible to my
trucks than those of the Libyan Sand Sea, and he warned
me against the Arabs of Tunisia, whom he believed to be
largely disaffected on account of their longstanding hostility
to the French. This was bad news to me; I had planned an
impregnable and improbable base in the Grand Erg Oriental,
and had counted on a network of Arab information similar to
the one which had served me in Cyrenaica. I hoped he was
mistaken.

A rendezvous was arranged with Nick Wilder on his way
back; he would give us fresh information about the southern
part of our area which he had just reconnoitred. I was warned
that the S.A.S. would probably be operating in the same parts
as ourselves, but their movements and indeed also their aims
remained obscure, for David Stirling kept his own counsel and
preferred not to disclose his plans to possible rivals.

David Stirling, young, tall, good looking and dashing, had
become (much against his naturally modest disposition) the
romantic figure of the war in the Middle East. He had raised
his First S.A.S. Regiment and trained it, at first for parachute
operations, then for land fighting in jeeps. With Mayne and
a band of friends they had ravaged the German airfields
before El Alamein and spread panic amongst the defeated
enemy troops after the battle. With a light heart and a
cool courage he inspired in his men a passionate devotion
and led them to thrilling adventures. Where we plodded, he
pranced.

He was captured near Gabes a few weeks later and spent the remainder of the war in captivity.

Yunnie had brought up from Zella the tail of P.P.A., and Hunter had also joined the assembly in Shweref, bringing back with him our Locke and his companions. In this way, by a succession of coincidences, my little band was reunited. I moved forward from Shweref, leaving no one behind.

We had lost Binney, captured in Wadi Zemzem, but we had received a powerful reinforcement which increased our officer strength by fifty per cent: Jean Caneri, our third officer, had turned up in Zella. At the time we left Cairo he was with Chapman, my former companion in the Jebel, engaged in sinking ships in Benghazi harbour. The method they used was to swim at night across the harbour carrying special mines (nicknamed Limpets) strapped to their chests. Having reached a ship, they unstrapped the mine and fixed it to the hull under the water line. The mine was fitted with magnets by means of which it adhered to the steel plates of the ship's hull. They then set the time fuse, swam back to shore, recovered their clothes and walked through the town and on to their hide-out ten miles out in the hills. In due course the mine blew a hole ten feet square out of the hull and the ship went to the bottom.

The liberation of Benghazi had put an end to these exhausting exercises. Caneri, fearing to report back to Cairo in case he should be snatched up once more by the decaying Libyan Arab Force, wandered forward instead and happened to be in El Agheila on January 8th when an L.R.D.G. heavy section convoy came up from Zella for supplies. Caneri had been attached to L.R.D.G. for several months and counted many friends amongst its personnel: he gossiped with these men, heard casually that P.P.A. was stationed in Zella, put his kit on board one of their trucks and reported for duty to Bob Yunnie two days later.

Caneri (we pronounced his name as "Canary") was French. Posted to the French Army in Syria at the declaration of war as a gunner sergeant, he deserted at the time of the fall of France, and came to Cairo where he had spent part of his childhood and had many friends. He promptly enlisted in the British

Army, and was commissioned and posted to the Libyan Arab Force after a period of service in the Abyssinian campaign. He had taken a law degree at the Sorbonne, but having served two years as a conscript he had had no opportunity of being called to the Bar. He was twenty-six years old when he joined us, and at that time spoke in a rather broken English.

I had now two officers according to my heart: experienced and determined men tied closely together by deep friendship, mutual understanding and a common purpose.

Our outlooks differed and were in a way complementary: Yunnie, matter-of-fact as he was, had a romantic side with a touch of flamboyant bravery which gave colour to our undertakings and inspired our men; Caneri, hard and some-what cynical, had a cold-blooded courage together with a disarming ingenuity: he was both liked and feared – and obeyed. He had a passionate love of tidy details which put order in our affairs where my haphazard negligence produced an incredible confusion. I had imagination, a broad view of our problems and a certain flair for picking out men suitable for our purposes, but without this persevering pair to implement them, most of my plans would have petered out. We had all three of us an obstinate continuity of purpose which urged us on unceasingly and never allowed us to relax.

I could open my heart to them both and yet lose none of my authority: I was thus spared the loneliness which induces a dangerous autocratic pig-headedness in so many commanders incapable of choosing outspoken confidants. With them I was by no means "always right"; I could not take their acquiescence for granted and I had to consider my decisions more carefully than if my orders had invariably been law.

As soon as we set out from Shweref I realized that the minor operations on which some of us had recently been engaged had borne fruit. Our men, no longer merely thrown together by the chance of recruiting, had now some common memories, excitements experienced together, private jokes, a certain pride in their achievements (somewhat magnified no doubt), a desire to do more, and the beginnings of confidence in their fellows and reliance on their commanders. Locke had distinguished himself in trying to drive his jeep down a precipitous face of Jebel Nefusa west of Nalut, where he had gone with Hunter and his patrol. The jeep had turned over and rolled down the slope, a total wreck, Locke and his companion being thrown out unhurt. Amidst Tripolitanian soldiers (in Italian service) who had turned up at this awkward moment, Locke had recovered his guns and all his equipment. To the Tripolitanians he had somehow conveyed that he was a German officer experimenting with a new type of car. Hunter and he had spent the next night in the comfort of an Italian post (January nights are bitterly cold fifteen hundred feet up the mountains) talking gibberish German to one another, and had slipped away quietly before breakfast. Strangely, Locke himself had given me a very sober account – Hunter had been more colourful in describing our pirate's exploits and gave him great praise for his resourcefulness and his presence of mind – but I can't say what stories he told his companions, to whom he was now a bit of a hero, and something of a mascot.

Driver Davies, the Yorkshireman, a storekeeper in civilian life, disgraced himself during the trip from Kufra to Zella by whimpering over a bout of malaria, but after his recovery it appeared that his short illness had brought out a latent forcefulness: he bossed his companions, cheered us all in our days of adversity, and showed so much strength of character and so much fun that he had to be made a corporal, then patrol sergeant and finally quartermaster sergeant.

We had lost one jeep down Jebel Nefusa, leaving us with three only, but Prendergast had arranged that Tinker, on completing his reconnaissance, should hand us over one of his. The two three-tonners were in good order.

We set our course through the Hamada el Homra (the red stony desert), about ten thousand square miles of blank on the map, as yet uncrossed by any of our patrols, which we expected to find very difficult going as it had somehow got a reputation for frightfulness. We were agreeably disappointed: the going was quite good over a rolling plain of firm sand strewn with stones. Coming after the black basalt boulders of the Kharug surrounding Hon, where trucks had to travel snakewise, and, however carefully driven, had their tyres shaved off by the razor-like edges of rock, the Hamada el Homra gave us a holiday drive. The reputation for frightfulness came from the complete absence of vegetation: it is a very empty stretch of desert, without a single bush for a hundred miles, but very lovely, the sand a pearly grey, with red stones about the size of a hand, set in it vertically on edge. When the sun is low on the horizon each slope according to the incidence of light comes out in a different colour, shifting, as the traveller proceeds, from pale coral pink to dark crimson.

One morning I noticed along the top of a slope to my left a multitude of small serrations bobbing up and down. Puzzled, as I thought, by a peculiar form of mirage, I drove idly up the slope: my serrations were the heads, just visible above the skyline, of a herd of gazelle bounding along in the same direction as we were going and keeping pretty well the same speed. There were, we estimated, more than two thousand of them, in one compact mass, bound on some migration of theirs across the inhospitable Hamada. Suddenly the whole herd took a right turn and joined the path of our trucks: in a moment the beasts were amongst us, so close that I had to brake sharply to avoid running one over. On every vehicle rifles came out, but such was the amazement of our men (to whom hitherto a dozen gazelle seen at one time had been a wonder) at the number and the fearlessness of the lovely animals that not a shot was fired. They ran with our moving trucks for a while, then another turn took the herd out of our path over the northern skyline.

Davies mused a long time over the incident. At our next stop he came over to me:

"They must have thought we were another herd of gazelle."

Out of the Hamada we drove into rocky hills looking for the petrol dump. With the "chart and the instructions" we discovered our treasure: cans spread out under rocks and covered with stones. While we were loading, the trucks of T2 Patrol, with Nick Wilder, came lurching down the wadi, like small ships in a choppy sea with the wind astern. They struck their sails and we exchanged the news. Wilder had found the gap in the range which several other patrols had searched for before him, and was now on his way back to Hon to report, refit and set out again. Much of his reconnaissance had been done wearily on foot, but driving, he told us, had been even more exhausting than walking. The going in the corridor thirty-five miles wide between Jebel Nefusa and the Grand Erg sand dunes was the most exasperating he had ever been over, and he sardonically wished us better luck than he had had, for we were bound for the same unattractive parts. We parted the next morning in our opposite directions.

In uncharted country, each patrol endeavoured to break a new route and to cover fresh ground on each voyage: the information brought back was the material from which Shaw and his surveyors built up maps on which layers of colours denoted the nature of the going. These maps were used by Army Headquarters to plan their movements over the desert and were also issued to the units concerned. Thus it happened that the next day we were running along the edge of an unknown escarpment, searching for a gully down which we could drive our trucks into the plain three hundred feet below. The gullies were all found to end in vertical drops; in desperation we chose to build ourselves a ramp at a spot where the cliff face itself had crumbled down somewhat. For five hours we rolled boulders and carried stones, then drove the jeeps down, then the thirty-hundred-weights and finally my heavy, overloaded, three-tonners slithered, lurched and bumped their way down. All the time Italian traffic was running up and down the Sinaun-Nalut track, two miles across the plain. We had a meal and after dark crept across the track and away to the west to rest under cover of very meagre bushes.

The next day we crossed the Tunisian border and immediately encountered the exasperating country Wilder had promised us. Our course lay to the west of his, skirting ochre-coloured dunes, outliers of the Grand Erg Sand Sea, over choppy, closely-packed, sandy hillocks twelve to twenty feet high, overgrown with repulsive bushes. The whole of Tunisia seems to be covered with the decaying carcasses of monstrous, dead animals. In the north, straight, broken-edged mountain ranges sticking out of the plains are sharp backbones from which the flesh has rotted away and flowed down in streams of pus to fill the cesspools of the "shotts" (a shott is a salt marsh); in the south we travelled as on dubious pelts, firm on top but supported underneath only by sagging putrid entrails. In the tracks of our bumping trucks I expected to see oozing viscous purple projections. In my childhood I had one day slithered down a high bank and landed smartly on my bottom on a very dead sheep covered in grass and leaves: the horrible long forgotten memory never left me as long as I stayed in Tunsisia.

We struggled on a few miles a day. The long three tonners alternately bellied on the crests and wedged in the troughs of the sand waves; when we struck easier patches of more undulating ground the brush, thick, dry and brittle, collected under the bellies of the jeeps, jammed the steering and caught fire over the exhaust pipes.

On January 24th we met human beings for the first time, a band of twelve Arabs with two camels, ragged, starved and diseased, sulky and suspicious creatures who accepted our hospitality but kept their shifty eyes averted. I took one of them, Abdel Kerim ben 'Ali el Bendiri, with us, nominally as a guide, in fact as a hostage. I had less difficulty in understanding their speech than I had expected, and our Senussis conversed with them quite easily.

The next morning I decided with Tinker to leave behind all our heavy vehicles and to carry out the reconnaissance northwards with jeeps only. We drove westwards under a hill called Qaret 'Ali, intending to establish our base a few miles inside the sand dunes of the Grand Erg, where it would be safe against surprise by enemy land forces. At our first attempt we realized that the technique which had taken us over the Libyan Sand Sea would not serve us here: the dunes here were made of dirty brown, powdery, silt-like sand, into which our steel channels sank as in water. We gave up the attempt and established our base on a long patch of hard ground, surrounded on three sides by high dunes, a position easy enough to defend as it could only be reached along a narrow neck. Vehicles trying to force an entry would have to negotiate this difficult gap under the fire of our trucks, well covered themselves by low hummocks. To make things more difficult we laid a few mines in the gap, leaving only a passage for our own use. We filled with water from brackish wells under Qaret el Jesseb, three miles to the south. I put Yunnie in charge of the party, handed him our hostage, wished him good luck and left, to be back in four or five days.

Our reconnaissance party was made up of Tinker, his navigator, and two of his New Zealanders in two jeeps, myself, Caneri, Petrie, Yunes and one man in two other jeeps: a nice party to handle, small enough to keep easily under control; as each one of us knew exactly what we were doing I had no worry about a tail that might go astray. Our low vehicles were practically invisible: the only enemy we had to beware of were armoured cars, and as long as we kept off the tracks, which they couldn't leave in this difficult country, we were quite safe. The local Arabs had reluctantly told us that the only German and Italian posts in the neighbourhood were at Duz, Jemma and Kebili. Ksar Rhilane, an old Roman fort twenty miles north of Qaret 'Ali was empty by their account. We first made sure of this, and found the only inhabitant within its crumbling walls an elderly Arab called 'Ali, a former sergeant-major in the French colonial troops, who spoke French, and preserved in his raggedness remains of military swagger. He told us that a number of vehicles similar to ours had been at the fort a few days previously and had driven off northwards (an S.A.S. detachment we concluded), and that two of these men, their jeep broken down and mislaid, had been living at the fort ever since – but they could not be found before we left. Separated in two groups to cover more ground, we made, as nearly in a straight line as we could, for Matmata, two miles short of which we arranged to meet again in the evening. Up, down and round we switchbacked over the hillocks, stopping only to clear the brushwood from under the chassis. In the early afternoon we reached higher ground and better going. Two unknown jeeps came dashing up a slope behind us: I turned to face them and put out a yellow flag, the agreed recognition signal for all our troops operating in Tunisia, but they took no notice, and stopped only when I fired a burst over their heads. They were six hearty paratroopers of the French section of the S.A.S., who had had originally three jeeps (but had smashed one), and now in their eagerness they were rushing off to Kebili for some vague purpose of their own, and wouldn't listen to my warnings of enemy troops, but drove off at an unreasonable speed, waving and shouting excited farewells.

At four o'clock in the afternoon we pulled up in a discreet wadi within sight of Matmata, a small stone-built town perched on one of the last spurs of the Nefusa range. Less than ten minutes later Yunes, posted as a look-out on top of a hill, waved Tinker in. He and I immediately walked towards Matmata over rocks and grassy slopes – this corner of Tunisia was like a real country – and before nightfall we had seen as much as we needed to make a fair sketch of the western approaches to the town. We had even been near enough to look into the sleepy streets, where, apart from a few Arabs, we had only seen two fat German officers, a very different picture from what I had expected of the fortress which guarded the western end of the formidable Mareth Line.

The main defences of the original Mareth Line extended westwards from the coast to Matmata. The gap through which Montgomery intended to launch his left hook extended from this town to the Jebel Tebaqa range: it was the main object of our reconnaissance. We had that day examined the approaches and found a possible route for an armoured division: it remained now to reconnoitre the actual battle ground. We knew that the planners at Eighth Army Headquarters were waiting for the results of our investigations and we made all the haste we could.

During our absence Yunes had been gossiping with some Arab shepherds, to whom he had given out that we were German officers concerned with the building of the new defences, and had given them hopes of employment. He had heard that some of our supposed colleagues were indeed engaged in building strong points along a line extending from Matmata to the eastern tip of Jebel Tebaqa. This was precisely what we had come to investigate; during the next day, roaming gingerly in the twenty mile gap between the two ranges, we saw I believe most of the work being done by the Germans at the time, which was not very much. They were not taking too seriously the possibility of an attack in force west of the Nefusa range. We knew better and felt very powerful in our four little jeeps.

Tinker had a gravity well beyond his years – I believe he was only twenty-two – and a great big, black, bushy beard gave him an elderly appearance. I treated him as a man of my own age, and such was the assurance of his manner that I tended to take his advice in many matters. Several months later I called on the L.R.D.G. in Egypt, where they had gone to refit, and saw most of my friends. Left alone in the mess I went over in my mind the names of those I had wanted to see and found that Tinker had not put in an appearance. An unknown, slim, clean-shaven youth came in, whom I had noticed previously keeping shyly in the background as if he was a new recruit. I asked him:

"Do you know if Lieutenant Tinker is in camp? I particularly want to see him."

Surprised, he laughed.

"I am Tinker. I wondered why you wouldn't speak to me Popski."

At the end of the fourth day of our reconnaissance we considered that we had the answers to the main problems set by Eighth Army: we had found a route – of terribly bad going, but just practicable, from Wilder's Gap up to the western end of the main Mareth Line; behind the line and as far as El Hamma we had found, with the exception of one wadi, the ground free of major obstacles, either topographical or man-made, and we knew the location of the defence works that were built at that time.

Six weeks later the New Zealand Corps, comprising the Second New Zealand Division, the Eighth Armoured Brigade and General Leclerc's force, reinforced later by the First Armoured Division, was to advance along the route we had reconnoitred and to attack Rommel's right wing on the ground over which we had just been wandering. They forced their way as far as El Hamma, outflanked Rommel, compelled him to withdraw his forces to Wadi Akarit and won the Battle of the Mareth Line.

Our share in the coming events was now to pass on our knowledge to Eighth Army, and accordingly we made for our wireless at Qaret 'Ali.

We separated once more: I took an easterly route along the

Nefusa foothills, Tinker went zigzagging towards Kebili, and promised to join us at our base the next day, calling at Ksar Rhilane on the way. With Caneri we struggled on for hours in a maze of hillocks till we emerged on the Kebili Fum Tatahwin road: it was lovely and smooth, the temptation great – we fell, and, ignoring the risk, whizzed along the road. I pulled up to ask a young shepherd how far to the water.

"Quite near," he said, and went on to gossip of other things. As we were leaving he said: "The two cars of your friends are at the well now," and pointed to two Italian scout cars which – unnoticed by us – were drawing water from Bir Soltan a quarter of a mile to the right of the road. I had a hurried conference with Caneri: we were in great spirits, our reconnaissance had been more successful than we had dared to hope, forty miles away only, the comfort of our big trucks would be ours this very night, and we could now afford to enjoy a little fun. I decided to shoot up the Italian cars and investigate the wells. Water supplies, I speciously argued to myself, were a matter of vital importance to a large force moving in the desert: Eighth Army would want to know all about Bir Soltan, and my mission would be incomplete without a report on this water.

We cocked our guns and I led slowly along the road, looking for the turning which led to the wells. The plan was to drive our two jeeps abreast and thirty yards apart, straight at the wells, and open fire at a hundred yards range. Carefully – round a bend – and uphill. My gunner tapped my arm, pointed ahead and said: "Do you see what I see?"

What I saw was the turret of a whacking big tank, hull down by the roadside a hundred yards away. I stuck out my arm for Caneri, turned sharp left off the road, put my foot down and went bouncing along the hillside out of sight. Caneri, who had seen nothing, had the sense to follow me and caught up when I had gone in a wide circle and crossed the road again three miles below the wells. The laugh was on us even more than we knew: I heard later that what I had seen of the turret was all there was – it had no tank underneath! Set up at some time as a machine-gun post to guard the wells, it was not manned.

At another well five miles from Ksar Rhilane where we

stopped for water, an ancient, toothless Arab, nearly unintelligible, made desperate efforts to warn us of some urgent danger. All we could gather was that something had been burnt and that the enemy was about. The poor creature could not know which of us was fighting whom. I thought there might have been a scrap between the French madmen and an Italian patrol from Duz. Anyway, it seemed reasonable not to drive into Ksar Rhilane without first making sure that the enemy wasn't in it: so two miles short of the Roman fort, we concealed our two jeeps in thick bushes, and while we waited quietly for the night to fall I told Caneri of plans I was making. That evening I would write my report to Eighth Army; the next day I would remain at Qaret 'Ali, waiting for Tinker's return. The following day Tinker and his New Zealanders would make for Hon and we would remain to start operations on our own account. I had noticed a telephone line connecting the half-built German strong points off Matmata: we would liberate a field telephone, tap the line, ring up Head-quarters in Gabes and find the times of the supply trains running from the harbour in Gabes to the railhead in Medenine. With this information we would arrange for a train to blow itself up, together with a bridge between Gabes and Katena. If the times turned out suitable, we might simultaneously make a noisy night display in the streets of Gabes as a diversion. I would arrange to give the Germans the impression that our raid had originated from French-held Tozeur, and we would then withdraw in peace for a while to a new hiding place south of Qaret 'Ali. For the next operation I was thinking of breaking past Gabes into central Tunisia. By the time I could be ready for it I thought Eighth Army would be on the Tunisian border, Gabes would be within fighter range of the R.A.F., and our place would be much further back in the enemy rear.

Night came. Caneri and Yunes walked away towards Ksar Rhilane. Busy in my mind with the details of my plans, I lay down on the ground to wait for their return. An hour and a half later the lights of a car showed below the skyline. We brought the guns of the jeeps to bear on the track and waited: I thought Caneri had been captured and that the enemy were now searching for us. Two headlights that might have been those of a jeep appeared over a rise. I made up my mind and flashed R – R – R on my torch. The headlights blinked T – T – T, an agreed reply, and we uncocked the guns. A jeep pulled up, Caneri climbed out, with him was the French lieutenant parachutist. I said:

"I am glad to see you are still alive and free."

He laughed. "I know. But we never got to Kebili. We smashed another jeep, piled the six of us on to the last remaining one and came back to Ksar Rhilane. Now it seems that the enemy has been active. I have heard rumours that three Messerschmidts strafed your camp at Qaret 'Ali yesterday morning and that some of your vehicles have been burnt out."

We drove to the Roman tower. 'Ali, the friendly old sergeant-major, late of the French Army, confirmed the rumour. Two of the Arabs we had met at Qaret 'Ali had ridden to the Italian post at Duz with the information of our leaguer.

I left Caneri and the six Frenchmen concealed outside Ksar Rhilane to intercept Tinker on his return and prevent him from falling into a trap, for if, as I expected, an Italian armoured patrol came down from Duz or Kebili to deal with the survivors of the Luftwaffe raid, the only track they could use ran through Ksar Rhilane. I drove off in the night with 'Ali to guide me to Qaret 'Ali.

The jeep crashed through the malevolent, man-high Tunisian weeds with a continuous crackle. The glare of the headlights gave them repellent, unnatural hues of metallic green and white as they sprang at us out of the night and vanished under the car. 'Ali understood his job; after an hour and a half we turned right into the defile leading to our leaguer; as I drove through my lights suddenly picked out the skeleton of a three-ton truck standing gauntly burnt out amongst flung litter; I drove round the leaguer, counting the wrecks: every one of my trucks and those of the New Zealanders stood burnt to the ribs. There was a deadly hush and no sign of our men.

At the far end of the leaguer we picked up footprints in the sand of many men, a trail leading into the highest dunes. I left the jeep and followed the trail on foot with a torch: up and up I trudged for a quarter of an hour, shouting my name, reached a crest, sank into a hollow, climbed another slope. I was challenged and shone my torch on a figure muffled in a blanket. Bob Yunnie led me to a hollow where his men were sleeping: they were all there, but two New Zealanders had limb wounds and couldn't walk.

He had saved a few pistols and tommy guns, some rations and a few blankets. Thirty cans of petrol which he had buried had been dug up by the Arabs during the night and stolen. All the rest was lost. The Arabs, including our hostage, had vanished.

The extent of my disaster filled me with sombre joy. My mind was swept clean of all the plans and the hopes with which I had been busy day and night during the last three months, and I had not even a flicker of regret for the strenuous preparations and the long efforts now suddenly wasted at the very moment they were about to bear fruit. From my long-cherished plans for defeating the enemy single-handed, my mind switched over in a moment to consider the new and desperate problems which I had now to solve. Exhilarated by the urgency and the difficulty of the task, my brain functioned with a delightful, effortless lucidity, which I had never experienced before, for I am usually a slow and muddled thinker, full of questionings and doubts.

Woefully cheerful, Yunnie told me that early the previous morning three Messerschmidts had dived from just over the high dunes which surrounded the leaguer. The rattle of their machine guns was the first warning he had had. Backwards and forwards they dived and machine-gunned, and flew away after five minutes, leaving his nine trucks ablaze and exploding. He had tried to save our wireless jeep, which had not been hit, but a burning petrol can projected from one of the three-tonners, landed on the truck and put an end to it. Two New Zealanders had bullet wounds and several other men, including Waterson, had suffered superficial burns while they were attempting salvage from the blaze. Expecting an Italian motor patrol, he had withdrawn with his men into the dunes, where they could only be attacked on foot.

We sat talking in low voices, the men asleep around us. A fire had been kindled by our Senussis and they brewed us some tea, for they had salvaged, together with their weapons, their teapots and glasses. While I questioned Yunnie and listened to his replies, a picture of our situation formed itself in my mind with a clarity of detail that owed nothing to any conscious effort of mine. This picture in outline was as follows: the nearest spot at which I could expect to find help was Tozeur, the French oasis on the other side of Shott Jerid. The distance from Qaret 'Ali to Tozeur was roughly one hundred and ninety miles over unknown desert – probably very rough. The enemy, mostly Italian, had known posts along our route at Duz, Kebili and Sabria. They knew of our presence in the area. The nomad Arabs were miserable but actively hostile: they might fight us themselves, and they would certainly attempt to ingratiate themselves with their Italian masters by reporting our movements. Though they were few in numbers we couldn't hope to move through their areas without their knowledge, and we should have to rely on them to show us the wells, and probably for food. We had no wireless.

Our vehicles were five jeeps, with no more than fifty gallons of petrol between them: probably enough to take three jeeps as far as Tozeur.

Counting the Frenchmen and the two S.A.S. men stranded in Ksar Rhilane, our party numbered fifty-one men, two of whom were wounded and unable to walk. The others were ill shod (most of us wore open sandals or gym shoes on our bare feet) and untrained for long marches.

The food available was sufficient for five or six days, on very short rations.

My immediate tasks, in order of urgency, were:

Communicate the results of our reconnaissance to Eighth Army.
Get medical attention for the wounded.
Get our men out of the dunes at Qaret 'Ali, before dawn

if possible, to avoid the risk of their being trapped by
an Italian land force, and then march them to Tozeur
to safety.

Warn Henry, who was coming up behind us with the
Rhodesian patrol, of the danger he was in of being
betrayed to the Luftwaffe by the local Arabs.

By the time Yunnie had finished his report I knew how I was
going to set about my business. It was fascinating, I thought, to
find all the answers without having to rack my brains; I hoped
this unexpected power of decision would remain with me for
ever, and I looked forward to the next few days with pleasure.
I had all the men woken up and sitting around me; with fresh
wood on the fire I kindled a bright blaze so as to light their
faces for me while I spoke to them; and to give them time
to collect their spirits I made the Arabs draw extravagantly
on our meagre supplies of tea and prepare a powerful brew
of Arab tea for everyone. I myself woke the two wounded New
Zealanders and helped them to the fire: they had had a shot
of morphia and slumbered heavily.

When I saw that I had everyone's attention I said:

"You may think that something has happened to Tinker
that he is not here with me. Tinker is all right. He will be
back tomorrow. While you were being strafed here we made,
quite a scoop, Tinker and I, and we want to get the news back
to Army quick. We have now got no wireless so we shall go
over to First Army to find one.

"Our mishap here was brought about by the local Arabs
who betrayed us. I know the two who did it. The Arabs here
are not like the Senussis; they are paid by the Italians and
the Germans.

"The nearest place where we can get in touch with First
Army is Tozeur, held by the French. We are going to walk
one hundred and ninety miles to get there. We shan't all
walk: Tinker and Caneri are going to drive in three jeeps,
carrying twelve men, including our two casualties. The rest
of us will walk. If possible when the driving party reaches
Tozeur they will raise transport and come back to collect
the walking party. But we mustn't count on it. I reckon we

can walk to Tozeur in eight days and we are going to start in two hours' time so as to get out of this place, which I don't like, before daylight. Also we haven't got much food and we don't want to waste it sitting on our bottoms.

"I shall drive the two casualties to Ksar Rhilane right now and drive back here in the early morning to collect the food and kit which the Arabs haven't looted. Sergeant Waterson will be in charge of the walking party from here to Ksar Rhilane, and Yunes will guide you by the shortest route which does not follow the tracks of my jeep.

"Bob Yunnie, Sergeant Garven and Sergeant Mohammed will remain here for no more than seven days, in case Henry and S Patrol call here on their way to Tozeur. He is to warn them of the danger of betrayal by the Arabs. If Henry does not call they will make their own way to Tozeur.

"With a little luck we shall get out of this jam without any worse trouble than very sore feet. I want you all to keep close together and allow no one to stray. This is not the Jebel. A lonely man will not have a chance amongst hostile Arabs.

"That is all. Thank you very much. Waterson will now call the roll."

My original intention had been to leave Sergeant Mohammed behind alone to convey the warning to Henry, but I had accepted Yunnie's offer to stay with him, and Sergeant Garven, a New Zealander, had also asked to be allowed to remain: he felt, I believe, that L.R.D.G. should be represented on this desperate rear party.

Yunnie, at that time thirty-three years old, was fundamentally a civilian. He held the methods and the discipline of the army in some contempt and preferred – passionately – to go his own way. He claimed now, as a privilege, to be allowed to remain behind on this risky mission: I thought it would compensate him, in a way, for his cruel disappointment at the loss of our equipment, for, he more than anybody else, had had the trouble of getting it together, and now it was all gone while he was still waiting for his first chance to use it.

He thought that, assisted by the craftiness of Mohammed they would be able to survive in spite of the treachery of the local Arabs. Mohammed had been with him on the two hundred mile trek behind the lines, when his Libyan battalion had walked from Ajedabia to Tobruq nearly exactly a year previously: and from that time he had put great faith in his ability.

The two wounded New Zealanders were carried to my jeep, and I drove immediately to Ksar Rhilane, where I left them with Caneri; then back again to Qaret 'Ali to rummage for food by daylight. Waterson and the walking party had left at four guided by 'Ali, on whom Yunes kept an eye.

Bob Yunnie, Mohammed and two men of P.P.A. were collecting tins when I arrived. Fortunately the Arabs had no use for tinned food, and had overlooked it in their very thorough looting, which had even included the theodolite, after it had been salvaged and hidden under a bush.

On my way back for the second time to Ksar Rhilane with our small stock of supplies and my two men, I followed the tracks of the walking party and overtook them about midday as they were resting and waiting for their dinner to be boiled: a large kid which Yunes had bought from some Arabs. They seemed all in good spirits and Waterson particularly ebullient. I believe that, like me, he enjoyed disasters.

At Ksar Rhilane Tinker was very impatient to get our reports sent over to Eighth Army. We decided that he would leave the same evening for Tozeur and First Army, and that my walking party would follow in the tracks of his jeeps. After sending off our messages to Eighth Army, he would try to raise transport and come back along his tracks to meet us and give us a lift. We found that we had enough petrol to send three jeeps to Tozeur, with a few gallons left over for my jeep and the French one which would carry supplies for the walking party and give us the protection of their guns, as long as the petrol lasted.

My walking party consisted of thirty-seven men: seventeen New Zealanders, twelve British, six French and two Arabs. As we were practically unarmed, our chances of avoiding being killed on our two hundred mile march were slender. On our right, and no more than five miles distant from our route, stood the Italian posts in Duz and Sabria. On our left the

sands of the Grand Erg prevented us from giving the enemy
a wider berth. All along the first hundred miles of our route
any Arab who decided to betray us would not have to ride
his camel more than a few hours before reaching an Italian
post where a reward would be paid for his information. I
had no fear of a motorized column, as the Italians possessed
no vehicles that could travel over the difficult country we
would be crossing, nor could their aircraft hurt us much
beyond compelling us to waste time under cover; but they
had mounted native troops against which we would be quite
powerless once they got on our tracks. And the nomad Arabs
themselves with their antique muskets could well snipe us
out of existence if ever they discovered how few weapons we
carried. In the latter part of our march we ran the risk of
encountering patrols of French Goums, who had a reputation
for shooting first and asking questions afterwards, and for
being rather indiscriminate in their choice of enemies.

My only chance of getting my men through alive lay in
bluffing our enemies, Italians and Arabs, and playing them
off, one against the other. This I proceeded to attempt without
delay. The Italians first; though three days had now elapsed
since the air attack, they had shown no signs of sending out
a patrol to investigate. I assumed that the reports they must
have received of vehicles moving around Ksar Rhilane made
them shy of risking a scrap with an unknown number of
heavily armed and highly mobile jeeps. I decided to give
them a fantastic idea of our numbers. I got 'Ali to invite a
few of the neighbouring shepherds to have tea with me at
the fort: then, while we were sipping, Caneri drove smartly
into the courtyard with two jeeps, came up to me, saluted,
pocketed a document I handed to him and departed with
a great noisy revving of engines. A moment later Tinker
repeated the ceremony with three jeeps, then the French
lieutenant with two vehicles, and so on till, in the course
of an hour, every one of the fifteen men we had with us at the
moment had come up before me and our five jeeps had been
displayed nine times over. Hurried alterations were made to
the jeep loads between each scene, although I felt sure that
to my untrained guests one jeep was as good as another. I

knew that in the early hours of next morning an alarmed
Italian commander in Duz would be pulled out of bed to
listen to reports of fifty jeeps mounting six guns each, all
passing through Ksar Rhilane in one afternoon. It would, I
hoped, put him on the defensive, clamouring on the telephone
for reinforcements from Kebili. A warning no doubt would
also reach Sabria, further on our course.

The show over, I went into a huddle with Yunes and 'Abdel
Salam to concoct a programme of deception for the use of the
Arabs we would meet on our march.

Waterson and his party walked in from Qaret 'Ali later in
the afternoon and that evening Tinker and Caneri, with the
two casualties and eight men, drove off to Tozeur, taking with
them by mistake two of the petrol cans which had been put
aside for my use.

The next morning I called my motley party together, gave
them my instructions successively in English, French and
Arabic, and we walked off in good order for a well, Bir Haj
Brahim, twenty-five miles away, where I wanted to spend
the first night. Two hours later we were a straggling column
stretched over a mile: Waterson and a group of enthusiasts
led the pace at a rate that I found hard to keep up. Now
and then I got into my jeep and counted the men as they
went by, then drove up again, carrying the last stragglers to
march with Waterson for a while. In this disorder we were
lucky to gather all our men to the well at nightfall. The
six Frenchmen insisted on riding in their jeep, and nothing
I said could shame them into taking turns at walking and
giving lifts to the more footsore of their companions. They
were quite unconscious of the precariousness of our position
and talked wildly of pushing ahead and clearing away the
Arabs for us.

We found some shepherds watering their cattle at the
well and tried on them the story we had prepared. Their
acceptance gave us hopes that we would also succeed in
deceiving warriors less obtuse than these simple-minded lads.
The next day we kept better order, stopping every hour and
collecting the stragglers each time, but we covered only fifteen
miles. We saw no Arabs at all the whole of that day.

On the third day we again did fifteen miles. Some of the men were now going barefooted rather than in open sandals which collect sand between foot and sole and make walking very painful. But their feet were tender and they made slow progress. We camped for the night seven miles from Sabria in sand dunes. The night was so cold that I burnt a hole in my leather jerkin sleeping on the fire; another man burnt his socks off his feet. These comical mishaps considerably helped our morale.

We had seen no Arabs during the whole day, but two men came up to our fire after dark: it seems there was a feud between the tribe which pastured its flocks near Duz and that which kept near Ksar Rhilane and to avoid daily clashes they left an empty no-man's-land to divide their grazings; thus it was our good fortune that gossip seeped through slowly, and rumours of our identity had not reached them.

Like all the tribesmen in southern Tunisia these men were destitute and lived miserably off their thin cattle for which they had no decent grazing. The French, the Italians and also some of their Arab brethren settling on the land further north, had slowly squeezed them out of the rich pastures on which their forefathers had lived in plenty. Hence a surly resentment against all the people in the north, dull grievances which I intended to exploit for our own ends. 'Ali of the Roman castle, who was glib and politically minded as befitted a man who counted himself well travelled and enlightened, had provided me with a knowledge of local politics, sufficient, I hoped, for my dealings with the half-savage tribesmen.

I entertained my visitors as nobly as my means allowed and asked them to inform their sheikh, whose tents were pitched some twenty-five miles to the south-west, of my visit on the following evening. For their pains I gave them a present of money, generous indeed but not so extravagant (I had inquired from 'Ali the Italian rates of pay) as to excite their cupidity. I gave them to understand that I had matters of importance and secrecy to disclose to their sheikh, counting on the Arabs' love of intrigue to keep their mouths shut.

My big bluff had to be made on the next day or never, because after that time I would be out of petrol, and, without the prestige of a car, I couldn't hope to impress the intended victims of my deceptions with my secret importance. My visitors no doubt could not have helped noticing the scarcity of our weapons: so I hinted broadly that with us all was not as it seemed, as our common enemies, the French, would in due course find out to their grief. With this suggestion of secret weapons I sent them home.

On the fourth day we made an early start and walked over twenty miles following the tracks of Tinker's jeeps, to come to rest in the early afternoon two miles from a spring, 'En bu Rdaf. The going over choppy hillocks overgrown with bushes was tiring for the walkers and alarmingly heavy on petrol for the jeeps. We had all suddenly become extremely ragged; every semblance of military smartness discarded, our appearance was that of a band of refugees. The raggedness, however, was not in our hearts: shadowed the whole day by Arab horsemen, we moved in a close group, ready to fight at any moment, the few of us who possessed a weapon disposed at the head and at the tail of our column. My jeep drove a few hundred yards ahead, the Frenchmen in the rear, driving and stopping alternately so as not to outstrip the men on foot. During the afternoon more and more horsemen showed up on both flanks: with old French Chassepot rifles or long Arab muskets slung on their backs, they became bolder as their numbers increased and I thought that it was only out of respect for the twin guns on our jeeps that they refrained from falling on us.

At the evening halt I found that no more than a few pints of muddy petrol were left in the tanks. We drained and strained the last drops from the French jeep and poured it into mine, hoping it would last long enough to enable it to perform its last task. I got ready for a ceremonial call: as I had carried my kit with me in the jeep all the time I had not suffered to the same extent as the others from the disaster at Qaret 'Ali; I managed to dress with some appearance of decency, and strapped on to me a .45 pistol, field glasses compass and empty pouches. Yunes and 'Abdel Salam had salvaged some of their kit together with their rifles, and we made them look spruce enough. They were the only ones in our crowd who wore army boots. I took Locke with me as my gunner and covered his nakedness – for he wore only a pair of khaki shorts – with my sheepskin coat and gave him my spare pair of desert boots, three sizes too big. I armed him with a tommy gun and an automatic – he had also saved his dagger – and briefed him in his new role. Thus arrayed, the four of us drove off to 'En bu Rdaf, the spring of water at which I had arranged to meet my visitors of the previous night. An Arab, impressed from the crowd of onlookers, guided us. At the spring, to my immense relief, I found both my messengers waiting for me: perched on the back of my jeep they escorted us to the tents of their sheikh.

A man of mean appearance with clever shifty eyes, he was sitting under a patched tent with the flaps up. As he rose to greet me I saw that he too had made an effort to smarten himself up: his threadbare burnous was white and fairly clean, but his followers were clad in the usual ragged brown homespun. Assuming my best party manners, I drew out as long as I could the exchange of courtesies, noticing hopefully some preparations for a meal. My host and his followers being unarmed, I unbuckled my belt and threw it in the jeep: my Senussis required no telling and had already placed their rifles under Locke's care. He remained sitting behind his guns and refused mutely invitations to alight.

We sat down under the tent on camel saddles covered with sheep-skins: our host, a poor man, owned neither wooden sofas nor rugs. As we had arranged, Yunes sat next to me to help me in my conversation and interpret when the local dialect became too obscure for my understanding; 'Abdel Salam, a wizened old man of great cunning and sagacity, sat amongst the followers to spread calculated indiscretions.

I wanted to impress my host with the importance of my own person, as well as with the greatness of my condescension in visiting him. My aim was to make him feel flattered and eager to learn the object of my visit; never to suspect that I wanted favours from him. For this reason I dragged out the conversation interminably in polite courtesies and general gossip until the meal was brought in. Yunes, with whom I had rehearsed the proceedings, seconded me admirably, while 'Abdel Salam carried on the good work in the background. We talked and talked, on a multitude of subjects, but never mentioned our purpose. Beyond the fact that I was a high-ranking German officer, and my two friends Tripolitanian sheikhs of high standing, I told him nothing of our intentions and aloofly ignored his pointed questions.

The meal of boiled goat and kuskus was silent as good manners required. When water had been poured over our hands, I asked my host to let down the flaps of his tent and admit inside only his trusted confidants.

I started then on the evening's business. The German command, I said, had become equally distrustful of the Italians and of the town Arabs in the north. As things were going the only consequence of us Germans winning the war in Tunisia would be to replace greedy Frenchmen by even greedier Italians in the possession of the land. What we wanted was a Tunisia controlled by warlike nomads under German supervision, a military base for us in which contented tribesmen would recover the fat pastures which had been filched from them by the French and their scheming town-Arab friends. Truly these town Arabs had now turned against the French and started a Free Tunisia movement but all they wanted was plunder. Our business was not to fight a painful war to the end that fat, deceitful, town dwellers should grow fatter and richer and finally turn us out of the land. Our friends were the faithful nomads, brave soldiers like ourselves; we intended that they should have a share of the rich loot of Gabes, Sfax, Sousse and Tunis, and then pasture their flocks in peace and amity on rich grass lands – no more on God-forsaken parched and barren sand dunes.

In this vein I talked for hours: I never knew I could say the same things in so many different ways. When I tired, Yunes took up the thread and described the fabulous wealth of Tunis (which he had never seen). In the gloom of the far end of the tent 'Abdel Salam murmured to a close circle of enthralled listeners.

What we wanted from the tribesmen, I told my host, was their help to evict all the settlers, French, Italian and Arab alike – when the time came, which was not yet. I had taken the opportunity of my present mission to call on him, a man of influence as I knew, to prepare him for the call. He would understand that the matter must be kept secret from our weak Italian allies. They had still their uses for us at the present time and should not be made suspicious.

Loot, intrigue, treachery, fat pastures, glory – I had exhausted the temptations I could offer my debased Arab host. Under his native composure I felt him excited; cupidity shone in his eyes. I thought he was ripe for further disclosures: I kicked quietly Yunes's leg to draw his attention to the change of subject and said, quite casually:

"I might as well tell you the truth about the occasion which has brought us here. The French in Tozeur have three companies of Tunisian Goum. We hear that the men are much disaffected to their French officers. We have got together the German soldiers I have with me, all picked men, and dressed them up as escaped British prisoners-of-war. In this guise we intend to drift into Tozeur, where the French, unsuspecting, will receive us well and quarter us in the barracks with the Goum. We will get to work amongst the men and one night the three companies will rise, cut their French officers' throats and seize the town. They will be led by my men, every one of whom carries a powerful German automatic pistol concealed under his clothes."

I had done it! I watched Yunes anxiously out of the tail of my eye. He expanded my speech and added a few details. Our host leaned over and in a low voice asked Yunes some questions which I failed to understand. Then Yunes very deliberately lit a cigarette for the host – not from his lighter, but with an ember picked out of the fire. We had arranged this to be a sign that, in Yunes's opinion, the bait had been swallowed.

I went on: "For the sake of likelihood we cannot take our cars into Tozeur. I would like to leave them here if you would care to look after them till I send someone back to collect."

The sheikh agreed and I thanked him casually. Standing up to stretch my legs I heard Yunes whisper to our host:

"These Germans are generous."

We talked of other matters, but I felt that he had something on his mind.

"Will Your Excellency walk with the men? I am very poor but I could provide you with a riding camel, not a good one, but still, one that would go."

I looked at him dreamily, as if I was turning over in my mind vast problems of strategy:

"I leave such matters to be settled by Yunes," I said, and strode out of the tent into the cold night.

When Yunes joined me later it appeared that we were to be provided with two camels, one intended for my personal use, the other to carry our stores. He had also obtained four sheep, one of which was being slaughtered at that very moment to provide supper for our hungry men. The three others would be carried on the camels. It was just as well that he had succeeded in refilling our larder, otherwise the next day would have seen the last of our rations.

Better still than transport and food, he had induced the sheikh to provide a khabir to go with us, a guide who would vouch for us and smooth out unpleasantness which might arise with Arabs of other tribes along our route.

I gave Yunes a gold coin for our deluded host, and I drove back to camp extremely weary and fighting down an unexpected urge to giggle. I said to Yunes:

"We have told many lies tonight. Please God we may be able to tell the truth sometimes after this."

"God be praised," he said piously. "These Arabs are extremely credulous," and he chuckled softly. I shook with uncontrollable laughter.

The next day, fifth out of Ksar Rhilane, we started late. We made camp for the six Frenchmen, who had long ago expressed their determination not to walk and who now asked to remain behind to guard the paralysed jeeps. Failing to convince them of the unwiseness of their choice, I arranged with the sheikh for food and warned them not to forget that they were supposed to be Germans. They laughed: "Anything rather than walk!" They couldn't speak a word of intelligible Arabic so perhaps they couldn't give us away.

The khabir turned up with two camels and three sheep, we

loaded our blankets and few remaining rations, and walked
away. We covered twenty miles before nightfall, one hundred
and fifteen from Qaret 'Ali. The sixth day I estimated also
at twenty miles. Waterson was like a bird, hopping about
and cheerful. He had taken special charge of Petrie, who
tended to brood but always kept in the van. Most of the New
Zealanders walked with these two. They showed no signs of
being upset. Some of my English lads dragged behind and
required encouragement now and then. Locke, completely
unperturbed, walked generally by himself, flapping his feet
in my large desert boots. The Arabs were quite at home
on the march and somehow their clothes suffered less than
ours. The cold, sharp during the night, became unbearable
towards morning, and as we couldn't sleep we walked away
before dawn.

On the seventh day we saw several horsemen hovering
about. The khabir grew nervous and talked of going home.
During the afternoon we heard a distant noise of aircraft and
we went to ground, dispersed amongst the hillocks. The noise
grew and grew and suddenly one of my men stood on top of
a hillock waving and cheering, and the next moment we were
all doing the same: two hundred feet overhead, fifty R.A.F.
bombers in close formation thundered over us on their way to
Tripolitania. We still had our noses in the air when I noticed,
on the ground this time, coming towards us a school of jeeps
wheeling up and down over the hillocks like porpoises in a
choppy sea. Tinker, in a hurry as usual, drove up to me. He
had four borrowed jeeps with him. Caneri with another four
jeeps was searching for us along a shorter route, in case we
had lost the original track. I sent Yunes to guide Tinker to
the two jeeps we had left with the Frenchmen, and we all sat
down and rubbed our feet; we had walked one hundred and
fifty miles. In an incredibly short time he was back with our
vehicles from the spring from which we had walked in three
days. We piled in, six and seven to a jeep, and drove off. That
night we slept on the shore of Shott Jerid. The next morning
we drove like birds over the mud flats at the western tail of
the Shott, fearful of hitting a quagmire and of being engulfed.
At eleven o'clock we hit the tarmac road which runs from

Touggourt to Tozeur, and a little after twelve we sat down to lunch in the gaudy dining-room of the Hotel Trans atlantique in Tozeur. We looked very incongruous, sitting in fours at our tables, with white linen, an array of cutlery and three glasses to each of us.

SIEGE AT PRINCES GATE
Jon E. Lewis

The Special Air Service of the British Army burst into the world headlines in May 1980 when it stormed the Iranian Embassy in London to free 26 hostages held by Arab gunmen. It was an unusually public appearance for the SAS, most of whose operations since its foundation in 1941 have been deep behind enemy lines, or in the more shadowy areas of counter-revolutionary warfare.

The man most responsible for the foundation of the SAS was David Stirling, a young and junior officer of the Scots Guards who tricked his way into the British Army Middle East HQ in Cairo in 1941 in an effort to talk to the Chief of Staff about "a matter of operational importance". He ended up in the office of the deputy Chief, Major-General Neil Ritchie, who, impressed with Stirling's audacity, gave him a hearing. The subaltern's idea was to destroy Axis aircraft in the desert while they were on the ground, using a small mobile land unit. Ritchie gave the scheme his approval and L Detachment, Special Air Service Brigade was born. (There was in fact no "Brigade"; it was a bluff to fool German intelligence into thinking that the unit was larger than it was, namely a handful of men, three tents and one three-ton truck). The badge of the SAS, the Sword Of Damocles and wings, with the motto "Who Dares Wins", was formally approved in 1942. Most of L Detachment's initial troopers were disbanded commandos who, under Stirling's training and leadership and in close liaison with the Long Range Desert Group, proved to be formidable desert raiders. In January 1943 the 1st Special Air Service Regiment was formally recognised, and three months later the 2nd SAS Regiment was formed. In the same year, Stirling himself was captured by the Germans in Tunisia. After Africa, the regiments fought in Italy and northwest Europe. With the war's end the SAS, along with several other "private armies", was disbanded.

In 1947, however, it was reformed as 21 SAS, with a Malayan Scouts (SAS) unit coming into being in 1950. As its name implied, its chief purpose was to fight in the jungles of Malaya against the communist insurgency. The scouts were officially recognized as the 22nd SAS in 1952. Since that time, 22 SAS has been involved in campaigns in Borneo, Aden, and Oman (see pages 235 ff). Following the massacre of Israeli atheletes at the Munich Olympics in 1972, its counter-revolutionary warfare training and role was stepped up considerably, with the Regiment playing an active, if covert, part in the war against the Provisional IRA in Ireland and mainland Britain. It has also worked alongside the CRW units of other nations, including the West German GSG9 at Mogadishu. It therefore went in to break the siege of the Iranian Embassy at Princes Gate in 1980, the story of which is related below, with a wealth of CRW experience.

A T 11.25 AM ON the morning of Wednesday 30 April 1980, the tranquillity of Princes Gate, in London's leafy Kensington district, was shattered as six gunmen wearing shamags over their faces sprayed the outside of No.16 with machine gun fire and stormed through the entrance. The leading gunman made straight for an astonished police constable standing in the foyer, Trevor Lock of the Diplomatic Protection Group, while the rest, shouting and waving their machine pistols, rounded up the other occupants of the building.

The gunmen – Faisal, Hassan, Shai, Makki, Ali and Salim – were members of Mohieddin al Nasser Martyr Group, an Arab group seeking the liberation of Khuzestan from Ayatollah Khomeini's Iran. No. 16 was the Iranian Embassy in Britain. The siege of Princes Gate had begun.

The police were on the scene almost immediately, alerted by an emergency signal by Trevor Lock, and were soon followed by Scotland Yard specialist units including C13, the anti-terrorist squad, and D11, the elite blue beret marksmen. The building was surrounded, and Scotland Yard hastily began putting in motion its siege negotiation machinery.

While no siege is ever the same as the one before or after it, most follow a definite pattern: in stage one, the authorities try to pacify the gunmen (usually with such provisions as cigarettes and food), and allow the release of ideological statements; in stage two, the hostage-takers drop their original demands, and begin negotiating their own escape; stage three is the resolution.

The Princes Gate siege moved very quickly to stage one, with Salim, the head Arab gunman announcing his demands over the telephone just after 2.35 pm: autonomy and human rights for the people of Khuzestan, and the release of 91 Arab prisoners held in Iranian jails. If his demands were not met he would blow up the Embassy, hostages and all, at noon the following day.

The SAS meanwhile had been alerted about the siege within minutes of its start. Dusty Gray, an ex-SAS sergeant now a Metropolitan Police dog handler, telephoned the Officers' Mess at Bradbury Lines, the SAS's HQ next to the River Wye in Hereford, and said that the SAS would probably be required at the Iranian Embassy, where gunmen had taken over. That night SAS troopers left for London in Range Rovers, arriving at a holding area in Regent's Park Barracks in the early hours of Thursday morning. The official authority from the Ministry of Defence approving the move of the SAS teams to London arrived at Bradbury Lines some hours after they had already left.

Over the next few days the Metropolitan Police continued their "softly, softly" negotiating approach, while trying to determine exactly how many hostages were in the Embassy and where they were located. Scotland Yard's technical squad, C7, installed microphones in the chimney and walls of No. 16, covering the noise by faking Gas Board repairs at neighbouring Enismore Gardens. Gradually it became clear that there were about 25 hostages (as they discovered at the end of the siege, the exact count was 26), most of them Iranian embassy workers. Also hostage were PC Trevor Lock and two BBC sound engineers, Sim Harris and Chris Cramer. The latter, who became seriously ill with a stomach disorder, was released by the gunmen as an act of good faith. It was a bad mistake by the Arab revolutionaries: a debriefing of Cramer gave the SAS vital information about the situation inside the

Embassy as they planned and trained in a new holding area only streets away from Princes Gate itself.

Inside the holding area a scale model of the Embassy had been constructed to familiarize the SAS troopers with the layout of the building they would assault if the police negotiations were to break down. Such training and preparation was nothing new. At the Bradbury Lines HQ, SAS Counter-Revolutionary Warfare teams use a Close-Quarter Battle house for experience of smallarms fire in confined spaces. (One exercise involves troopers sitting amongst dummy "terrorists" while others storm in and riddle the dummies with live rounds).

As the police negotiating team located in a forward base at No. 25 Princes Gate (of all places, the Royal School of Needlework) anticipated, the gunmen very quickly dropped their original demands. By late evening on the second day of the siege, the gunmen were requesting mediation of the siege by Arab ambassadors – and a safe passage out of the country. The British Government, under Margaret Thatcher, refused to countenance the request. To the anger of the gunmen, BBC radio news made no mention of their changed demands, the broadcast of which had been a concession agreed earlier in the day. Finally, the demands were transmitted – but the BBC got the details wrong.

For some tense moments on Saturday, the third day of the siege, it looked as though the furious Salim would start shooting. The crisis was only averted when the police promised that the BBC would put out the demands accurately that evening. The Nine o'clock news duly transmitted them as its first item. The gunmen were jubilant. As they congratulated themselves, however, an SAS reconnaissance team on the roof was discovering a way into No. 16 via an improperly locked skylight. Next door, at No. 18, the Ethiopian Embassy, bricks were being removed from the dividing wall, leaving only plaster for an assault team to break through.

On Sunday 4 May, it began to look as though all the SAS preparation would be for nothing. The tension inside the Embassy had palpably slackened, and the negotiations seemed to be getting somewhere. The gunmen's demands were lessening all the time. Arab ambassadors had agreed to attend a meeting of their COBRA committee in order to decide who would mediate in the siege.

And then, on the morning of Bank Holiday Monday, 5 May, the situation worsened rapidly. Just after dawn the gunmen woke the hostages in a frustrated and nervous state. Bizarrely, Salim, who thought he had heard noises in the night, sent PC Lock to scout the building, to see whether it had been infiltrated. The hostages in Room 9 heard him report to Salim that there was nobody in the Embassy but themselves. Conversations among the gunmen indicated that they increasingly believed they had little chance of escape. At 11.00 am Salim discovered an enormous bulge in the wall separating the Iranian Embassy from the Ethiopian Embassy. Extremely agitated, he moved the male hostages into the telex room at the front of the building on the second floor. Forty minutes later, PC Lock and Sim Harris appeared on the first-floor balcony and informed the police negotiator that their captors would start killing hostages if news of the Arab mediators was not forthcoming immediately. The police played for time, saying that there would be an update on the midday BBC news. The bulletin, however, only served to anger Salim, announcing as it did that the meeting between COBRA and the Arab ambassadors had failed to agree on the question of who would mediate. Incensed, Salim grabbed the telephone link to the police, and announced: "You have run out of time. There will be no more talking. Bring the ambassador to the phone or I will kill a hostage in forty-five minutes."

Outside, in the police forward post, the minutes ticked away with no news from the COBRA meeting, the last negotiating chip of the police. Forty-two minutes, forty-three minutes . . . The telephone rang. It was Trevor Lock to say that the gunmen had taken a hostage, the Iranian Press Attaché, and were tying him to the stairs. They were going to kill him. Salim came on to the phone shouting that the police had deceived him. At precisely 1.45 pm the distinct sound of three shots was heard from inside the embassy.

The news of the shooting was immediately forwarded to

the SAS teams waiting at their holding area. They would be used after all. Operation Nimrod – the relief of the Embassy – was on. The men checked and cleaned their weapons, 9 mm Browning HP automatic pistols and Heckler & Koch ("Hockler") MP5A3 submachine guns. The MP5, a favourite SAS weapon, first came to prominence when a German GSG9 unit used it to storm the hi-jacked airliner at Mogadishu. It can fire up to 650 rpm. The order for the assault teams to move into place was shortly forthcoming.

At 6.50 pm, with tension mounting, the gunmen announced their demands again, with the codicil that a hostage would be shot every forty-five minutes until their demands were met. Another burst of shots was heard. The door of the Embassy opened, and a body was flung down the steps. (The body belonged to the Press Attaché shot earlier in the day. The new burst of shots was a scare tactic.) The police phoned into the Embassy's first floor, where the telephone link with the gunmen was situated. They seemed to cave in to Salim's demands, assuring him that they were not tricking him, and that a bus would be arriving in minutes to take the gunmen to Heathrow Airport, from where they would fly to the Middle East. But by talking on the phone Salim had signalled his wherabouts to the SAS teams who had taken up their start positions on the roof, and in the two buildings either side of No. 16, the Ethiopian Embassy and the Royal College of Physicians. At around this time, formal responsibility – via a handwritten note – passed from the Metropolitan Police to the SAS.

Suddenly, as the world watched Princes Gate on TV, black-clad men wearing respirators appeared on the front balconies and placed "frame-charges" against the armoured-glass window. There was an enormous explosion. The time was exactly 7.23 pm. At the back of the building and on the roof, the assault teams heard the order "Go. Go. Go." Less than 12 minutes had elapsed since the body of the Press Attaché had appeared on the Embassy steps.

The assault on the building came from three sides, with the main assault from the rear, where three pairs of troopers abseiled down from the roof. One of the first party accidentally swung his foot through an upper storey window, thereby alerting Salim to their line of assault. The pair dropped to the ground and prepared to fight their way in, while another pair landed on the balcony, broke the window and threw in stun grenades. A third pair also abseiled down, but one of them became entangled in the ropes, which meant that the rear assault could not use frame charges to blow-in the bullet proof glass. Instead a call sign from a rear troop in the garden sledge-hammered the French windows open, with the troopers swarming into the building on the ground floor. They "negotiated" a gunman in the front hall, cleared the cellars, and then raced upwards to the second floor and the telex room, where the male hostages were held by three gunmen. Meanwhile the pair who had come in through the rear first floor balcony encountered PC Lock grappling with Salim, the head gunman, who had been about to fire at an SAS trooper at the window, and shot the gunman dead.

Almost simultaneous with the rear assault, the frontal assault group stormed over the balcony on the first floor, lobbing in stun grenades through the window broken by their frame charges. Amid gushing smoke they entered and also moved towards the telex room. Another SAS team broke into the building through the plaster division left after the bricks had been removed from wall with the Ethiopian Embassy.

Outside, at the front, the SAS shot CS gas cartridges into an upstairs room where one of the gunmen was believed to be hiding. This room caught fire, the flames spreading quickly to other rooms. (The trooper caught in the abseil rope suffered burns at this point, but was then cut free and rejoined the assault.)

The SAS converged at the telex room, as planned. The gunmen had started shooting the hostages. The Assistant Press Attaché was shot and killed, and the Chargé d'Affaires wounded before the SAS broke in. By then the gunmen were lying on the floor, trying in the smoke and noise to pass themselves off as hostages. What then happened is the subject of some dispute, but the outcome was that the SAS shot two of the gunmen dead. Afterwards, some of the hostages said that the gunmen tried to give themselves up, but were killed anyway. In the event, only one gunman escaped with his life, the one guarding the women in Room 9. The women refused to identify him as a terrorist, and he was handed over to the police. After a brief assembly at No. 14 for emotional congratulations from Home Secretary William Whitelaw, the SAS teams sped away in rented Avis vans. Behind them the Embassy was a blaze of fire and smoke.

The breaking of the siege had taken just 17 minutes. Of the 20 hostages in the building at the time of the SAS assault, 19 were brought out alive. The SAS suffered no casualties. Although mistakes were made in the assault (part of the main assault went in via a room which contained no gunmen and was blocked off from the rest of the Embassy), the speed, daring, and adaptability of the SAS assault proved the regiment an elite amongst the counter-revolutionary forces of the world.

THE BULL OF SCAPA FLOW
Wolfgang Frank

The Second World War was barely six weeks old when, on 13 October 1939, the German submarine Unterseeboot-47 *penetrated the British naval base at Scapa Flow, sinking the battleship* Royal Oak. *It was an audacious blow, one made all the sweeter for the Kriegsmarine in that Scapa Flow had been the site of the scuttling of its High Seas Fleet in 1918. The crew of* U-47 *returned home to Wilhelmshaven national heroes.*

Günther Prien, the commander of U-47, *was a natural U-boat ace and had already claimed the first U-boat victory of the war, a cargo ship on 5 September. An ardent Nazi, Prien had been an unemployed merchant seaman before volunteering for the U-boat arm (all German submarine crew were volunteers) in 1938. He had been appointed commander of* U-47 *just before the outbreak of war.*

After the success of the Scapa Flow raid, U-47 *was sent to the North Atlantic where it wreaked havoc amongst Allied shipping. A type VIIIB submarine,* U-47 *was armed with an 8.8 cm deck gun, a 2 cm anti-aircraft gun and five torpedo tubes (one stern, four in the bows). Its crew was 44 strong. Most of its attacking was done at night, on the surface, with the deck gun, since torpedoes were expensive and the boat could only remain underwater for short periods.*

The following account of the illustrious career of U-47, *including the Scapa Flow raid, is by Wolfgang Frank, the press officer for the U-boat arm during the 1939–45 conflict. He both knew most of the U-boat aces personally and occasionally accompanied them on their voyages.*

It is worth pointing out that the most important consequence of the Scapa Flow raid was that it enabled the head of the U-boat arm, Captain

Karl Dönitz, to persuade the Fuhrer – hitherto uninterested in naval matters – to endorse a massive U-boat building programme. As Dönitz realized, single U-boat raids, though spectacular and morale-sapping for the enemy would not greatly influence the war effort: large numbers of U-boats, organized in flotillas, or "Wolf Packs", to strangle the sea-lanes to Britain could. By the war's end some 600 submarines of the same type as U-47 had been built.

I N SEPTEMBER, 1939, one of the "canoes" operating east of the Orkneys found herself off the Pentland Firth, the passage between Scotland and the Orkneys. A strong westerly current caught the boat and swept her through the turbulent narrows. Finding that his engines were not powerful enough to pull him free, the captain, making a virtue out of necessity, carefully surveyed the movement of ships and the defences in the area. On his return he made a detailed report to Dönitz, who at once saw the possibilities of a special operation. After much deliberation he ordered one of his best young officers, Lieut. Günther Prien, to report on board the depot-ship *Weichsel* at Kiel.

As Prien entered the Commodore's cabin he found Dönitz in conference with his own flotilla-commander and Lieut. Wellner, the captain of the "canoe". Charts lay spread on the table before them and Prien's eye was immediately caught by the words "Scapa Flow". The Commodore addressed him.

"Do you think that a determined CO could take his boat into Scapa Flow and attack the ships there? Don't answer now, but let me have your reply by Tuesday. The decision rests entirely with you, and without prejudice to yourself." It was then Sunday. Prien saluted and withdrew, his heart beating fast. He went straight to his quarters and settled down to a thorough study of the problem. He worked away hour after hour, calculating, figuring, checking and re-checking. On the appointed day he stood once again before the Commodore.

"Yes or no?" – "Yes, Sir." A pause. "Have you thought it all out? Have you thought of Emsmann and Henning

who tried the same thing in the First World War and
never came back?" – "Yes, Sir." – "Then get your boat
ready."

The crew could make no sense of the preparations for
their next patrol. Why were they disembarking part of their
food supplies and taking so little fuel and fresh water with
them? Apart from giving essential orders, the captain was
uncommunicative, and on the appointed day the U-boat
slipped quietly through the Kiel Canal into the North Sea.
The nights were dark, the seas running high. While on passage
the crew watched their captain closely; although funnel-smoke
was sighted several times he never attempted to attack. At last,
early in the morning of 13th October, the Orkneys were in
sight. Prien gave the order to dive and when the U-boat was
resting easily on the sea-bed, he ordered all hands to muster
forward. "To-morrow we go into Scapa Flow," he began, and
went on talking quietly, making sure that every man knew
what he had to do. Then he ordered every available man off
watch to turn in; they would need all their strength when the
time came.

At four o'clock in the afternoon the boat came to life
again and the cook served a specially good meal. Jokes were
bandied about and Prien wrote in his log, "the morale of the
ship's company is superb." At seven-fifteen all hands went to
diving-stations, and the chief engineer began to lift the boat
off the bottom; the ballast-pumps sang and the boat began
to move as the motors stirred into life. Prien took a first
cautious glimpse through the periscope. All clear. He gave
the order to surface. The wind had dropped but the sky
was covered with light clouds; although there was a new
moon, the Northern Lights made the night almost as bright
as day.

As they moved into the narrows a powerful rip-tide suddenly
caught the boat, just as Prien had expected. He needed every
ounce of concentration now and a good deal of luck. The
rudder was swung from port to starboard and back again,
with full use of diesel engines, to keep the bows steady
against the stream. At one moment he had to go full astern
to avoid colliding with a blockship. Then he suddenly bent

down and shouted through the hatch, "We are inside Scapa Flow!*

At this point his log read, "I could see nothing to the south, so turned away along the coast to the north. There I sighted two battleships and beyond them some destroyers at anchor. No cruisers. I decided to attack the big ships." As the U-boat crept closer still, he could make out the details of the ships. The nearest to him was of the *Royal Oak* class. He went closer, until the bows of the second ship appeared beyond the first. She looked like the *Repulse*. He gave his orders, "Ready all tubes! Stand by to fire a salvo from Nos. 1 to 4!' Endrass, his first lieutenant, was taking aim; the forecastle of the *Repulse*†️ came into the cross-wires. "Fire!" He pressed the firing key.

The U-boat shuddered as the torpedoes leaped away. There was a moment's agonizing pause. Would they hit? Then a tall column of water reared against *Repulse*'s side. But *Royal Oak* lay motionless as before. A miss? Impossible. Defective torpedo? Unlikely. Minutes went by but the silence of the bay remained unbroken. Had the ships been abandoned? Was the whole of Scapa still asleep? Why no counter-attack from the destroyers? It is almost impossible to believe what happened next. Calmly deciding to make a second attack, the captain took his boat in a wide circle round the anchorage *on the surface*, while the spare torpedoes were being loaded into the tubes. For nearly twenty minutes he cruised round the main base of the British fleet while down below the sweating hands pushed torpedo after torpedo into place. As though the situation were not tense enough already, Prien suddenly noticed one of his junior officers, Sub-Lieutenant von Varendorff, calmly walking round the deck. "Are you crazy?" hissed the captain. "Come up here at once!" Once again Prien moved to the attack – this time at closer range – and once again the torpedoes raced towards their target.

* The entry into Scapa Flow was made through Kirk Sound, which was inadequately blocked.
† Prien mistook the old seaplane-carrier *Pegasus* for *Repulse*, which was not in Scapa Flow. Only *Royal Oak* was hit in both attacks. For the next five months the Home Fleet had to use remote anchorages on the west coast of Scotland, until the defences of Scapa had been put in order.

smoke and water towered into the air while the sky was filled with falling wreckage – whole gun-turrets and strips of armourplating weighing tons apiece. The harbour sprang to life. Morse signals flashed from every corner, searchlights probed and swept, a car on the coast road stopped, turned and flashed its headlights on and off as though signalling, as it dashed back the way it had come.

"Emergency full ahead both!" ordered Prien. "Group up motors. Give me everything you've got!" As the water bubbled and boiled beneath the U-boat's stern, he saw a destroyer coming swiftly towards him, sweeping the water with her searchlight. She began to signal with her Aldis lamp; Prien bit his lip as the bridge beneath him shuddered to the vibration of the screws. His wake showed up all too clearly yet he could not afford to reduce speed. Suddenly the miracle happened; the destroyer dropped astern, turned away and disappeared. A moment later he heard the crash of her depth-charges in the distance. The U-boat scraped past the end of a jetty and then – "We're through! Pass the word, we're through!" A roar of cheers answered him from below. Prien set course for the south-east – and home.

During the long hours of waiting before the attack, the crew had passed round a comic paper; one of the cartoons in it showed a bull with head down and nostrils smoking. "Harry Hotspur," someone had said; that was also their name for their captain. Now, on the way home, Endrass had an idea. Armed with paint-brushes and some white paint a small working party clambered on to the casing and painted on the side of the conning-tower the boat's new crest – the Bull of Scapa Flow.

While crossing the North Sea they listened to the wireless. "According to a British Admiralty report," said the announcer, "the battleship *Royal Oak* has been sunk, apparently by a U-boat. British reports say that the U-boat was also sunk." The men in *U47* smiled. In the afternoon came an official announcement from the German Admiralty: "The U-boat which sank the British battleship *Royal Oak* is now known to have also hit the battleship *Repulse* and to have put her out of action. It can now be announced that this U-boat was commanded by Lieutenant Prien." For the first time the name of Prien was heard by the German people. Prien in Scapa Flow – where twenty years before, the German High Seas Fleet had gone to the bottom!

As the U-boat made fast to the jetty Dönitz could be seen standing next to Grand Admiral Raeder, the cornflower-blue lapels of his uniform clearly visible. The Grand Admiral came on board to congratulate the crew; offering his hand to each man he conferred upon every one of them the Iron Cross, Second Class, while the captain was awarded the First Class of the Order. "Lieutenant Prien," said Admiral Raeder, "you will have an opportunity of making a personal report to the Führer." Turning to Dönitz he then announced before them all that the Commodore had been promoted to Rear-Admiral. Henceforth he would be the Flag Officer Commanding U-boats. That same afternoon Prien and his crew were flown to Berlin. Hitler received them in the Reich Chancellery and conferred upon the captain the Knight's Cross of the Iron Cross.

In June, 1940, *U 47* was patrolling to the west of Scotland, still commanded by Lieut. Prien, the "Bull of Scapa Flow". The weather was calm and mild, the nights so light that one could read a book on the bridge at midnight.

Early one morning the haze lifted to reveal a ship – their first target for days. Just as *U 47* altered course to attack, the target turned too and came straight down at her. Prien lowered his periscope and dived as fast as he could to 180 feet, while the ship rumbled unwittingly overhead. Almost at once he surfaced again, ordering the gun's crew to their stations; but as they were closing up round the gun, an after look-out suddenly reported more smoke astern of the U-boat and Prien realised that a convoy was approaching. He abandoned his original plan and, after sending out a hasty sighting-report to head-quarters, he submerged again.

As soon as *U 47* was running smoothly at periscope-depth, he took a quick look through the lens as it broke surface for a few seconds. He could hardly believe his eyes. Forty-two ships were steaming majestically towards him in open order, seven columns of six ships of all shapes and sizes, escorted by two ancient-looking destroyers and three modern ones. For three hours, still submerged, Prien tried to close on the convoy, but his boat was too slow; steadily he lost bearing on the ships, until they were out of periscope sight. He started to surface but almost immediately a trawler hove in sight and he had to dive; at his next attempt a Sunderland zoomed out of the sun like a fat bumble-bee and forced him below again. Prien now realised that to catch up with that convoy he would have to chase it for at least ten hours, and by then it would be so close to the coast that he would never get near it for aircraft and surface-escorts. As he sat weighing up his chances and scanning the horizon, masts and smoke suddenly appeared to port and a straggler from the convoy came hurrying along, zigzagging violently. So he stayed below the surface, and everyone kept deathly still, as if the U-boat herself were holding her breath like a living thing. "All tubes ready!" Every man was standing tensely at his post. Suddenly the ship turned away; with a curse Prien called for the last ounce of power from his motors as he stood after his prey. "No. 5, stand by . . . fire!" Some seconds later there was a clanging crash. "We've hit her near the funnel!" called Prien triumphantly. "She's the *Balmoral Wood** – look and see how big she is, I'd put her at 5,000 or 6,000 tons." As the water closed over the sinking ship, all that could be seen on the surface were a few large crates, some of which had burst open to reveal aircraft wings and fuselages. "Well, *they* won't be dropping any bombs on Kiel, anyway," commented one of the crew.

All next day Prien carried out a searching sweep on various courses, but sighted nothing. "The Atlantic seems to have been swept clean," he wrote in his log. But his luck changed with the dawn of the following day, for a 5,000-tonner without lights came steaming past, barely 5,000 yards away. Despite the growing daylight, Prien tried to approach on the surface but he was soon forced under by a Sunderland; however, he was determined to get in an attack and once again he surfaced. This time his first hasty look round revealed warships ahead and

* This ship was torpedoed and sunk on 14 June 1940.

merchant ships astern of him; quickly he sent out a sighting signal and dived again, realizing that he had chanced upon the meeting-place of a convoy with its escort. He moved in to attack but soon saw that the twenty ships in convoy were screened by at least four escorts of the *Auckland* and *Bittern* class, while a Sunderland flew above them. His original plan of attack would be of no avail against such a strong escort, so he waited awhile before surfacing and then made a wide sweep round, so as to try his luck from the other side. As night fell he closed in, once more at periscope-depth, and began to look for a likely target. The weather was favourable; white caps of foam on the waves would make it difficult for the enemy look-outs to spot his periscope, and although the sky was cloudy, visibility was good.

Despite all this, it looked as though the U-boat had in fact been sighted, for one of the escorts turned towards *U 47* and came down like a pointer sniffing into the wind for game. The range dropped quickly – 300 yards, 250, 200 . . . Prien was tempted to fire at the escort, but she suddenly turned away and disappeared on a course parallel to the U-boat. With a sigh of relief Prien ordered, "No. 1 ready . . . fire!" His target was a great tanker, deeply laden, which had caught his eye earlier in the day. He did not wait to see the torpedo hit, but turned immediately to his next victim, which was slightly nearer – a ship of about 7,000 tons. "No. 2 . . . fire!" While the U-boat was still heeling, Prien suddenly saw a column of water spouting up alongside a ship he had not aimed at. There had been a slight mishap in the torpedo compartment; the torpedo-artificer had been thrown off his balance by the movement of the boat and had saved himself from falling by catching hold of the firing-grip. As a result No. 3 tube had fired a fraction after No. 2 – but the torpedo had hit a second tanker.

Fifteen minutes later the U-boat surfaced and Prien sprang up to the bridge; it was not yet quite dark and the sea was getting up. Over on the port quarter lay the big tanker with a heavy list, her bows well below the surface, her decks awash. Prien sent for the silhouette-book and soon identified the battered wreck as that of the tanker *Cadillac*,

12,100 tons.* The other ship, of which nothing could now be seen, was presumably one of the *Gracia* class of 5,600 tons. The third had also disappeared. Now for the rest of them!

But it was not to be; a storm blew up and after two days' fruitless search Prien realised that he had lost the convoy. A day later, however, he sighted and sank the Dutch tanker *Leticia*,† 2,800 tons, bound for England from Curaçao with fuel-oil. Late that night, in a freshening sea, yet another tanker was sighted and Prien ordered the gun to be manned, having decided to stop the ship with a couple of well-placed rounds and then sink her at his leisure. "Only five rounds of ammunition left, Sir," warned the coxswain. – "Never mind, we'll use them just the same." Time passed but there was no sign of the captain of the gun. Prien called down the hatchway, "Control room! Where's Meier?" There was the sound of running feet below, then the voice of the control room petty officer. "Meier is lying in his bunk, Sir, and says there's absolutely no point in trying to aim a gun in this weather." Prien could hardly believe his ears; the bridge watch did their best to hide their amusement. "Give him a direct order from the captain to report immediately on the bridge!" When Meier at last appeared he did not trouble to hide his feelings. "In *this* sea, with only a couple of rounds?" – "They *must* hit, Meier!" – "Aye, aye, Sir." Indifferently he moved towards the gun and Prien gave the order to open fire. The tanker turned sharply away as the first shells screamed towards her, but two of them hit her; Meier was excelling himself. "Hit her in the engine-room!" ordered Prien. Another hit – but the target was still moving away. The last of the five rounds went into the breech, and this time the shell-burst was followed by a cloud of grey smoke and a yellow flash. Soaked to the skin, Meier returned to the bridge; the tanker had stopped and the crew were hastily abandoning ship. Throwing a quick word of congratulation to his still impenitent gunner, Prien brought *U 47* into a good firing position and loosed off a torpedo. His log

* Probably the tanker *San Fernando*, torpedoed and sunk on 21 June 1940.
† Sunk on 27 June 1940.

reads: "The torpedo hit and the ship began to sink. Despite the gunfire and the torpedo-hit, her radio operator continued to signal '*Empire Toucan* torpedoed in position 49°20' North, 13°52' West' and later 'Sinking rapidly by stern'. Finally he jumped overboard with a flare and was seen swimming away from the ship." Prien immediately steered towards the flare but when he reached the spot, there was nothing to be seen. A brave man had died. . . .

Weeks went by as Prien and his brother captains hunted and sank, watched and waited, shadowed the convoys and "homed" other boats on to them, in fair weather and in foul. When at length the U-boats returned to France for repairs and provisioning, their crews were sent to the new rest-centres at Carnac and Quiberon near Lorient, where they could relax on the beach, bathe, ride and do exactly as they pleased. Here they could let the world go by, as they took the pretty daughters of France by storm and quaffed the local wines; all too soon they would once more be at sea, the perpetual thunder of the diesels around them and the waves foaming and crashing on their decks.

Prien, too, was soon back at sea. One dark and rainy night, he and half a dozen other boats encountered a convoy, which they attacked from all sides at once. This was one of the earliest organized wolf-pack actions of the war, and will go down to history as the "Night of the Long Knives". Torpedo after torpedo raced from its tube to detonate against some ship's side. Ten thousand tons of petrol went up in a fiery ball of white-hot flame a thousand feet high; an ammunition ship exploded with a deafening roar and literally disintegrated; all around was nothing but the bright glow of flames. Some ships stood on end before finally disappearing, some listed heavily and turned turtle, others broke apart, to die a painful death. Everywhere, like a pack of wolves, the U-boats were at the convoy. With all his torpedoes gone, Prien reckoned up the tonnage he had sunk by identifying his victims from the "picture book". Then he took a signal-pad and wrote, "Have sunk eight ships in the convoy totalling 50,500 tons. All torpedoes fired."

The dawn came slowly, marking the end of the "Night of

the Long Knives". The other commanders were also making
their reckoning: Kretschmer, Schepke, Frauenheim, Endrass,
Bleichrodt, Moehle and Liebe. In two days of operating
together they had achieved the staggering figure of 325,000
tons sunk.* Within a few days *U 47* had returned to her base.
Prien, as the first U-boat captain to top the 200,000-ton mark,
now became the fifth officer in the armed forces to receive
what was then the highest decoration – the Oak Leaves to
the Knight's Cross.

AFTERWORD
The luck of U-47 ran out on 8 March 1941, when it was sunk by HMS
Wolverine, *with the loss of all hands. During its career the boat had
sunk 28 ships totalling 160,939 tons.*

* "Night of the Long Knives" – 18/19th October, 1940.

OPERATION THUNDERBALL
Yeshayu Ben-Porat, Eitan Haber and Zeev Schiff

Just after midday on 27 June 1976 Air France Flight 139 was hijacked en route to Paris from Tel Aviv by members of the German Baader-Meinhof gang and the Popular Front for Liberation of Palestine (PFLP). Fifteen hours later, the jet – which had 258, mostly Israeli, passengers and crew aboard – landed at Entebbe, in Uganda. There the four hijackers were joined by other Baader-Meinhof and PFLP members, and personally welcomed by President Idi Amin Dada. On the following day, the 28th, the hijackers, led by Wilfred Böse of Baader-Meinhof, announced their demands to the waiting world: 53 of their comrades, held in prisons in Israel, France, West Germany, Switzerland and Kenya, must be released. Or they would start shooting the hostages.

At first, the Israeli government of Yitzhak Rabin was inclined to negotiate, since non-Jewish hostages were also involved. The Israeli attitude changed, however, when the hijackers released all the hostages who were not Israeli or Jewish, and it became clear that Idi Amin Dada was intransigent in his support for the hijackers. On 3 July, the Israeli cabinet accepted a dramatic rescue plan proposed by Major-General Dan Shomron, general officer comanding paratroopers and infantry.

Shomron's plan called for crack Israeli para teams to land on the runway at Entebbe in Hercules transport planes, from which the paratroopers, led by Lieutenant-Colonel Jonathan "Yoni" Netanyu, would fan out to secure their targets, most importantly the old terminal where the hostages were held. Crucial to the success of Operation Thunderball, as Shomron's plan was now called, was speed and surprise. As a ruse to fool the Ugandan airport guards, the para team detailed to take the old terminal was to drive there from the runway in a black

Mercedes disguised as Amin's personal car. Meanwhile, above the air-field an Israeli Boeing would act as a mobile communications centre.

The account here of Operation Thunderball, is extracted from Entebbe Rescue *by Israeli authors Ben-Porat, Haber and Schiff, and begins with the first Israeli Hercules transports landing on the runway at Entebbe, 23.01 hours, 3 July 1976.*

T HE LEAD HERCULES was still taxiing slowly along the runway as a dozen soldiers leaped out and dispersed, several yards apart, on either side. Each of them turned to a nearby runway beacon and placed mobile flashlights alongside them – a precaution in case the control tower shut off the power before the other three planes landed. More soldiers charged out of the belly of the plane as it stopped moving, taking positions around it to combat any possible Ugandan reaction.

Colonel Natan Aloni was standing by the ramp of the first Hercules as it dropped open to allow in a flow of cool night air. At a distance, he could see the control tower – code-named "Aviva." With the stream of air came an army of tiny tropical flies and mosquitoes which beat against the faces of waiting infantrymen. The temperature was 60°.

Aloni, a veteran soldier, had correctly estimated that the hard work would be over as soon as the plane had landed safely. They had already come several hundred yards down the runway, and no one had opened fire. From here on, he was confident that Operation Thunderball could proceed exactly as planned. Shouting "Forward," he ran in the direction of "July" – New Terminal. The force under his command had to seize the control tower to ensure a clear takeoff at the end of the raid.

The mobile beacons placed by paratroops from the first plane were already illuminating the area next to runway "Yuval."

It was cramped and uncomfortable inside the Mercedes. As the pilot swung the nose of the plane around, Tzur Ben-Ami pressed down on his accelerator and the car leaped forward. Old Terminal was over to the right bathed in a pool of light.

The nine men in the Mercedes knew its location, approximately 1,500 yards away, from rehearsals the day before.

Yoni shouted to the other drivers to keep in line, then ordered Tzur to drive slow enough not to arouse suspicion. Ten or fifteen seconds had already elapsed since they had left the plane, and the Mercedes was approaching the old control tower when Yoni and Tzur spotted two figures a couple of hundred yards from them.

"Pay attention now," Yoni ordered as his men gripped their weapons. The Mercedes moved straight ahead, the two Land Rovers close behind. Rain was spattering the windshield.

The two Ugandan guards were now only fifteen yards from them. During rehearsals, Yossi had insisted that Ugandan troops would not stop a Mercedes, and would certainly never fire on it; after all, these were the cars their officers used. Now, therefore, he was no less surprised than his comrades when one of the Ugandans signaled the car to halt. They were only four yards away.

The Mercedes crawled one yard nearer. This soldier could endanger the entire mission, but there was no mistaking his uplifted right arm.

A pistol poked out the right-hand window. The Ugandan fell, but wasn't dead. Nobody had heard the shot that hit him.

"Right, step on it," ordered Yoni.

Tzur Ben-Ami responded immediately.

Michael Golan steered straight into the pool of light that was Entebbe. He glided in to land and taxied straight to his preset offloading point, behind a twenty- or thirty-foot-high hillock next to one of the runways. Flicking on his microphone, Michael confirmed: "I am at 'Katie.'"

Four flight controllers were on duty in the tower. Five minutes earlier, a passenger plane had asked permission to land. Now, something strange was happening to the radar screens – so foreign journalists were told later. The dancing white spots known as "snow" obscured their entire radius of sweep. Having little choice, the controllers sat back to wait patiently till the electronic disturbance abated.

"There's another light plane in the air," one of the controllers remarked, his voice clearly heard over the radios

in the Hercules' cockpits. The men were instantly panicked.

Brigadier Dan Shomron had another worry. When the first
Hercules braked at its assigned spot, Shomron jumped off
the ramp to choose a location for his command team. The
sudden silence of the Ugandan airport hit him hard. For one
terrible moment, he was sure that the hostages must have been
moved from Old Terminal – a fear reinforced by the memory
of a crack United States army detachment that reached an
American prisoner of war camp in Vietnam only to find it
empty. The silence persisted as the second Hercules trundled
along the runway to its parking spot.

In the defense minister's office far off in Tel Aviv, the silence
seemed almost painful. The ministers sat along the walls and
around the desk, some smoking, others leaning toward the
intercom as if their attentiveness might coerce it into speech.
But the intercom wouldn't cooperate.

Asher Ben-Natan's bottle of Napoleon brandy still stood on
the desk. No one touched it. Military secretaries Braun and
Poran sat with poised pens, ready to record any word coming
from the intercom.

Somebody coughed, and Yitzhak Rabin turned toward
him, instantly indignant, in tacit reproach for disturbing the
moment.

Shimon Peres closed his eyes and his companions got the
impression that he was offering up a silent prayer. He knew
that the next ten or twenty seconds were the most critical
of all – for the hostages, for the soldiers on the ground in
Entebbe, for the army, and for the government of Israel.

Not far from Peres, Mota Gur was listening over his
intercom to the command net on the ground in Entebbe.
He could hear the first reports coming in to Dan Shomron,
but was waiting for a clear picture from his head of Staff
Branch, Yekutiel Adam. In the past there had been occasions
when Mota had been grateful for his deputy's characteristic
lack of loquaciousness, but right now he was dying to know
what was happening in Entebbe.

*   *   *

The Israeli air force Boeing had just landed at Nairobi. The plane appeared to be an El Al jet on a scheduled flight from Johannesburg to Tel Aviv, via Nairobi. Inside the craft, doctors were installing the last items of equipment, ready for what was to come.

Kenyan security men moved in to surround the plane.

The third Hercules was a few feet above the runway when the lights went out. Pilot Ariel Luz was shocked, but only for a fraction of a second. He made a hard landing and let his plane roll forward, hoping to spot the beacons placed by the paratroops from the first plane. Then he applied his brakes, but the heavy craft only rolled to a stop on the grass beside the asphalt runway.

Michael Golan was puzzled. Only a moment ago, the runway lights had been on; now it was pitch dark. He was worried that Ugandan soldiers could creep out from the terminal buildings to attack the three planes already on the ground.

Kuti Adam, circling above in another plane, was desperate for news. He could hear Dan Shomron, could listen to reports from the teams spreading out over the airport, could grasp that the aircraft were landing without difficulties so far – but he knew nothing about the most critical stage of all. Operation Thunderball would stand or fail by what happened to the Mercedes and its companion Land Rovers. If the terrorists or Ugandans realized there were Israelis in the cars, Old Terminal could become a charnel house. Yoni Netaniahu and his men had seconds in which to reach all three entrances to the building – and Kuti Adam still had no word of them.

The fourth Hercules came in to land between the paratroop torches. In the third plane, the pilot was in a cold sweat. Beyond his windows, he saw that his front wheels had stopped three feet from a six-foot-deep trench. Three feet more and Operation Thunderball would have been over for him, his crew, and his passengers.

The Mercedes and its two Land Rover escorts were now speeding into the area between the old control tower and the terminal, close enough to see the covered walkways at the entrances, exactly as described in their preliminary briefing.

Three or four seconds ago, the second Ugandan – the one who hadn't been shot – had vanished from sight. Now he surfaced again, close to the control tower. He hadn't panicked, and he opened fire immediately. A paratroop sergeant in one of the Land Rovers loosed a burst from a Kalashnikov and the Ugandan fell.

"Faster," Yoni shouted.

Tzur Ben-Ami pressed the pedal down as far as it would go. Then the Mercedes jerked to a stop, its four doors already swinging back hard on their hinges, as the occupants shot out from the car. The spot could not have been better chosen – near enough to Old Terminal for a fast entry, but just far enough not to alert the terrorists unnecessarily.

Yoni, Yossi, and their team raced like men possessed toward the three entrances to Old Terminal.

"Those soldiers must be organizing a revolution against Amin," Jaaber commented on hearing two or three shots in the distance outside the building. This was the burst that had cut down the second Ugandan sentry.

Michel Bacos was washing his hands.

Yitzhak David straightened up on his mattress.

Lisette Hadad pulled her blanket over her head and rolled off the mattress onto the floor. Yosef Hadad grabbed a nearby chair and lifted it over his head.

Jean Jacques Maimoni, who was sitting at the far end, lifted his mattress over his body.

Yossi was the first to reach the doorway. The distance from the Mercedes took him at most three seconds. Yoni ran alongside, with the others close on his heels. Behind the rail that ran the length of Old Terminal, Yossi spotted a terrorist who had come out of the building. He fired. The terrorist bent over and ran back in the direction of the doorway.

Wilfried Böse heard the shot and came out to see what was happening. Yossi shot again, but missed. Böse leaped backward and pointed his carbine in the direction of the hostages.

"Retreat!" shouted Böse, turning his head. Yossi shot him.

"Get in," yelled Yoni. "Through the doors!"

Jaaber stood at the far end, gesturing at the terrorist girl in an unmistakable question: "What's going on?"

The girl threw her hand grenade on Jean Jacques' mattress.

Sara Davidson threw herself flat on the floor, then crawled with Uzzi and her two sons toward the corridor to the washrooms. It wasn't far, and it offered the protective sanctuary of a wall. The washrooms were already crowded with terrified hostages who had pressed themselves flat to the floor.

Hana Cohen had lost sight of her son Yaakov. In the chaos, she didn't notice that he wasn't running with her husband and daughter into the corridor. The three of them sprawled on the floor, Pasco Cohen covering his two women with his own body.

Yaakov Cohen tipped over the bench on which he had been sleeping, and covered himself with a mattress.

Ilan Hartuv ran for the corridor.

Yossi raced under the awning and up to the first door. To his horror, he found it was locked. In a fraction of a second, he spun around and hurtled toward the second entrance. He could still hear Yoni egging the others on: "Forward! Forward!" A terrorist suddenly appeared in Yossi's way. He pressed hard on the trigger of his gun – but nothing happened. Empty magazine! Three soldiers hurtled past and into the second doorway. Yossi switched magazines in record time and jumped in after his men. Coming through the doorway, he noticed the terrorist girl standing inside the hall to the left of the door. Another instant and Yossi would have shot her, but the man behind him beat him to it. Hit by a burst, she spun onto the floor near a window. Beyond the group of hostages, who were hugging the floor, a terrorist aimed his Kalashnikov down at the spread-eagled bodies. One of the French crewman screamed: "Don't shoot!"

The terrorist hesitated a second, and it was his last. From ten yards away, Yossi fired a burst that killed him outright.

Across to the right another terrorist managed to fire. He loosed three or four shots that echoed around the hall, then dropped. Amnon Ben-David hit him. He tried to rise and Amnon shot him again.

The paratroopers who had burst through the two open doorways could now take in a sight of utter confusion. A mad mixture of people, beds, mattresses, blankets, overnight bags. The hostages were terrified. After all, it had happened in fifteen seconds – far too quickly for anyone to grasp!

Ron Vardi and his comrades clung to the sides of a command car as it careened across the empty space to the new control tower. Off to one side was a fire station. As Ron watched, it was suddenly pitch black. Somebody had killed the airport lights. At the foot of the tower, the combat team could hear the crackle of shots from elsewhere on the field, but their target was deserted. The four flight controllers were no longer at their stations. An officer scanned the panels, searching for a switch that would restore light to the runways.

Lieutenant Shlomo Lavi raced at the head of his force, riding in two Rabbi field cars, into the Ugandan air force parking area. According to plan, his men were to prevent any attempt by the MIG pilots to get their craft airborne and attack the departing Hercules. Shlomo's mission proceeded smoothly. In minimum time the area was secure, without opposition.

Around the field, men of the Golani and the paratroop detachments were already deployed across main access routes and roads to block any reinforcements from a nearby army camp almost within earshot of Entebbe International.

At the center of the airport, Dan Shomron was losing patience. Still not a word from Yoni Netaniahu, though he could hear the crackle of light-arms fire – rarely a good sign.

Yoni's Land Rover team headed straight for the second floor. Their mission was to secure the building against any attempt to interfere with the transfer of hostages to the aircraft. The first soldier racing up met two Ugandan soldiers on the stairs. They froze. Above them, on the second floor, were more of their comrades. There was some resistance, but it was over in less than a minute and the Israelis were free to mount guard on the roof, where they could survey the entire surrounding area.

The force now inside Old Terminal had a rough idea of the number of terrorists, all of whom had to be taken care of if the evacuation was to proceed safely. While Yossi and his squad went in to the passenger hall, another team ran along the front of the building to the old VIP Room at the far end. As they arrived, the terrorists off duty came tumbling into the corridor.

Two white Europeans came out of a nearby room. For a split second Ilan Gonen held his fire, thinking that these must be passengers off the Aerobus.

"Who are you?" Ilan shouted in English.

No answer. The two men continued their slow walk.

In the defense minister's office, shots could be heard over the intercom. Were it not for the tension and anxiety, Rabin, Peres, and the others might have found time to marvel at the wonders of modern technology that could let them listen to a battle two thousand miles away. Yet, apart from a few crisp orders issued by Dan Shomron, and terse conversations between the plane and the ground below, there was no way of knowing how things were going or whether the hostages were safe. Amos Aron was sending a message to President Ford over the phone to Ambassador Dinitz in Washington: AT THE TIME OF DELIVERY OF THIS MESSAGE, OUR FORCES . . . Dinitz listened in astonishment.

It was only at 11:07 P.M. that Kuti Adam's voice finally came through in the chief of staff's private bureau and the defense minister's room elsewhere in the building.

"Everything's okay. You'll have a precise report immediately."

Everything's okay?

What had happened at Entebbe?

Were the hostages safe?

Were the terrorists dead?

What about casualties?

The prime minister and his defense minister leaned forward, almost unable to bear the tension, praying to hear Dan Shomron's voice.

Mota Gur no longer hesitated. He called Dan directly.

"What's happening there?"
"Everything's all right. I'll report later. I'm busy now."
Again, everything's all right. . . . What's all right?

Yosef Hadad held the chair over his head as protection against terrorist bullets. A bullet hit his chair, and he thought his end had come. Out of the corner of his eye, he could see Böse lying in a pool of blood.

Pasco Cohen lay on top of his wife and daughter, with more hostages on top of him. He lifted himself for a moment to make sure that Zippy wasn't suffocating. A bullet penetrated his thigh, then tore an artery near his bladder.

"I'm wounded," he told Hana quietly, "look after the children."

As Pasco collapsed on the floor of the corridor, Jean Jacques Maimoni panicked at the sight of the hand grenade that had landed on his mattress. The boy jumped to his feet and ran, bent over, toward the washroom corridor. Two bullets hit his back and sent him sprawling on the floor, dead. Yitzhak David, who lifted his body in an attempt to pull Jean Jacques down, took a bullet in his shoulder.

"Who are you?" Ilan Gonen yelled again. But the two Europeans went on walking, as though all the hubbub and chaos had nothing to do with them. The soldier pointed his gun barrel at them. Spotting the flash of a grenade fuse, he let loose a burst, then dropped flat on the floor. The grenade exploded in the corridor, tearing the bodies of the two Europeans but not harming the paratroopers.

Sara Davidson thought she could hear voices speaking Hebrew. They were coming nearer! A loudspeaker boomed through the enclosed space: "This is *Zahal* – the IDF! We've come to take you home! Lie on the floor and wait for instructions! This is *Zahal!*"

Yosef Hadad shouted in a voice clearly heard throughout Old Terminal: "They're ours! They're ours!"

Somebody else lifted a head to call: "Israeli soldiers? Israeli soldiers!"

Baruch Gross peeked into the hall from the washroom

corridor and almost stopped breathing. Before him stood an Israeli soldier. There could be no mistake! But the man's gun was pointing at him. Baruch didn't lose his head: "*Yisrael!*" he shouted the Hebrew word, "*Yisrael!*" The gun barrel turned, and it seemed to Baruch that his life was also turning.

"Lie on the floor," boomed the bullhorn, "we have come to get you and it will be all right!"

Thirteen-year-old Benny Davidson couldn't believe it. Only at noon he had jokingly told his parents and brother that "the army will come to free us tonight at midnight." So he had said it – so what? He didn't mean it, and certainly didn't believe it. And now, one hour before midnight, Israeli soldiers had appeared in Old Terminal. Sara Davidson dropped on top of Ron, while Benny mumbled a prayer.

Hana Cohen didn't lose her head. She was too good a nurse for that. Tearing Pasco's shirt, she bandaged the wound, but the makeshift dressing turned red. The wound was deep. Pasco was losing too much blood.

Yossi ran through Old Terminal checking to see that all the terrorists were dead. Then he called a sixteen-year-old hostage named Michael, and asked him to identify them. Once that was done, Yossi reported to Brigadier Dan Shomron, somewhere on Entebbe's field. Shomron passed the news on to Yekutiel Adam in the Boeing. Adam relayed the message to General Gur. "The transgressors are eliminated," he said quietly. "I repeat, transgressors eliminated."

Four words were all it took to relieve the tension in Shimon Peres' study. A smile flittered across Yitzhak Rabin's face, and Shimon Peres' eyes sparkled. But they still didn't know very much.

The men in the room could now allow themselves a few words of quiet conversation, but their voices were muted. Suddenly the phone rang; General Zeevi from Paris. He was still waiting for new instructions. Who the hell could negotiate this way? Could he please speak to the prime minister?

This time Rabin told Gandhi that there was no more need for French mediation, and he hoped that the general would forgive him for not saying anything sooner. As a military man of many years' standing, Gandhi could understand Rabin's earlier predicament. And he would be delighted to accept the honor of personally informing President Giscard d'Estaing.

On the second floor of Old Terminal, paratroops checked room by room, looking for terrorists or Ugandan troops. Their instructions were to allow the Ugandans to escape, provided of course they didn't offer resistance. Scores of black troops made use of the opportunity to get away, and quickly.

Almost all the Israeli vehicles were now headed toward the old control tower. First place was given to the half-track armored personnel carrier, from which a torrent of lead from bazooka rockets and machine-gun bullets poured onto the tower. Its occupants had been firing on the Israelis for the past few minutes, and the paratroopers could not but admire the courage of the unknown defenders. Finally it seemed that stage two could begin: the hostages could be moved out to the plane that would take them home.

Only now did Yossi realize that he hadn't heard Yoni's voice for at least sixty seconds. He scanned the interior of Old Terminal, but there was no sign of his commanding officer. Running from the building, he found Yoni almost immediately. He lay unconscious on the ground by the building, a doctor and a corpsman in attendance, trying to save his life. He had been shot in the very first minutes after leaving the Mercedes – a bullet in the back, fired from the old control tower, the place that had worried him during yesterday's rehearsal. Yoni had dropped to the ground, mortally wounded, a moment after guiding his men to target.

Yossi, startled to realize that he was now in command of the main force in Operation Thunderball, begged the doctor: "Do everything you can!"

Inside the lead Hercules, Dr. Yosef was getting anxious. He knew that the aircraft now made a huge static target as it sat being filled with fuel. It was vulnerable even without the flashes of firing that the doctor could see through the small portholes. With him were nine more doctors and orderlies, waiting up front for the hostages, praying they weren't wounded – but ready to do their jobs if they had to.

Yitzhak David rubbed his shoulder. Blood was pouring from it. Ilan Hartuv suddenly noticed the sticky red stream, and raised his voice over the din: "Our leader is hurt. Someone come and bandage him." Michael helped Ilan bind the wound and brought him over to the mattress where, until yesterday, his mother had slept. It was empty, but next to it lay Ida Borowitz, her son Boris stooping over her.

Ida's body was covered with blood. Nobody had noticed her die, but the body of a terrorist lay beside her. Had he shot her? Had he decided to die with one of the hostages? Boris hugged the dead body of his mother and wailed: "*Imaleh, Imaleh* – Mother, Mother!" There were tears in the eyes of the people around him, yet the time had not yet come to mourn the dead.

Sergeant Hershko Surin was due to begin demobilization leave the next day, Sunday. His three years of conscript service were almost over. Twelve hours before ending his military career, Hershko dashed into Entebbe Old Terminal. Climbing the stairs to the second floor, he met two Ugandans. One of them was faster than Hershko. Sergeant Surin dropped to the ground, wavering between life and death, his body paralyzed.

By the outer wall of Old Terminal, a doctor labored to save Yoni Netaniahu. It was useless. The brilliant young lieutenant colonel who had come home to serve his people was dying. Yossi Yaar and the others lifted him gently onto a stretcher. For a moment it seemed that Yoni's will to live might overcome. He raised his head as though wanting to say something – then dropped back on the stretcher.

Yossi ordered his men to collect the casualties strewn across the floor. The bodies of Ida Borowitz and Jean Jacques Maimoni were laid on stretchers, as were the ten people injured in the course of the lightning-fast raid. Bullhorns summoned all the hostages back from corridors and side rooms into the main hall. The stunned men, women, and children shuffled in. The paratroopers had to slap a few to bring them out of shock.

The pilot of the first Hercules started his engines and began to move his craft slowly and cautiously toward Old Terminal, stopping 500 yards away. Yossi ordered his men to prepare the evacuation of the wounded and the hostages, although shots were still being exchanged between Israeli soldiers and Ugandans. When it seemed that the gunfire had finally stopped, Yossi picked up a bullhorn and instructed the hostages to check and see that all members of their families were accounted for.

Uzzi Davidson collected together Sara, Benny, and Ron. Yitzhak David, lying on a stretcher, grasped his wife's hand.

Ilan Hartuv was very worried. His mother was still in Mulago Hospital, but what could be done about that?

Outside the terminal, soldiers took position in two lines, forming a funnel straight to the gaping hatch of the Hercules. Yoni's solution for shock and panic would still be used, even if he wasn't there to supervise it. Yet there was another reason: no one wanted a hostage to run into an engine.

Command cars, jeeps, Rabbi field cars, and a Peugeot pickup truck pulled into the area in front of the building as the 104 hostages were started moving toward the waiting plane. There was some panic. Families clung together and rushed for the vehicles. One young girl came out dressed only in bra and panties, as there had been no time to dress. A soldier threw her a blanket, and she wrapped it around herself as she scrambled onto a command car. Shots were still being fired.

Eighteen minutes had passed since the Mercedes began its journey across Entebbe Airport. Now Yekutiel Adam's voice boomed out from a radio in the General Staff "pit," and from the intercoms in Gur's and Peres' rooms: "Mount Carmel. I repeat, Mount Carmel!"

The prime minister and defense minister knew now that the tough part of the mission was almost over. "Mount Carmel" was the code word denoting the start of evacuation from Old Terminal.

Defense Ministry spokesman Naftali Lavi dialed the home of a military correspondent of one of the daily papers. "It's worthwhile to stay awake tonight," he said – but refused to elaborate.

"What's happening?"

Naftali could not explain, so he merely said, "They'll trade terrorists for hostages tonight."

The journalist couldn't swear to it, but there seemed to be a note of mockery in the spokesman's last remark.

The 500 yards now appeared secure, so Yossi gave the signal for the vehicles to move. Across the way, the engines of the Hercules were holding to a steady, muffled roar. Hostages who hadn't found places on the vehicles began to walk toward the plane.

Hana Cohen swept Zippy up in her arms and began to run. Yaakov caught up with her and ran alongside. Pasco, lying on a stretcher, waved weakly to his son as he was lifted inside the Hercules. A team of doctors and orderlies set to work at once to save his life, pushing Hana, who wanted to help, gently aside. Before she even found a seat, she could see a blood-transfusion bag in place as the precious fluid dripped into Pasco's body. The wound was evidently more serious than she had realized.

Dr Yosef leaned over the stretcher that bore the unconscious body of Lieutenant Colonel Jonathan Netaniahu. There was nothing more that could be done. Yoni was dying, and the doctors were powerless to prevent it happening.

Soldiers helped hostages off the vehicles by the ramp of the Hercules, guiding them across the 500-yard walk. Their stunned charges were encouraged to move at a brisk pace, yet there was no need for panic.

Inside the cockpit, the pilot and his crew were already making their pre-takeoff instrument check. Behind them, at the bottom of the ramp, officers and men of the Thunderball force quietly asked each hostage to check that all his family were accounted for. When Captain Bacos approached the ramp, an officer politely asked him to check his family – the crew of Air Force 139. No one was missing. Only Ilan Hartuv remained silent. He was leaving his mother behind in a Ugandan hospital, with no way to save her – but what else could he do? It would be futile to remain in Entebbe. Now, in the doorway of the Hercules, he could only hope that the president of Uganda would extend his protection to Dora Bloch. Still stunned by the events of the last half hour, Ilan pressed forward into the belly of the plane. Like the others, he was still finding it difficult to believe that the week of captivity was nearly over.

Far away across the airport, Lieutenant Shlomo Lavi and his men detailed to guard the Ugandan MIGs were firing at Ugandan soldiers coming from the direction of the terminal. The opposition was heavy enough to force Lavi's team into equally heavy return fire.

Michael Golan, in the cockpit of the second Hercules, was still behind the hillock next to a runway. The MIGs were parked in a lower area of the airport and he couldn't see them, although he did notice flames and a column of smoke ascending into the night sky. It was Shlomo Lavi's men blowing up eleven MIGs – seven 21s and four 17s. Perhaps half the order of battle of the Ugandan air force was now smoke and ashes.

A spirited radio conversation began between Michael and the other three pilots. Minutes ago an attempt had started to refuel the Israeli planes from Entebbe Airport storage tanks. They had brought three pumps and a group of men who had served in Uganda and knew exactly where the airport fuel stocks were kept. One of the planes was already linked up, but the pump was supplying fuel at low pressure. It seemed as if the process was going to take 45 minutes, and the pilots were growing nervous. Finally, the Golani detachment commander radioed a suggestion to Dan Shomron to stop the refueling: "We have succeeded. Why should we take more risks here?"

Kuti and Benny heard the conversation and agreed, ordering immediate takeoff. Never mind reloading the pumps! All of them together are only worth ten thousand dollars! Let Amin have them. Get those planes airborne!

The lead Hercules, with its load of dazed hostages, lumbered onto the long runway, gathered speed, and climbed heavily into the night. In the cockpit, the hands of the clock indicated

11:43; precisely forty minutes after the first plane landed at Entebbe.

"'Hear, O Israel . . .'" One of the passengers recited the ancient prayer, and Baruch Gross picked up the refrain.

WIRELESS RIDGE
John Frost

The British Army's Second Battalion of The Parachute Regiment fought in all the major battles of the 1982 land war between Britain and Argentina for the Falkland Islands (Malvinas). After spearheading the landings at San Carlos on 21 May, the battalion fought its way to Port Stanley against determined Argentinian resistance, via Bluff Cove, Goose Green and Wireless Ridge. The most famous of these battles is undoubtedly Goose Green (where 2 Para commander, Lieutenant-Colonel "H" Jones, won a posthumous Victoria Cross for his charge against an enemy position), but the engagement at Wireless Ridge on 13–14 June was no less dramatic. The Ridge, a spur on the north side of Port Stanley, was heavily defended by troops from the Argentine 7th Infantry Regiment and the Argentine 1st Parachute Regiment. The story of the battle is told here by Major-General John Frost, CB, DSO, MC, who served with 2 Para in WWII, commanding the Battalion from October 1942 until his capture at Arnhem, 1944, where he led the defence of the bridge.

The origins of The Parachute Regiment lie with an initiative of Winston Churchill who, after noting the success of German paratroop operations during Germany's invasion of Holland and Belgium, suggested the formation of a British airborne elite force. The first units began training in June 1940, with volunteers from the units forming The Parachute Regiment in August 1942.

2 PARA'S TASK WAS to capture the Wireless Ridge features, keeping west of the telegraph wires, and Colonel Chaundler's plan called for a two-phase noisy night attack. In Phase 1, A Company would take the northern spur where the ponds were, C Company having secured the start-line. Once this was secure Phase 2 would come into operation, and B and

D Companies would pass through from the north to attack the main Wireless Ridge feature itself. B Company would go to the right (the western end of the ridge), while D Company attacked the rocky ridge-line east of the track.

The mortars would move forward from Mount Kent to a position in the lee of the hillside south of Drunken Rock Pass, and this would also be the site for a static Battalion Headquarters during the attack. H-hour was again to be at about 0030. The importance of digging in on the objectives was emphasised once more, since Wireless Ridge was dominated by both Tumbledown and Sapper Hill, and if enemy troops should still be there at dawn they could make 2 Para's positions untenable.

The orders were straightforward, and the plan simple, involving the maximum use of darkness. As the "O" Group ended the company commanders were told that they would now fly up to Mount Longdon to look at the ground over which they would operate.

The CO went on ahead with the Battery Commander to meet Lieutenant-Colonel Hew Pike, CO of 3 Para, and Major William McCracken, RA, who controlled the artillery "anchor" OP on Mount Longdon. They discussed and arranged for co-ordinated fire support, with 3 Para's mortars, Milan teams and machine-guns all ready to fire from the flank, and Major Martin Osborne's C Company, 3 Para, in reserve.

Back at the gully all was peaceful in the bright sunshine. Suddenly this was shattered as nine Skyhawks appeared further to the north, flying very low in formation and heading due west towards Mount Kent. The effect was electric, for no one expected that the Argentines could still flaunt their air power in this way.

At "A" Echelon, behind Mount Kent, there was no doubt as to who the jets were aiming for. As they came screaming up over the col and rose to attacking height, the formation split: three went for the area where the artillery gun-line had recently been, three went for 3 Commando Brigade HQ, and three attacked "A" Echelon. All the machine-guns opened up, claiming one possible hit as the bombs rained down. Amazingly, there were no casualties from this minor blitzkrieg. But the accuracy of the attack, and its obvious definiteness of purpose, left people wondering if the enemy had left concealed OPs behind, watching Mount Kent, or if satellite photography had shown up the various targets or, possibly, if Argentine electronic-warfare equipment had picked up radio signals from Brigade HQ.

The air raid created delays to all helicopter movement, but eventually the CO was able to fly on to Brigade HQ, while the company commanders were dropped on to Mount Longdon for their own recces. Colonel Chaundler had already been updated on the actual strength of the enemy, which was greater than had been thought, and a new Argentine position had been detected to the east of the pond-covered spur, on a knoll overlooking Hearnden Water and the mouth of the Murrell River.

While the CO was at Brigade HQ, the company commanders were able to study Wireless Ridge in detail from the commanding position on Longdon. It at once became obvious that much of the information so far given to them was inaccurate. What was thought to be C Company of 3 Para proved to be nothing of the sort: Major Dair Farrar-Hockley noticed that it was an *enemy* position of about company strength, situated dangerously on the flank of the 2 Para axis of attack, west of the northern spur. It was also clear that Wireless Ridge proper was heavily defended, with positions which stretched a long way to the east beyond the line of telegraph poles that marked the 2 Para boundary. Strangely, no harassing fire was being brought to bear during the day on any of the Argentine positions, and their soldiers were free to stand about in the open.

The company commanders flew back to Furze Bush Pass, but clearly a major change in plan was necessary. The CO returned from Brigade HQ as evening approached and was told of the situation. "Go away and have your supper. Come back in forty-five minutes and you will have a new set of orders," he said. Meanwhile the move-up of mortars and the adjustment of artillery had been delayed, and as a result the changes to the fireplan had to continue into the night, directed by the OP on Longdon and using illuminating rounds.

Unfortunately for the company commanders, normal battle procedure had already ensured that relevant details of the first plan had permeated to the lowest level. Platoon and section commanders had had time to issue clear and well constructed orders to their subordinates, but now their efforts were all useless, for by the time the company commanders returned with the CO's revised plan, it was too late to go into new details. Such a sudden last-minute change did little for the men's faith in the system, but it was unavoidable and, in any case, the soldiers had by now become stoical, while the cynics among them were not disappointed by this evidence of fallibility at higher levels. Nevertheless, the battalion was able to adapt and change its plans and moved off on time. But Phil Neame had his misgivings about what the SAS to the east of his line of advance was *meant* to be doing, and there was no knowledge of what the SAS was actually *going* to do. Furthermore, no one really knew what was beyond Wireless Ridge to the south, in the Moody Brook area, and everyone would have liked to have known exactly when the 5 Brigade attack on Tumbledown was timed to begin.

The battalion's new plan was for a four-phase noisy night attack. In Phase 1 D Company would capture the newly discovered enemy position west of the northern spur; A and B Companies would then assault the pond-covered hilltop; Phase 3 called for C Company to take the knoll to the east; and finally D Company would roll up the enemy on Wireless Ridge itself, with fire support from A and B Companies, starting in the west and finishing at the telegraph poles.

Fire support was to be lavish in comparison to Goose Green: two batteries of 105-mm guns, HMS *Ambuscade* with her one 4.5-inch gun offshore, and the mortars of both 2 and 3 Para, totalling sixteen tubes. Ammunition was plentiful, and the battalion's mortars had been moved complete from Mount Kent by helicopter, and were thus fresh for action. The Machine-Gun Platoon had also been flown forward. Between the six guns they had enough ammunition to provide a massive weight of fire, and the men were fresh and rather proud of

their earlier achievement behind Mount Kent against the
Skyhawks. The Milan Platoon was already forward with the
battalion – the experience of Goose Green had demonstrated
the capability of this precision guided missile against static
defences. Finally the light tanks of the Blues and Royals
would be there, Scimitars with their 30-mm automatic cannon
and Scorpions with 76-mm guns, and both equipped with
very high quality night-vision equipment and having superb
cross-country performance. All available support was allotted
first to D Company, then to A and B in their assault, and
finally to D Company again as it traversed the ridge.

As night closed in the tanks, the mortars and the Recce
Platoon, which was to secure the start-line, moved up. By
now the promise of the day had vanished and snow and sleet
were falling, considerably limiting the effectiveness of all the
gunsighting equipment, and reducing visibility.

At about 0015 a storm of fire from the supporting artillery
and mortars was unleashed upon the Argentine positions. A
and B Companies passed by, led by C Company patrols to
the new start-line secured by Corporal Bishop's patrol in the
relatively safe ground overlooking Lower Pass. At 0045 hours
on Monday 14 June, D Company moved over its own start-line
further to the west, and headed towards the identified enemy
position.

As the company moved forward, the tanks of the Blues
and Royals and the machine-guns provided fire support while
the artillery increased its rate of fire. Enemy mortar fire in
retaliation became heavy. In the rear of the company, Private
Godfrey of 12 Platoon had a near miss as a piece of shrapnel
cut through his windproof and dug into his boot. He dived for
cover – straight into an Argentine latrine!

The weight of supporting artillery and mortar fire was
singularly effective, for the enemy on the D Company objective
could be seen running away as the company pushed forward,
although 155-mm air-burst shelling increased as the Paras
began to clear the Argentine trenches, now-abandoned except
for a few enemy killed by the barrage. The darkness of the night
and the extent of the enemy position caused the company to
spread out, creating problems of control. Lieutenant Webster

of 10 Platoon counted up to twenty trenches on his right, with more over to the left, where 2nd Lieutenant Waddington's 11 Platoon found the other half of the assault formation.

Occasionally as they moved forward, men would suddenly disappear into the freezing water of an ice-covered pond. Privates Dean and Creasey of 11 Platoon went in up to their necks, and had to tread water to stay afloat until their platoon sergeant, Sergeant Light, dragged them out.

Fire support for the company was immaculate. The tanks used their powerful image-intensifier night-sights to pinpoint targets. Once enemy positions were identified, they fired. As soon as the battalion's machine-gunners saw the strike they, too, opened up. Occasionally the machine-gun fire was too close for comfort, even for D Company, and in the end 10 Platoon Commander called for it to stop.

The opposition had fled, and D Company took its first objective in record time, remaining *in situ* while A and B Companies began their part of the battle. Enemy artillery fire was increasing, however, and Neame therefore decided to push forward for another 300 hundred metres into relative safety, to avoid the worst of the barrage.

Several of those waiting to move on the A and B Company start-lines were reminded of scenes they had seen from films of the First and Second World Wars. As shells landed all around, men lay huddled against the peat, with bayonets fixed. There could be no denying that, for the soldiers, fear of the known was in this case worse than blissful ignorance of the unknown. In the shelter of the peat bogs some smoked, watching the display of illuminants above.

Just as the time came to move, the shelling claimed its first victim, for Colour Sergeant "Doc" Findlay was killed in the rear of A Company, and soldiers from Support and HQ Companies were also wounded. The advance began, the two companies moving southwards parallel to each other, on either side of the track. The men crossed the stream in the valley north of their objective with the tanks firing over their heads. The effect upon the enemy was devastating. In their night-sights the tank crews could see Argentine soldiers running or falling as the accurate fire took effect. The boost to morale that this form of suppressive fire gave was considerable; fundamentally, the battle was being won by supporting arms, the infantry being free to do their own job, which is actually clearing and securing the ground.

On the left, all was going well with A Company. Command and control had been well practised back at Goose Green and now the junior officers and section commanders were quite expert in maintaining direction. Silence was unnecessary and orders were shouted backwards and forwards. The enemy were still shelling as the companies advanced, but now counter-battery fire was being provided by our own artillery. From his own position the CO could see the two companies in extended formation, moving quickly up the hill, the whole battlefield brightly lit by starshell. .

Co-ordinating the two assaulting companies' advances was difficult, however. The track provided a boundary of sorts, but controlling upwards of 200 men during a noisy battle over difficult terrain is not easy. Colonel Chaundler had another worry. Earlier, before the battalion had moved up, he had been shown a captured Argentine map which indicated a minefield directly in the path of the assaulting companies. There was only fifteen minutes to go before 2 Para set off – far too late for a change of plan. The CO only had time to brief OC B Company, while John Crosland had none in which to warn his men, and in any case was told to push on regardless, since there would be no time to clear the mines. Only afterwards did Major Crosland tell his men that they had actually moved directly through the minefield without knowing it. Miraculously, no one was blown up on the way.

The ponds on the spur claimed a victim, however, when Private Philpott of 5 Platoon suddenly plunged into over six feet of water. He was dragged out and his section commander, Corporal Curtis, immediately organized a complete change of clothing from the other men in the section, which probably saved Philpott's life.

The two companies consolidated on the objective. There was some firing from the trenches, swiftly silenced as the men of both companies ran in to clear them. Once more the enemy had fled, leaving only twenty or so of their number

behind, quickly taken prisoner as they were winkled out of
their holes. Radios were still switched on, and several dead lay
around the positions. As the men dug in, the enemy shelling
increased and it was to continue for the rest of the night at
the same level of intensity. Most thought it was worse than
Goose Green, but fortunately the abandoned enemy bunkers
provided reasonable shelter, although a number of casualties
occurred in A Company.

It was now C Company's turn. Already they had had a
minor scare on the A and B Company start-line when a
Scorpion tank had careered towards Company Headquarters
in the darkness. It was hopelessly lost and its commander had
to be evacuated after a dose of "hatch rash" – the effect of
placing the head in the path of a rapidly closing hatch. The
confused vehicle was soon heading in the right direction, but
now under the command of Captain Roger Field, who had
seized this opportunity to revert to a more honourable role
than foot-slogging.

With A and B Companies now firm, C Company was
ordered to check out the Argentine position further to the east
that had been spotted from Mount Longdon on the previous
day. Major Roger Jenner was glad to be moving again, for it
seemed that the supporting artillery battery had developed a
"rogue gun" and every sixth round meant for the enemy was
coming in uncomfortably close to his company. He and his
men set off, taking cover occasionally on the way as shells fell
close by. There had been no firing from the company objective
during the battle, and soon the platoons were pushing round
the side of a minefield on to the knoll.

As the Recce Platoon advanced, they could hear noises
of weapons being cocked. The bright moonlight left them
uncomfortably exposed on the hillside. On the forward edge of
the slope were two parallel lines of rock, and on the second line
the platoon found a series of shell scrapes, suggesting recent
occupation by a body of troops. Once again it seemed that the
enemy had left hurriedly, leaving tents and bits of equipment
behind in the process. Away over to the east Jenner's men
could see the bright lights of Stanley airfield, and could hear a
C-130 landing. The company was ordered to dig in, but since

an enemy attack on this feature was extremely unlikely the CO changed the orders, and C Company moved up to the pond-covered hill.

If any particular group deserves special praise for what was done that night, then it must be the tanks of the Blues and Royals. Their mere presence had been a remarkable boost to morale during all the attacks that had taken place, and the speed and accuracy of their fire, matched by their ability to keep up with the advancing Paras, had been a severe shock to the enemy. Lance-Corporal Dunkeley's tank, which Captain Field had taken over following the injury to its commander, had alone fired forty rounds from its 76-mm gun.

2 Para was performing superbly, its three first objectives taken with great speed and a minimum of casualties, despite heavy and accurate enemy artillery fire. Whenever the enemy in trenches had sought to return fire they had been met by a withering concentration of fire from the rifle companies' weapons which, coupled with very heavy support, had proved devastating. It is not known whether the Argentines had gathered that they were facing the men from Goose Green, but there can be no question that 2 Para knew.

D Company was now ready to go into the final phase of the attack and began moving forward again to the west end of Wireless Ridge. The tanks and support weapons moved up to join A and B Companies on the hilltop overlooking the D Company objective, and endured the artillery fire as well as anti-tank fire from Wireless Ridge to the south.

12 Platoon was now in the lead. Lieutenant John Page, who had taken over from the tragically killed Jim Barry, looked for the fence, running at right-angles to the ridge, that would guide him to the correct start-line for the assault. Unfortunately there was little left of the fence marked on the maps, and Corporal Barton's section, at the point of the platoon, could only find a few strands of wire to follow. The number of ice-covered ponds added to the difficulty and the intense cold was beginning to affect men's reactions, as they worked their way south to the western end of Wireless Ridge.

Once more, massive fire-power began to soften up the enemy, who apparently still had no intimation that they were about to be rolled up from a flank. The initial idea had been for D Company simply to sweep eastwards along the ridge without stopping, with 11 Platoon on the left, 12 Platoon on the right and 10 Platoon in reserve. There was still uncertainty as to whether Tumbledown to the south had been taken or not, and clearly a battle was still in progress on that mountain as the Scots Guards fought to drive out the Argentines on its summit. But Neame and his D Company had no intention other than to push on regardless, although they knew that if Tumbledown was still in enemy hands by daylight then 2 Para would be extremely vulnerable.

The bombardment of the western end of the Wireless Ridge continued as the platoons advanced. It seemed to have been effective, since no enemy were encountered at all, although, to be certain, 11 Platoon cleared any bunkers they came across on the reverse slope with grenades.

The first part of Wireless Ridge was now clear and across the dip, where the track came up, lay the narrower rocky outcrops of the remainder of the objective. Fire was concentrated on these areas from A and B Companies as tanks, Milans and machine-guns provided an intense concentration on to three enemy machine-gun posts that remained.

Efforts to switch artillery support further forward and on to the area of Moody Brook had unfortunate results. Five rounds of high explosive crashed on to the ridge around and very near the leading D Company platoons. 3 Section of 11 Platoon was caught in the open and, despite screams to stop the firing, it was too late. Private Parr was killed instantly, and Corporal McAuley was somersaulted into some rocks, completely dazed, and had to be picked up by a stretcher party.

There was a considerable delay while a livid Major Neame tried to get the gunners to sort themselves out. It seemed that one gun was off target, as C Company had noted, but at the gun-lines they did not know which, since in the dark it was impossible to note the fall of shot, even if there had been time, and the other battery was not available owing to shortage of ammunition. In the meantime the CO was growing increasingly impatient, urging the D Company commander to press on.

As soon as the gunners could guarantee reasonable support, and with increased efforts from the Blues and Royals, Neame was off again. All through the wait constant harassing fire from the enemy had been landing around the company, so none were sorry to move. Despite the fire pouring on to the ridge-line ahead, enemy machine-gunners continued firing from well sited bunkers, and were still staunchly in action as the platoons advanced.

They moved with 11 Platoon on the left, 12 Platoon ahead on the ridge itself, with the company commander immediately behind and, in the rear, 10 Platoon. 12 Platoon came across an abandoned Argentine recoilless rifle, an anti-tank weapon, as they crossed the start-line, which may well have been the weapon that had earlier been engaging the tanks on the A and B Company positions. The platoon moved down into the gap between the two parts of the ridge line, but as the soldiers passed by some ponds, very heavy machine-gun fire began from their front and illumination was called for as the platoon answered the firing. Corporal Barton came across some orange string, possibly indicating a minefield, but his platoon commander urged him on regardless.

The enemy appeared to be surprised by the direction of the assault, and as the Paras advanced, they could hear an Argentine voice calling out, possibly to give warning of this sudden attack from the west. 10 Platoon came across a lone enemy machine-gunner who lay wounded in both legs, his weapon lying abandoned beside him.

Corporal Harley of 11 Platoon caught his foot in a wire, which may have been part of a minefield, and, fearing that it might be an Argentine jumping mine, unravelled himself with some care. The platoon pushed on, skirmishing by sections until they met a concertina of wire. Fearing mines, Sappers were called for from Company Headquarters, but these could do little in the darkness except tape off the suspect area. In fact channels could be discerned between the concertinas, and these were assumed, correctly, as it turned out, to be safe lanes.

While 11 Platoon was extricating itself from the minefield, Neame pushed 12 Platoon on and brought 10 Platoon out to the left to maintain the momentum. Suddenly an intense burst of firing brought the company to a halt. It was a critical moment. For a short time, *all* commanders had to do everything in their power to get things going again, with platoon commanders and sergeants and section commanders all urging their men on. It was a real test of leadership as several soldiers understandably went to ground.

A brief fire-fight ensued, with 12 Platoon engaging the enemy as they pushed forward on the right overlooking Moody Brook below, where lights could be seen. The moment of doubt had passed, however, and once more the men were clearing bunkers and mopping up with gusto. 10 and 12 Platoons now moved on either side of the company commander. Maximum speed was needed to keep the enemy off balance as they fell back, conducting a fighting withdrawal along the ridge. The tanks continued to fire, directed by the company commander. Unfortunately his signaller had fallen into a shell hole and become separated, thus creating considerable frustration for the CO, who wanted to talk to Neame about the progress of his battle.

During 12 Platoon's brief fight Private Slough had been hit and died later in hospital, and another soldier was wounded.

Enemy artillery fire continued to make life uncomfortable. Fortunately D Company's task was no longer difficult, as most of the enemy bunkers had now been abandoned. 12 Platoon reached the telegraph wires and consolidated there, while the other platoons reorganized further back along the ridge. Shell fire intensified and snipers began to engage from enemy positions further to the east along the ridge.

Neame went up to see the platoon commander, Lieutenant Page. Snipers in the rocks were still firing on the platoon and it seemed that the enemy might be about to counter-attack from the direction of Moody Brook, to the right.

On several occasions the company commander was nearly hit, and his perambulations began to be the cause of some comment. Sergeant Meredith shouted to him, "For God's sake push off, Sir – you're attracting bullets everywhere you go!"

100 metres or so to the east, Argentines could be heard shouting to each other, as though rallying for a counter-attack.

John Page called for fire support, and then ordered his own
men to stop firing, for by so doing they were merely identifying
their positions. They felt very isolated and vulnerable.

For two very long and uncomfortable hours the company
remained under pressure. Small-arms fire mingled with all
types of HE fell in and around 12 Platoon's position as the men
crouched in the abandoned enemy sangars and in shell holes.
John Page continued to move around his platoon, organizing
its defences, and suffering a near-miss in the process. He was
hit by a bullet, which passed between two grenades hanging
on his webbing and landed in a full magazine in his pouch.
He was blown off his feet by the shock. "It was like being
hit by a sledgehammer and having an electric shock at the
same time," he later described the moment. As he lay there a
round exploded in the magazine, but fortunately the grenades
remained intact, and he was soon on his feet.

Meanwhile the CO was still trying to get in touch with
Neame to know the form. Lieutenant Webster, OC 10 Platoon,
was momentarily elevated to commanding the company since
he was the only officer left near Company Headquarters. As
he talked to the CO, voices could be heard below in the
direction of Moody Brook. Corporal Elliot's section opened
up and automatic fire was returned by perhaps ten to fifteen
men. 11 Platoon moved forward to join 10 Platoon in a
long extended line along the ridge, the men firing downhill
towards the enemy position. Eventually the CO got through
to the company commander, who had had a hair-raising time
walking along the ridge to discover what was happening. He
now informed the CO of his fears of imminent attack.

Sporadic enemy fire from Tumbledown added to D Company's danger, and all the earlier fears of the consequences
of delay to the 5 Brigade attack came to the fore. The CO
offered to send tanks up but Neame declined, since they would
be very exposed on the forward slope fire positions they would
be forced to adopt. He would have preferred another company
to hold the first part of Wireless Ridge, which as yet remained
undefended.

The company reorganized, leaving Corporal Owen's section
forward as a standing patrol while 10 and 11 Platoons found

dug-outs on the reverse slope. 12 Platoon stayed in its positions near the telegraph poles.

There was little more that the Companies on the northern spur could now do to support D Company. Two of A Company's trained medical orderlies had been wounded by the shelling that still continued, so the platoons had to look after their own casualties – once again the value of the medical training for all ranks was vindicated. Fortunately the helicopters in support that night were fully effective, evacuating casualties with minimum delay, and other casualties were taken back to the RAP on one of the tanks. The enemy artillery fire gave the remainder every incentive to dig, and the possibility of being overlooked by Mount Tumbledown in the morning was an additional spur.

For A and B Companies it was now a matter of lasting the cold night out, which was not without incident. Privates (Jud') Brookes and Gormley of A Company's 1 Platoon had been hit by shrapnel. The rule was to switch on the injured man's easco light, normally used for night parachute descents, to ensure that he would not be missed in the dark. Sergeant Barrett went back to look for Brookes, whose light was smashed.

"All right, Brookes – me and the Boss will be back to pick you up later."

"Ee, Sarge," he replied in a thick Northern accent, "Ah knows tha f – will."

Unknown to them, the men of 3 Platoon were actually sitting next door to thirteen Argentine soldiers, who were taking cover from their own shell-fire. Only later in the morning were they found and taken prisoner.

In B Company, the state of Privates Carroll and Philpott of 5 Platoon was a cause for concern, since both were now suffering from hypothermia after being immersed in one of the ponds. Their section commander, Corporal Steve Curtis, decided to tell the platoon commander. As he ran out into the shelling, a round exploded close by, shredding his clothes almost completely yet, amazingly, leaving him unharmed.

The mortar teams had been busy all night. By now they had moved on to the side of the A and B Company hill to avoid shelling, which had been uncomfortably close at their first position in the bottom of the valley to the north. Improvised bins had helped to reduce the tendency of the mortar tubes to bed into the soft peat, although not completely, and another problem was that tubes would at times actually slip out of their base-plates under recoil. To prevent this, mortarmen took turns to stand on the base-plates as the tubes were fired, and by the end of the night four men had suffered broken ankles for their efforts. The fire they had been able to provide was very effective, however, and all concerned had been determined that, this time, there would be no question of running short of ammunition or of being out of range. The 3 Para mortars on Longdon did sterling work providing illumination.

The Machine-Gun Platoons, too, had been hard at work, their six guns providing intense heavy fire throughout the night. Resupplied by the tanks and by the splendid work of WO2 Grace's Pioneer Platoon, they had had no worries about ammunition. But gradually the guns broke down, and by dawn only two of the six were still in action.

In Battalion Headquarters the second-in-command, the Operations Officer and Captain David Constance had taken turns at duty officer. At one point the second-in-command, Major Keeble, had been able to see the flashes of the enemy 155-mm guns as they fired, but no amount of reporting back produced any countermeasures. Once the drone of a low-flying Argentine Canberra jet was heard, and amidst the din of artillery even larger thuds reverberated as the aircraft dropped its bombs. Private Steele of the Defence Platoon was unlucky: as he lay on the ground a piece of shrapnel caught him in the back. He hardly felt it, thinking that it was only a piece of turf from the explosion – only later did he discover a rather nasty wound where the metal had penetrated.

The CO's party had not escaped either. A stray round hit Private McLoughlin, a member of the Battery Commander's group, and actually penetrated his helmet at the front. The helmet deflected the round, however, and McLoughlin walked away unharmed.

The snipers were in great demand. Their night-sights enabled them to identify the enemy infra-red sights and to use the signature that then appeared in the image itensifier as an aiming-mark. The Commando Sappers had had a relatively minor role to play in the battle, since there were no mines that it was imperative to clear. But, as at Goose Green, they provided a very useful addition when acting as infantry.

On Wireless Ridge at first light, 12 Platoon was still being sniped at from behind and to the right. Further back along the ridge, Corporal Owen had searched a command post. While rummaging in the bunker, he found a map showing all the details of the Argentine positions, as well as some patrol reports. These were quickly dispatched to Company Headquarters and on to Brigade.

Private Ferguson, in Owen's section, suddenly noticed four or five men below them. The corporal was uncertain as to who they could be – possibly 12 Platoon – and told Ferguson to challenge. The latter yelled "Who's there!", and was instantly greeted with a burst of fire that left them in no doubt. Grenades started to explode around Owen and his men as the enemy counter-attacked. The section opened fire, and Corporal Owen shouted for the machine-guns to engage.

10 Platoon meanwhile were firing on either side of the section, and Owen himself blasted away with eight M-79 rounds. The section was soon short of ammunition, and the men began to ferret for abandoned Argentine supplies. Just then the remainder of the platoon moved up to join the section; though uncertain as to exactly where the enemy were, they were determined to prevent the Argentines from regaining the ridge.

Private Lambert heard an Argentine, close in, shouting, "Grenado, grenado!"

"What a good idea," he thought, and lobbed one of his own in the direction of the voice. There were no more shouts.

11 Platoon also saw a group of four men to its front. 2nd Lieutenant Chris Waddington was unable to make out who they were and, thinking they might be 10 Platoon, shouted to them to stop. The four men took no notice, so he ordered a flare to be put up – the figures ran off as the platoon engaged with small arms and grenades. The orders not to exploit beyond the ridge-line meant that not all the enemy positions had been cleared during the night, and it seemed that some stay-behind

snipers had been left there, and it was probably these that had given 12 Platoon so much trouble. But the counter-attack, such as it was, had fizzled out. Artillery fire was called down on Moody Brook to break up any further efforts at dislodging D Company. Down below the ridge a Landrover could be seen trying to get away. Lance-Corporal Walker fired at it and it crashed.

11 Platoon now came under extremely accurate enemy artillery fire, possibly registered on the flashes of their weapons. Major Neame therefore ordered them to cease firing with small arms, intending to continue the battle with artillery alone. Moody Brook was deserted, however. In the distance the men of D Company noticed two Argentine soldiers walking off down the track as if at the end of an exercise.

In the light of dawn it appeared to the Paras on the ridge that a large number of enemy troops were moving up to reinforce Sapper Hill to the south-east. Neame called for artillery with great urgency, but no guns were available. After a further twenty minutes or so, by which time the enemy had reached the top, the target was engaged. Meanwhile other Argentines could be seen streaming off Tumbledown and Harriet – 5 Brigade had won its battles.

As D Company began to engage this new target the CO arrived. He confirmed Neame's orders to fire on the enemy retiring towards Stanley, and the company now joined in with machine-guns in a "turkey shoot". John Greenhalgh's helicopters swept in and fired SS-11 rockets and, together with two other Scouts, attacked an Argentine battery. The enemy AA was still active, however, and all the helicopters withdrew.

The retiring Argentines on Tumbledown had made no reply to the helicopters, and their artillery had stopped. It was obvious that a major change had occurred. The news was relayed to the Brigadier, who found it difficult to believe what was happening. But the CO realised how vital it was to get the battalion moving into Stanley before the enemy could rally, and A and B Companies, together with the Blues and Royals, were ordered to move as fast as possible up on to Wireless Ridge. The Brigadier arrived, still disbelieving until

Colonel Chaundler said, "It's OK, Brigadier, it's all over."
Together they conferred as to what to do next. D Company
ceased firing on the fleeing enemy on the far hillside, and the
order was given that men were only to fire if fired upon first.
Permission was then given for the battalion to move on.

B Company, by now on the ridge, was ordered down into
Moody Brook. Corporal Connors's section of 5 Platoon led
the way, still expecting to come under fire from the "Triple
As" on the race-course. The other two sections covered him
forward. He cleared the flattened buildings of the old barracks
and Curtis's section took over, clearing the bridge over the
Murrell River and the building on the other side, while all
the time their platoon commander was exhorted, "Push on,
push on!" They remained cautious, fearing booby traps or a
sudden burst of fire.

A Company now took the lead as B Company, covering A's
advance, moved south on to the high ground on the far side of
the valley, above the road, passing through three abandoned
gun positions on the way. The tanks of the Blues and Royals
moved east along Wireless Ridge to give support if it should be
necessary. A Company was well on the way down the road into
Stanley, with C and D Companies following, when Brigade
announced a cease-fire. Cheers went up, and red berets
quickly replaced steel helmets. Bottles of alcohol miraculously
appeared to celebrate with. Relief, elation, disbelief – all in
turn had their effect.

Major Dair Farrar-Hockley led his men towards the race-
course, past the abandoned guns that had been spotted so
many hours earlier yet had remained operational in spite of
requests for artillery fire. According to civilians afterwards,
the Argentines still on the outskirts of Stanley simply broke
and ran when they heard that "the Paras" were coming.
The leading elements of the battalion arrived in Stanley at
1330 hours, on Monday, 14 June some five hours before the
official cease-fire, with 2nd Lieutenant Mark Coe's 2 Platoon
the first into the town. They were the first British troops into
the capital.

Eventually all the companies were brought into the western
outskirts, finding shelter amongst the deserted houses, a few

of which had suffered from stray shells. One or two dead Argentine soldiers still lay in the street where they had been caught by shell-fire. On the race-course the Argentine flag was pulled down and Sergeant-Major Fenwick's Union Jack once more served its purpose.

THE SEA DEVILS
J. Valerio Borghese

Without doubt the most effective Italian special unit of WWII was the Underwater Division of the 10th MAS (motor torpedo boat) Flotilla, the pioneers of the manned or "human" torpedo. First developed by Sub-Lieutenants Tesei and Toschi of the Italian Navy in 1936, the human torpedo was an electric underwater chariot – ridden by a crew of two frogmen – with an explosive warhead, which was detached and clamped to the hulls of enemy ships by means of magnets.

Initially, 10th MAS operations with the human torpedo were dogged by ill-luck and equipment malfunction, but in September 1941 the unit succeeded in spectacularly sinking two British naval tankers and a cargo ship carrying high-explosives at Gibraltar.

Yet the Gibraltar raid, though a tonic for the Italian Navy after the defeats at Taranto and Cape Matapan, was but a prelude to the 10th MAS's next exploit, the attack on the British Mediterranean fleet at Alexandria Harbour, 18–19 December 1941. The event is described below in an extract from Sea Devils, *the autobiography of Count Julio Valerio Borghese, the onetime head of the Underwater Division of the 10th MAS. In the attack itself Borghese commanded the submarine which transported the human torpedoes to the target area.*

THE OPERATION AGAINST Alexandria was most carefully thought out. The most important requirement was the maintenance of absolute secrecy, that indispensable co-efficient of success in any action, and particularly in those where the vulnerability of a handful of half-naked men, plunged underwater in the dark depths of an enemy harbour, had to overcome armour-plates, barriers and a hundred methods of watching for and spotting them, and also thousands of people on dry land, operating from cover and behind defences on mole and ships, whose business it was to discover and destroy the assailant.

Wide use was made of air reconnaissance for the obtaining of information and photographs with a view to keeping us informed about the usual moorings of vessels and the nature of the protective measures employed (net obstructions, etc.). Great care was also taken in preparing materials: the human torpedoes, which were now in good shape, as had been verified during the last mission to Gibraltar, were brought to the highest level of efficiency.

The *Scirè* was again appointed to carry out the approach. Her gallant crew, now thoroughly accustomed to such experiences, remained unchanged. All its members, after their usual period of rest in the Alto Adige, were in excellent physical trim.

The senior group of pilots had been given a long training by myself in carrying out exercises similar to the performances they would have to accomplish at Alexandria (they were, however, not told the final object of the courses and defence negotiating they were ordered to do). In other words, practice took place at night in the actual conditions prevalent in the enemy harbour, their difficulties being, wherever possible, increased. Thus, while the operators were being trained to economize their strength in view of the prolonged and difficult nature of the assigned task, we ourselves were obtaining the data necessary for the study of the plan of operations and had the opportunity of verifying, as if we had made a survey on the spot, the methods to be adopted for the job, the periods required to complete the various stages and the precautions needed to circumvent difficulties and elude enemy detection, as well as, lastly, to check the degrees of skill acquired by individual operators.

One day we called them all together; Forza made the following very brief speech to them: "Now, boys, we want three crews for an operation in the very near future; all I can tell you about it is that it differs from the Gibraltar operations in the fact that return from it is extremely problematical. Is there anyone who would like to take part in it?" Without an instant's hesitation they all volunteered. Accordingly, we of the Command had the delicate task of making a selection. Finally, the crews were as follows: Lieutenant Luigi Durand de la Penne and P.O./diver Emilio Vianchi; Engineer Captain Antonio Marceglia and P.O./diver Spartaco Schergat; Gunner Captain Vincenzo Martellotta and P.O./diver Mario Marino.

These men were chosen because they were the pick of the bunch. De la Penne, leader of the group, was a veteran of the previous missions to Gibraltar and the rest were all equally vigorous, steady and resolute fellows, in mind as in body. It was pure chance that the three officers represented three different services of the Navy: deck, engines and guns.

The reserve crew consisted of Surgeon Sub-Lieutenant Spaccarelli and Engineer Lieutenant Feltrinelli, both belonging to a lower age group than the others but equally keen.

The usual instructions were given: absolute secrecy was to be maintained without exception for anyone, whether comrades, superior officers or, naturally, relatives; training, now openly designed for this particular operation, was to be intensified; each man's private affairs were to be settled in view of his imminent departure for a length of time which could not be foreseen; at worst, it might be for ever, at best there would be some years of imprisonment.

Meanwhile, all the wheels of the machine began to go round. This kind of operation, if it were to have any decent chance of success, had to be thought out to the last detail; the whole of an extensive organization had to be got ready; there were a thousand details to be studied and put into practice: from the collection of hydrographic and meteorological data to intelligence as to enemy vigilance; from the taking of aerial photographs of the harbour to the arrangement of safe and extremely rapid channels of radio liaison with the submarine, so that the latter could be informed, immediately before the operators were dropped, as to the number and disposition of units on the night of the operation; from the determination of suitable ciphers to getting materials ready for action; from composition of the series of operational orders to the training of operators so as to bring them to the maximum of physical efficiency by the pre-arranged day; from the study of navigation and the best routes of approach for the submarine and those for the forcing of the harbour by the pilots, to research on new devices for causing the enemy maximum damage should the occasion arise; in a word, the proceedings were exactly the opposite of what the phrase "assault craft" might be supposed to mean; there was to be nothing in the nature of making a dash, nothing was to be left to chance, all impulsiveness was to be held in check; on the contrary, everything was to be coolly calculated and every technical and ingenious resource was to be exploited to the fullest extent possible.

During this preparatory phase, we were afflicted by the grievous loss of a valued collaborator; this was Lieutenant Sogos, belonging to the Command of the Tenth. While he was in transit to Athens for consultation with the military authorities there, his young and promising life was cut short by a wretched traffic accident.

At last the time came to start. On the 3rd of December the *Scirè* left La Spezia, ostensibly on an ordinary cruise, so as not to arouse curiosity among the crews of the other submarines at the base.

My gallant, steady and reliable crew neither knew nor wished to know where we were going, so as not to be burdened with a secret which, like all secrets, would be difficult to keep; they only knew that we were on another dangerous operation, perhaps as dangerous as the former ones, perhaps more so; they had confidence in their commander and in their vessel, to which each of them had devoted every care during the period of preparation, knowing well that it was on the proper functioning of the elements of which it was composed that the outcome of the venture, its success and the very lives of all aboard depended.

We had scarcely left harbour, at twilight, so as to elude any indiscreet watchers, when a lighter approached us; it was carrying the human torpedoes 221, 222 and 223, which had just left the works at San Bartolomeo in the pink of condition, as well as the operators' clothing and breathing sets; such was the slight equipment necessary to transform three pairs of men into three engines of destruction.

The operators checked over their craft with a sort of tender solicitude. Each possessed his own; he had done his training with it and knew its good points, its shortcomings and its caprices; he placed it in the appropriate cylinder (de la Penne's was forward, those of Marceglia and Martellotta astern), settling it in such a way as to avoid risking shocks and injury to it. Finally, late at night, everything was fixed to rights; we took leave of the lads, who would rejoin us at the last moment by 'plane, and set out, hugging Tino Island, along the safety route through the minefields. It was 2300 hours on the 3rd of December, 1941. "Operation EA 3", the third attempt of the Tenth Light Flotilla against Alexandria and the ships of the British Eastern Mediterranean Fleet, had begun.

We proceeded normally along the courses set until we made the Sicilian coast; here a curious episode occurred which is worth relating. The Cape Pelorias signal station sent out a Donath (nocturnal signalling lamp) message in clear: "Submarine *Scirè*." A piece of madness! Did they want everyone to know that the *Scirè*, the only submarine in the Italian Navy equipped to carry assault craft, was at sea? Not much of a secret, apparently, though such trouble had been taken to keep it! Off the San Ranieri (Messina) lighthouse a launch belonging to the Naval Command approached us. I was handed an envelope; we immediately resumed navigation. The note was from the Supreme Naval Command informing me of the position of the allied vessels then at sea in case I met them. And the Messina Naval Command told me that an enemy submarine had been seen a few hours before close to Cape dell'Armi, firing torpedoes at one of our convoys.

I had, in fact, to pass near Cape dell'Armi; I decided to give it a wide berth and cruised along the coast of Sicily as far as Taormina. There I sighted a submarine which appeared to be motionless. I kept my bows turned towards it (one can never take too many precautions) and signalled it. I couldn't make head or tail of the answer: the vessel was clearly one of the enemy's. The situation being what it was, both of us being surfaced and visible to each other (it was a bright moonlight night), and considering my orders and my special task, as well, finally, as the fact that my adversary had two guns and I had none, I sent a signal to the Messina Naval Command that I had seen an enemy vessel and continued straight on my course towards the Eastern Mediterranean. And the enemy submarine? Well, she started off on a course parallel to my own! We proceeded in this way, side by side, with about 3000 metres between us, like the best of friends, for about an hour; after this, the other submarine, as unexpectedly as it had joined me, left me to myself and turned back towards Taormina. Strange things happen at sea in time of war! The next day we encountered a melancholy spectacle. We were passing through waters strewn with wreckage and flotsam of every description, including many life-belts; one of our convoys had been surprised during the past few days. On the 9th we reached Leros and entered Port Lago, which I knew well, having made a long stay there, years before, while in charge of the *Iride*. It is a magnificent natural inlet, protected on three sides by high, rocky mountains, while on the other lies a pleasant little village, built entirely during the last few years, with its inn, church and town hall; it looked like a corner of Italy transferred to this Aegean island. I moored at the pier outside the submarine barracks; and was at once visited by Spigai, a career colleague of mine, in command of the 5th Submarine Flotilla at Leros. He put himself at my disposal with the affection of a good comrade. The first thing I did was to cover the *Scirè*'s cylinders with enormous tarpaulins; we were ostensibly a submarine belonging to another base which had put in here on account of serious damage sustained while fighting and was in need of prolonged repairs. Leros was full of Greeks and no precaution could be excessive. Six technicians flown from Italy for the purpose proceeded, meanwhile, to give the "pigs" a final check-over.

On the 12th, the 10 operators arrived, also by air. To keep them out of sight, they were given quarters in the transport *Asmara*, which was moored in the deserted bay of Parteni, at the opposite end of the island; the same anchorage had been used by Faggioni's detachment and the Suda *E*-boats. The lads spent the last few hours before their operation in the peace and quiet of that isolated roadstead, with nothing to distract them and no dangers to be encountered; on the 13th, I paid them a visit and we studied the operational plan in detail, also examining the latest aerial photographs of the harbour and the data I had been receiving (only very few messages up to now); we also gossiped a little, possibly to distract our minds for a while from the subject on which we had been concentrating our whole attention for the last month.

Admiral Biancheri, Commander-in-Chief of the Aegean naval sector, arrived at Leros from Rhodes. He wanted us to carry out exercises and tests in his presence, there and then, at Port Lago! I took advantage of my orders giving me full authority during the operation to decline the invitation. The admiral expressed his disappointment and his convinced opinion that "we shan't do any good if we cut training short".

I could not lose time. The favourable lunar phase had begun, the nights being absolutely dark; weather reports were good. I resolved to start on the 14th of December. I kept in continuous touch with Forza, who had gone to Athens on the 9th to take charge of and co-ordinate air reconnaissance services, intelligence reports, the issue of weather bulletins and radio liaison with the *Scirè*.

The plan of operations provided for the arrival of the *Scirè* on a certain evening, a few thousand metres from the entrance to Alexandria harbour; as it was assumed that everything would be in darkness (owing to the black-out), it had been arranged that, in order to facilitate the submarine's landfall, the coast being low-lying and without conspicuous features, and to allow her to identify the harbour (for the success of the operators' raid would depend largely on the precision with which the point of their release was determined), on the evening before, and also on the one of the action, our aircraft would bomb the harbour. The submarine would then release the operators. The latter, proceeding on courses laid down beforehand, as soon as they arrived in front of the harbour, would have to overcome the obstructions and attack the targets previously assigned to them by the commander of the *Scirè*, who would base his orders on the latest data transmitted to him by radio. After attaching the charges to the hulls of the targets, the operators were to lay a certain number of floating incendiary bombs with which they had been supplied. These bombs would go off about an hour after the warheads had exploded and were intended to set alight the oil which would by then have spread from the ships which had been attacked; it was expected that this would cause fire to break out in the harbour, affecting all the vessels therein, together with the floating docks, the harbour installations and the warehouses . . .; thus putting the chief enemy naval base in the Eastern Mediterranean utterly out of action.

The *Scirè*, directly the operators had been dropped, was to start back. The pilots had been told which zones of the interior of the harbour were considered the least vigilantly watched, where they were to land on conclusion of the operation and what routes they were to take to get clear of the harbour area in the shortest possible time. Plans had also been laid for their rescue: on the days following the action the submarine *Zaffiro* (commanded by Giovanni Lombardi) would shuttle for two consecutive nights 10 miles off Rosetta in the Nile delta; such operators as eluded immediate capture would be able to reach her by any boat they could find on the coast.

The *Scirè*, with the pilots aboard, left Leros on the morning of the 14th. She proceeded without incident and, so to speak, in secret; by day we submerged, surfacing only at night, to charge the batteries and freshen up the atmosphere aboard. The task of the *Scirè* was, as usual, to find a method of getting as close as possible to the enemy harbour, without arousing prohibitive alarm or allowing her presence to be suspected. Discovery would mean arousing anti-submarine measures; a remorseless pursuit would begin, which would prevent us from carrying out the operation. We therefore took the strictest precautions. And as we might be detected by hydrophones as a result of normal sounds aboard the submarine, we had to proceed noiselessly, muffling the machinery. The intelligence we had received on setting out was to the effect that Alexandria harbour was surrounded, like all other harbours in time of war, by minefields. To quote the report: "*Fixed and mobile defences ascertained*: (a) minefield 20 miles NW of harbour; (b) line of 'lobster-pots' arranged at a depth of 30 fathoms in a circle with a radius of about six miles; (c) line of detector cables closer in; (d) groups of 'lobster-pots' in known positions; (e)

net barriers relatively easy to force; (f) advanced observation
line beyond minefield."

How could all these dangers be circumvented? How could
the minefields be evaded if we did not know the security routes?
Or the "lobster-pots"? Or the detector cables?

In order to reach the target we were obliged, after a certain
stage, to trust to luck; there was nothing else to do. But luck
can be "assisted", especially when the matter in hand is a
complex one. I had therefore decided that, as soon as we
reached a depth of 400 metres (which would probably be
where the minefields started), we would proceed at a depth of
not less than 60 metres, since I assumed that the mines, even
if they were anti-submarine, would be located at a higher level;
if the submarine should then collide with one of the mooring
cables, I felt sure that the latter would slide along her sides,
which were accurately streamlined and carefully cleared of
all adherent matter, without getting caught up anywhere, till
it fell harmlessly astern. There was nothing else I could do
to elude the peril of the mines, except, naturally, to trust
to luck.

The other difficulty was that of taking the submarine to
the *precise* point prearranged; in other words, to navigate with
the exactitude of a draughtsman working with compass and
ruler, despite the drifting caused by underwater currents,
which are always difficult to deal with, and despite, above
all, the impossibility of ascertaining one's position from the
moment when, at dawn of the day appointed for the operation,
the submarine would be obliged to submerge (so as not to
be detected from the enemy base) and proceed at a great
depth (to avoid mines), until the time came to release the
operators.

The solution of this problem of underwater navigation
cannot be reached without perfect control of the speed of
the vessel; the course has to be laid and kept to with great
precision (so as to eliminate errors due to faulty steering) and
finally position has to be determined from variations in depth
quota, the only hydrographic factor which can be ascertained
in a submerged submarine; here we are in a sphere closer to
that of art than to the science of navigation.

Everyone aboard gave me effective help, officers, petty officers and seamen. Each man, in his own special department, took care that his services should be regularly maintained and that his machinery should function in such a way as to prevent any unforeseen accident which might compromise the success of the operation.

Ursano, my second-in-command, had the general supervision of routine aboard; Benini and Olcese, the two efficient navigation officers, helped me in following the course and with the tricky business of dealing with codes and communication; while Tajer, the chief engineer, regulated the performance of the machinery (engines, electric batteries, air supply, etc.) and kept the respective services in order. The petty officers were first-rate: Ravera was chief mechanic, Farina chief torpedo-gunner, and Rapetti chief electrician; the wireless operators kept us in continuous touch with Rome and Athens; all were praise worthy in the discharge of their various duties. Last but not least there was the cook (a seaman to whom this task had been allotted; he was a mason in civil life) who became the martyr aboard; he was on his feet 24 hours out of 24 at the tiny, red-hot electric stoves, whatever the sea was like, concocting from dry rations dishes to satisfy the tastes and digestions of 60 people, as well as hot drinks for those on night watch and solid meals to keep up the spirits of the operators.

The latter, meanwhile, in perfect serenity (for the die was now cast) stored up their energy by resting. De la Penne, with his big fair head of rumpled hair, was generally to be found lying in his bunk asleep. Even as he slumbered he would every now and then stretch out an arm, put his hand into a drawer and extract a large fruit cake, which he ate up at a great rate. Then he would blissfully turn over and go back to his dreams.

Martellotta, permanently in good spirits, occupied another bunk. "Peace and good will!" was his invariable greeting; a heartening phrase. Marceglia, a giant of a man, with a tranquil temperament and something stately about him, was absorbed in study: his *basso profondo* tones were rarely heard and, when they were, it was to make some technical request or utter some comment on the operation. Feltrinelli, Bianchi, Marino, Schergat, Favale and Memoli all managed to find acceptable accommodation among the ship's equipment and spent their days in unbroken repose, only interrupted for the necessary more than substantial meals.

Public health was in the hands of Spaccarelli, surgeon, diver and reserve crew leader; every day he put the pilots through a thorough medical examination; it was essential to have them in the pink of condition on the day of the operation, which was now at hand.

The pilots remained very calm: the difficulties and dangers of which they were naturally well aware did not make them uneasy but merely increased their determination; anxiety and strain were inevitable, but did not find expression; talk went on at the ordinary level of cheerful tranquillity characteristic of life aboard; there were periods of gay hilarity, when facetious repartees were exchanged.

They were really extraordinary fellows, those lads; they were about to undertake action which would require the exploitation of their whole physical and moral energy and put their lives in peril at every moment, hour after hour; it would be a mission from which, *at best*, they could only hope to emerge as prisoners of war, and yet they preserved the attitude of a team of sportsmen off to play their customary Sunday game.

Meanwhile the *Scirè* encountered, on the 16th of December, a heavy storm.

In order to avoid exposing materials, and above all our operators, to excessive strain, I remained submerged even at night, the moment our supplies of air and electricity had been taken in.

The same day I wrote:

In consequence of the bad weather and the lack of exact information as to the number and size of the enemy units in harbour, I decided to postpone the operation for 24 hours from the night of the 17th/18th to that of the 18th/19th. (From my official report.)

On the 17th of December I added:

In view of the ship's position and the favourable weather conditions I decided that the operation should take place on the evening of the 18th, hoping that I should meanwhile receive precise intelligence regarding the presence of vessels in harbour.

This was a hope that was soon realized. The same evening we obtained at last, to our great delight, confirmation from Athens that both the two battleships were at Alexandria.

The word was now: forward! Throughout the day, on the 18th, the *Scirè* proceeded through a zone which we presumed to be mined, at a depth of 60 metres, over bottoms which rose rapidly as we approached the coast, till we slipped over them like a silent and invisible tank, "continually regulating our movements in accordance with the rise of the sea-bed, till at 1840 hours we found ourselves at the prearranged point, 1.3 miles by 356° from the lighthouse at the west mole of the commercial harbour of Alexandria, at a depth of 15 metres".

Preparations were made for release of the operators. As soon as I had discovered, by a survey taken through the periscope, that the darkness was complete, I surfaced just sufficiently to enable the trapdoor to be opened ("outcrop level", as it is technically known) and came out on the conning tower. The weather was perfect: it was pitch-dark; the sea very smooth and the sky unclouded. Alexandria was right ahead of me, very close. I identified some of its characteristic buildings and determined my position; to my great satisfaction I found that we were within a metre of the pre-arranged point. This was an exceptional result after 16 hours of blind navigation! Immediately afterwards, with the pilots wrapped in their rubber suits and wearing their breathing sets, the ceremony of leave-taking began; we neither spoke nor embraced one another: "Commander," was all they said, "give us the good-luck kick, will you?" And with this strange rite, into which I put all I knew, so that my good wishes might be evident, the farewell ceremony terminated.

The first to go up were the two leaders of the reserve crews,

Feltrinelli and Spaccarelli. Their job was to open the cylinder doors, to save the operators the fatigue of doing so.

One by one, de la Penne and Bianchi, Marceglia and Schergat, Martellotta and Marino, covered from head to foot in their black suits, their movements encumbered by their breathing gear, went up the ladder and disappeared into the darkness of the night and the sea. I submerged to the bottom.

A few minutes later the hydrophones told us that the three crews were on their way. "God be with them," I prayed, "and speed them well!"

Inside the submarine we waited for the sounds of blows struck against the deck, the agreed signal to be made when the doors of the cylinders, now empty, had been closed and the reserves were ready to be taken aboard again. When at last we heard them, I surfaced. Feltrinelli told me, in a voice broken by emotion, that as he could see no sign of Spaccarelli, he had gone astern to look for him: by pure chance he had stumbled against something soft on deck; he had discovered by groping (for we must not forget that the scene took place underwater at night) that it was the missing Spaccarelli, who seemed lifeless. I instantly sent up two other divers, who had been kept ready for any emergency; Spaccarelli was lifted up and lowered down the ladder into the interior of the submarine. I descended to the bottom again and began to head for home, following precisely the same course which had proved to be safe during my approach.

The unfortunate Spaccarelli was forthwith relieved of his mask, breathing set and diver's suit and put to bed; he was quite blue in the face, his pulse was imperceptible and he was not breathing; he showed every normal symptom of having been drowned.

What was to be done? The mission's surgeon was not much use to us in this extremity, for he himself was the victim. I arranged for two men to give him continuous artificial respiration; I rummaged in the medicine chest and had him injected with the contents of all the phials that, judging from the description of the ingredients, seemed capable of exercising a stimulating action on the heart and circulation; others gave him oxygen (the air aboard was emphatically unsuitable in this case); all the resources of our extremely slender store of medicaments and of our still slenderer knowledge of medicine were brought into play in the attempt to achieve what appeared to be an utter impossibility, the resuscitation of a dead man.

Meanwhile the *Scirè*, with this dramatic episode taking place aboard her, slipped along the sea-bed, further and further away from Alexandria. We took care not to reveal our presence in any way; discovery would have been fatal to the six adventurous lads who were at that very moment engaged in the crucial phase of the operation. But the submarine was not responding very well to my directions: the cylinder doors astern had been left open, a circumstance which made it difficult for me to keep my depth and maintain trim. As soon as we were some miles from the coast I surfaced to close them. I noticed that the Ras el Tin Lighthouse was functioning; a number of lights which I had not seen before showed at the entrance to the harbour; units were evidently going in or out; I hoped the operators would be able to take advantage of the fact. As for the cylinders, I found that they could not be closed on account of damage to one of the doors.

I continued on my course of withdrawal, remaining submerged, for the zone we were now crossing had been notified as constituting the minefield. After three and a half hours' continuous artificial respiration, a number of injections and some applications of oxygen, our surgeon, who had till then shown not the smallest sign of life, drew his first wheezing breath; it was a deep, hoarse sound, resembling a death-rattle. But it meant he was alive and we could save him! A few hours later, in fact, though his condition was still serious, he got back the use of his voice and was able to tell us that while he was making a terrific effort to close the starboard cylinder door, which stubbornly resisted every attempt he made, the effects of the oxygen he was breathing and those of water pressure at the depth involved had caused him to faint; luckily he fell on deck and did not slip overboard, as might very easily have happened, for there were no rails or bulwarks to the vessel (they had been removed to prevent the mine-cables from catching on them).

At last, on the evening of the 19th, since we were now presumably clear of the minefields, the *Scirè* surfaced, after 39 hours of submersion, and set course for Leros. On the evening of the 20th we received the following wireless communication from the Naval Supreme Command: "Photographic reconnaissance indicates two battleships hit." There was great enthusiasm aboard; no one had doubted it would be a success, but to have our expectations confirmed so soon gave us great satisfaction.

On the evening of the 21st, as soon as we had docked at Port Lago, we took Spaccarelli ashore to the local naval hospital. He was now out of danger but still required a good deal of attention in consequence of the severe shock he had experienced.

The return of the *Scirè* from Leros to La Spezia proceeded without any notable incidents, except that on Christmas Day, while the submarine was off Bengazi and the crew were listening to the Pope's speech on the loudspeaker, an aircraft of unidentified nationality came a little too close to the vessel and got within range of our four 13.2 machine-guns; the natural retaliation was the dropping of five bombs about 80 metres astern of us, which did no damage. Our Christmas pies!

On the 29th of December the *Scirè* arrived at La Spezia. Admiral Bacci, now chief of the North Tyrrhenean Sector, was waiting for us, on the pier; he brought us greetings and congratulations from Admiral Riccardi, Under Secretary of State for the Navy.

I was glad of this tribute to my gallant crew, who had worked so hard, with such efficiency and courage, in bringing our submarine back to harbour after 27 days of operational service, 22 of them at sea, and had covered without mishap 3500 miles, thus contributing to a great victory for Italy.

How had it fared with the operators, whom we had left in the open sea, outside Alexandria harbour, astride their fragile torpedoes, plunged beneath the waves in the darkness of night, surrounded by enemies in ambush? The three crews had left

the submarine in company and commenced approach along
the pre-arranged routes.

The sea was very calm, the night dark. Lights in the harbour
permitted the pilots to determine their position, which they
found to be precisely as planned. They went ahead so coolly
that at one point, as de la Penne relates in his report, "as
we were ahead of schedule, we opened our ration tins and
had a meal. We were then 500 metres from the Ras el Tin
Lighthouse."

At last they reached the net defences at the harbour's
entrance.

> We saw some people at the end of the pier and heard them talking;
> one of them was walking about with a lighted oil-lamp.
>
> We also saw a large motorboat cruising in silence off the
> pier and dropping depth-charges. These charges were rather a
> nuisance to us.

While the six heads, only just above water, were looking,
with all the concentrated attention of which they were capable,
for a gap in the net, three British destroyers suddenly appeared
at the entrance to the harbour, waiting to go in: guide lights
were switched on to show them the way and the net gates
were thrown wide open. Without a second's hesitation our
three assault craft slipped into the harbour with the British
destroyers: they were in! They had lost sight of one another
during this manœuvre, but they were now close to their targets.
The latter had been distributed as follows: de la Penne was
to take the battleship *Valiant*, Marceglia the battleship *Queen
Elizabeth* and Martellotta was to look for the aircraft-carrier;
if she were not in harbour, he was to attack a loaded tanker
in the hope that the oil or petrol which would issue from it
would spread over the water and thus furnish excellent fuel
for the floating incendiary bombs the operators were to scatter
before abandoning their "pigs".

We will now take up the stories of the individual crews.

De La Penne – Bianchi. Inside the harbour, after passing the
interned French warships, the presence of which was well

known, de la Penne sighted, at the presumed anchorage, the huge dark mass of the target assigned to him, the 32,000 ton battleship *Valiant*. As he approached her, he encountered the anti-torpedo net barrier: he got through it *surfaced* "in order to lose as little time as possible, for I found that my physical condition, owing to the cold, would be unlikely to let me hold out much longer". (His diver's suit had been leaking ever since he had left the submarine.) He had no difficulty with negotiation of the net: he was now 30 metres from the *Valiant*; it was 19 minutes past two. He touched the hull, giving it a slight bump; in performing the evolution necessary to get beneath the hull, his "pig" seemed to take on extra weight and went to the bottom in 17 metres of water; de la Penne dived after it and discovered to his amazement that there was no sign of his second pilot. He rose to the surface to look for him, but could not see him; everything was quiet aboard the battleship; no alarm had been given. De la Penne left Bianchi to his fate, returned to the bottom and tried to start the engine of his craft to get it underneath the hull, as it had meanwhile moved some distance away. But the engine would not start; a rapid check-over soon showed what the trouble was: a steel wire had got entangled in the propeller.

What was to be done? All alone, with his craft immobilized on the sea-bed a few metres from the target, de la Penne resolved to try the only possible expedient: this was to drag the "pig" by main force, finding his direction from the compass, beneath the battleship. Speed was essential, for he feared that at any moment the British might pick up his second pilot, who had probably fainted and would be floating about close by . . .; the alarm would be given, depth-charges would be dropped, his operation and those of his companions would be doomed to certain failure, for they would be at work only a few hundred metres away. With all his strength, panting and sweating, he dragged at the craft; his goggles became obscured and the mud he was stirring up prevented his reading the compass, his breath began to come in great gasps and it became difficult to breathe at all through the mask, but he stuck to it and made progress; he could hear, close above him, the noises made aboard the ship, especially the sound of an alternating pump, which he used to find his direction. After 40 minutes of superhuman effort, making a few inches at every pull, he at last bumped his head against the hull. He made a cursory survey of the position: he seemed to be at about the middle of the ship, an excellent spot for causing maximum damage. He was now almost exhausted; but he used the last vestiges of his strength to set the time fuses; in accordance with the orders he had received he regulated them so as to cause the explosion at five o'clock precisely (Italian time, corresponding with six o'clock local time). He did not release his incendiary bombs, for when they rose to the surface they would reveal the presence and the position of the threat now established under the hull with the fuses in action. He left his craft on the sea-bed under the vessel and swam to the surface. The moment he got his head above water he removed his mask and sank it; the fresh, pure air revived him; he began to swim slowly away from the ship. But someone called out to him, a searchlight picked him out, a burst of machine-gun fire brought him to a halt. He swam back towards the vessel and climbed out of the water on to the mooring-buoy at the bows of the *Valiant*. He found there his second pilot Bianchi, who, after fainting, had risen to the surface like a balloon and on regaining consciousness had hidden himself on the buoy so as not risk causing an alarm which would have disturbed the work of his leader. "Aboard they were making facetious remarks, believing that our operation had failed; they were talking contemptuously about Italians. I called Bianchi's attention to the probability that in a few hours they would have changed their minds about the Italians." It was then about 3.30. At last a motorboat turned up and the two "shipwrecked" men were picked up by it and taken aboard the battleship. A British officer asked who they were, where they had come from and expressed ironical sympathy with their lack of success. The two operators, who were now prisoners of war, made clear who they were, by handing over their military identity cards. They refused to answer any other questions. They were taken in the motorboat, separated from each other, to a hut ashore, near the Ras el Tin Lighthouse. Bianchi was the first to be cross-examined: on leaving the hut he made a sign to de la Penne indicating that he had said nothing. It was then the latter's turn: naturally, he held his tongue; the Britisher, who had a revolver in his hand, seemed to be an excitable sort of fellow, "I'll soon find a way to make you talk," he said, in excellent Italian. The men were taken back aboard the *Valiant*: it was then four o'clock.

They were received by the commanding officer, Captain Morgan, who asked them where the charge was located. On their refusing to answer, the two men, accompanied by the officer of the watch and escorted by an armed picket, were placed in one of the holds forward, between the two gun-turrets, not very far from the point at which the charge would explode.

We will now let de la Penne take up the tale.

Our escort were rather white about the gills and behaved very nicely to us; they gave me rum to drink and offered me cigarettes; they also tried to make us talk. Bianchi sat down and went to sleep. I perceived from the ribbons on the sailors' caps that we were aboard the battleship *Valiant*. When there were about 10 minutes left before the explosion, I asked if I could speak to the commanding officer. I was taken aft, into his presence. I told him that in a few minutes his ship would blow up, that there was nothing he could do about it and that, if he wished, he could still get his crew into a place of safety. He again asked me where I had placed the charge and as I did not reply had me escorted back to the hold. As we went along I heard the loudspeakers giving orders to abandon ship, as the vessel had been attacked by Italians, and saw people running aft. When I was again in the hold I said to Bianchi, as I came down the ladder, that things had turned out badly and that it was all up with us, but that we could be content, since we had succeeded, in spite of everything, in bringing the operation to a successful conclusion. Bianchi, however, did not answer me. I looked for him and could not find him. I supposed that the British, believing that I had confessed, had removed him. A few minutes passed (they were infernal ones for me: would the explosion take place?) and then it came. The vessel reared, with extreme violence. All the lights went out and the hold became filled with smoke. I was surrounded by shackles which had been hanging from the ceiling and had now fallen. I was unhurt, except for pain in a knee, which had been grazed by one of the shackles in its fall. The vessel was listing to port. I opened one of the port-holes very near sea level, hoping to be able to get through it and escape. This proved to be impossible, as the port-hole was too small, and I gave up the idea: but I left the port open, hoping that through it more water would enter. I waited for a few moments. The hold was now illuminated by the light which entered through the port. I concluded that it would be rash to stay there any longer, noticing that the vessel was now lying on the bottom and continuing slowly to list to port. I climbed up the ladder and, finding the hatchway open, began to walk aft; there was no one about. But there were still many of the crew at the stern. They got up as I passed them; I went on till I reached the Captain. At that moment he was engaged in giving orders for salvaging his ship. I asked him what he had done with my diver. He did not reply and the officer of the watch told me to be silent. The ship had now listed through 4–5 degrees and come to a standstill. I saw from a clock that it was a quarter past six. I went further aft, where a number of officers were standing, and began to watch the battleship *Queen Elizabeth*, which lay about 500 metres astern of us.

The crew of that battleship were standing in her bows. A few seconds passed and then the *Queen Elizabeth*, too, blew up. She rose a few inches out of the water and fragments of iron and other objects flew out of her funnel, mixed with oil which even reached the deck of the *Valiant*, splashing everyone of us standing on her stern. An officer came up and asked me to tell him on my word of honour if there were any other charges under the ship. I made no reply and was then again taken back to the hold. After about a quarter of an hour I was escorted up to the officers' mess, where at last I could sit down, and where I found Bianchi. Shortly afterwards I was put aboard a motor-boat, which took me back to Ras el Tin. I noticed that the anchor, which had been hanging at the bows, was now underwater. During transit an officer asked me whether we had got in through the gaps in the mole. At Ras el Tin we were locked in two cells and kept there until towards evening. I asked whether I could be given a little sunlight, as I was again very cold. A soldier came, felt my pulse and told me that I was perfectly all right.

Towards evening we were put into a small lorry and transported therein to a prisoner-of-war camp in Alexandria. I found some Italians in the camp who had heard the explosions that morning. We lay down on the ground, without having had any food, and, though we were soaked through, we slept till the following morning. I was taken to the infirmary for treatment of my knee injury and some Italian orderlies gave me an excellent dish of macaroni. The next morning I was removed to Cairo. (From the report handed in by Lieutenant Luigi de la Penne on his return from prison.)

In 1944, after de la Penne and Bianchi had come back to Italy from prison, they were awarded the gold medal for gallantry in war. And he who pinned the medal on the chest of de la Penne was none other than Admiral Morgan, formerly commanding officer of the *Valiant* and at that time chief of the allied naval mission in Italy.

Marceglia – Schergat. Approach commenced in company with de la Penne on the pre-arranged course. About midnight they saw the guide lights at the entrance to the harbour switched on; it was clear that units were either going in or coming out. Violent shocks were felt against the casing of the "pig", as though it had crashed against some metallic obstacle, accompanied by strong contraction of the leg muscles of the pilots: these were the effects of depth-charges dropped by the enemy at the entrance to the harbour to prevent "unwelcome visits". As they slipped into the entrance channel they noticed, much to their surprise and satisfaction, that the net gates had been opened. Shortly afterwards, towards one o'clock, they had to take rapid evasive action to avoid being run down by three destroyers which were just coming in. Marceglia resumed the pre-arranged course: "in no time at all found myself face to face with the whole massive bulk of my target." He came upon the anti-torpedo net, got through it and, now that the way was clear, submerged beneath the hull, in line with the funnel. With the aid of his second pilot, Marceglia precisely carried out manoeuvre: he clamped a loop-line connecting the two bilge keels and attached the warhead of his torpedo to the central point of the line, so that it hung about a metre and a half below the hull; then he set the fuse in motion. It was then

3.15 a.m. (Italian time).

I tried to analyse my sensations at that moment. I found that I did not feel particularly thrilled, but only rather tired and just starting to get cold. We got astride our craft again: my diver made me urgent signs to surface, as he was just about all in. I pumped in air to surface; the craft only detached itself from the bottom with difficulty, then at last it started to rise, at first slowly, later more rapidly. So as not to burst out of the water too suddenly, I had to exhaust; the air bubbles attracted the attention of the watch aft. He switched on a searchlight and we surfaced right into its rays. We ducked down on the craft to make the target as small as possible and prevent our goggles from reflecting the light. Shortly afterwards the searchlight was switched off; we started on our return, which took us past the bows of the ship; a man was walking up and down the fo'c'sle deck, I could see his cigarette glowing; everything was quiet aboard. We got out of the obstructed zone and, at last, took off our masks; it was very cold; I couldn't prevent my teeth chattering. We stopped again and began distributing our incendiaries after setting the fuses. (From a report by Engineer Captain Antonio Marceglia.)

They then set off for the spot on which they were to land: it was the area which, according to our maps and intelligence reports, was the least strictly guarded and furnished the most convenient access to the city.

While still some distance from land they set going the fuse of the craft's self-destructor and sank her; they swam ashore, removed their breathing sets and rubber suits, cut everything to pieces and buried the strips under the rocks. Then they waded ashore: it was 4.30 a.m.; they had been in the water exactly eight hours.

Marceglia and Schergat succeeded in leaving the harbour area unobserved. Posing as French sailors, they entered the city of Alexandria; after wandering about for some time, they made their way to the station to take the train for Rosetta and try to rejoin the submarine which would be lying about 10 miles out to sea at certain pre-arranged times, a night or two later. But at this point their troubles began: the sterling with which they were supplied did not circulate in Egypt; they wasted a lot of time trying to get it changed and were not able to leave until the evening. At Rosetta they spent the night in a squalid little inn, hiding from frequent visits by the police; next day, in the evening, they made for the seashore, but were stopped by the Egyptian police, recognized as Italians and turned over to the British naval authorities.

Their attempt to evade capture was thus frustrated.

Marceglia's operation may be characterized as a "perfect" one, meaning by this phrase that it was performed without a hitch at every stage and nothing unforeseen happened. In a letter he wrote me some years later he observed: "As you can see, Sir, our performance had nothing heroic about it; its success was due solely to the preparations made, the specially favourable conditions under which it took place and above all the determination to succeed at all costs."

Preparations, determination and luck were rewarded with the gold medal for gallantry in war, which both Marceglia and Schergat obtained on their release from prison.

Martellotta – Marino. Martellotta writes in his report:

> Aboard the submarine *Scirè* at 1630 on the 18th December 1941, I received from Lieutenant-Commander Borghese the following operational orders: "Attack to be made on a large loaded tanker and six incendiaries to be distributed in its immediate neighbourhood."
>
> The presence which had been notified of 12 loaded tankers in harbour at Alexandria, with a total tonnage of 120,000, was sufficient indication of the importance of the order received: the fire which might be started would be capable of reaching such proportions as to bring about the entire destruction of the harbour itself, with all the units present and all the shore installations.
>
> Nevertheless, I felt obliged to reply: "Sir, I shall obey your orders; but I should like you to know that my diver and I would rather have attacked a warship."
>
> The Captain smiled at this remark of mine and, to please me, since he was aware that there was a possibility of an aircraft-carrier having returned to the harbour, he modified the original operational orders to read: "Search to be made for the aircraft-carrier at its two normal anchorages and attack

to be made on it if found; otherwise, all other targets consisting
of active war units to be ignored and a large loaded tanker to be
attacked with distribution of the six incendiaries in its immediate
neighbourhood."

Martellotta had a certain amount of trouble in opening the
door of the cylinder and asked Spaccarelli to help him (this
was the difficulty which involved Spaccarelli in the adventure
related above); he finally joined the other two crews and
continued approach in their company as far as the entrance
net gate.

I felt shocks from depth-charges and violent pressure against my
legs, as though they were being crushed against the craft by some
heavy object. I put on my mask and, so as to avoid injury from the
frequent shocks being inflicted at vulnerable parts of my body, I
ducked in such a way as to lie low in the water, but with heart,
lungs and head above the surface. I told Marino, my diver, to put
on his mask also and to take up a similar position, but facing aft,
since I was unable myself to keep an eye open in that direction,
engaged as I was in looking ahead and having only the limited
area of visibility which the mask allowed.
    We arrived in these positions at the entrance to the harbour
. . . We did not find obstructions, as we had expected, at the
pier-heads: the channel was clear.
    We went ahead very slowly. Suddenly, my diver, Marino,
thumped me on the shoulder and said: "Hard a-starboard." I
instantly swerved in the direction indicated, putting on speed,
but the craft struck the buoys of the fixed interior barrier, being
driven against them by the waves from the bow of a ship which
had caught me up as it entered the harbour. It was a destroyer,
showing no lights and going at about 10 knots; I distinctly heard
chains clashing at her bows and saw members of the crew on
deck getting ready to moor. It was then 0030 hours on the 19th
December. I got going again and, taking advantage of the waves
made by a second destroyer as it entered the harbour, I slipped
in with it, still surfaced and passing within about 20 metres of
the guardship.

Martellotta, therefore, was now inside the harbour; he

started looking for the aircraft-carrier at its two habitual anchorages; he could not find her (as a matter of fact she was not in harbour that night).

But he did sight a large warship; believing her to be a battleship, he initiated attack; he had already got under her hull when he discovered that she was, on the contrary, a cruiser and with great reluctance, in obedience to orders received, abandoned the attack; just as he was clearing her after-davits he was caught in the rays of a pocket-torch aboard her: some seconds of utter immobility ensued, during which he felt as if even his heart had stopped beating; then the torch went out. He made for the zone of the tankers. Martellotta was now beginning to notice signs of strain: his head ached and he had to vomit; he could no longer keep the mouthpiece of the mask between his lips; he took it off and went ahead surfaced. There were the tankers. "I sighted a large one, heavily loaded, which I guessed to be about 16,000 tons." Not being able to submerge, he decided to carry out the attack from the surface: while Martellotta kept the "pig" under the stern of the tanker, the second pilot, Marino, fastened the charge beneath the hull. By 2.55 the fuse had been set going. While this operation was proceeding, a smaller tanker had come alongside the one under attack.

When Marino rose to the surface and saw her, he said: "Let's hope she stays here another three hours and then she'll have her hash settled too." Next, we started off again, for distribution of the incendiaries: we moored them, after setting their fuses, about 100 metres from the tanker and 20 metres apart.

The operation having been carried out in detail so far, the final stage began: this would be the attempt to escape so as not to fall into the hands of the enemy. They got ashore at the agreed place without incident, destroyed, by way of preventive action, their breathing sets and divers' suits and sank the "pig" after setting the self-destructor fuse. Then they went ashore.

I set off with Marino to get clear of the harbour zone and enter the city: we were stopped at a control point and arrested by some Egyptian customs officials and police, who summoned a second lieutenant and six privates of the British Marines. We were taken to an office occupied by two lieutenants of the Egyptian police, who started cross-examining us; while I was answering the questions put to me in as evasive and vague a manner as I could, a British naval commander arrived and requested the senior of the two Egyptian officers to hand us over to the British. The Egyptian refused to do so in the absence of any authority from his Government, pointing out that, as he had found us to be Italians from the documents we carried and Egypt was not at war with Italy, he would have to get special instructions.

The British Commander, after obtaining the necessary authorization from his Admiral, made a personal application to the Egyptian Government for the instructions required and succeeded in getting us handed over.

My waterproof watch was on the table with the other articles taken possession of and I never took my eyes off it. Shortly after 5.54 a.m. a violent explosion was heard, which shook the whole building. A few minutes later, as we were getting into a car to follow the British officer, a second explosion was heard, further away, and after the car had started a third. At the Ras el Tin naval headquarters we were briefly interrogated, courteously enough, and then despatched to the concentration camp for prisoners of war at Cairo. (From the report of Gunner Captain Vincenzo Martellotta.)

Martellotta and Marino, on their release from captivity, were also awarded the gold medal for gallantry in war.

The Italian War Bulletin N. 585 of the 8th of January, 1942, gives the following account of the success of the operation:

On the night of the 18th December assault craft of the Italian Royal Navy entered the harbour of Alexandria and attacked two British battleships anchored there. It has only just been confirmed that a battleship of the *Valiant* class was seriously damaged and put into dock for repairs, and is still there.

The following Bulletin, N. 586 of the 9th of January, rounds off the information as follows:

In the operation conducted by assault craft of the Italian Royal

Navy in the harbour of Alexandria and reported in yesterday's Bulletin we now have definite further intelligence that, in addition to the *Valiant*, a second battleship of the *Barham* class was also damaged.

Such was the modest announcement of a naval victory unparalleled throughout the war for precision of execution and importance of strategic results. At the cost of six men captured, there had been sunk, in addition to a large tanker, two 32,000 ton battleships, the last of those at the disposal of the British in the Mediterranean. Crippled by the charges applied to their hulls by the daring members of the Tenth Light Flotilla, the vessels were at a later date, after much expenditure of energy and materials, refloated, patched up for the time being and then transferred to quiet and distant yards for refit: but they made no further contribution to the war and immediately after the cessation of hostilities they were removed for demolition.

The losses of the *Valiant* and the *Queen Elizabeth*, following those of the *Ark Royal* and the *Barham* in the Mediterranean and almost contemporaneous with the destruction of the *Repulse* and the extremely recent *Prince of Wales* in Indonesia at the hands of Japanese aviators, brought about a most critical situation for the British Navy, which was only retrieved after a long lapse of time and then only by means of American assistance.

The strategic position in the Mediterranean was now reversed: for the first (and last) time in the course of the war the Italian Navy achieved crushing superiority and dominated the Mediterranean; it could therefore resume, with practical immunity, supplies to the armies overseas and carry out transport of the German *Afrika Corps* to Libya, thus causing the defeat, a few months later, of the British Army, which was driven out of Cyrenaica.

Even more could have been done: Italy's naval superiority at that time was such as to permit her armed forces to undertake a direct attack against the pivot of the war in the Mediterranean (and perhaps not only in that theatre of war), namely, Malta. An invasion force transported by a convoy protected by the entire Italian Fleet, when our battleships would be opposed by *no* such British vessels, would have eliminated that obstacle in the heart of the Mediterranean, which had done us so much harm already and was to do us even more later on. Such an operation would have disposed of the difficulties which the Italian Navy had to encounter, for months afterwards, in supplying our African army.

In view of the disproportion between naval forces, the operation would certainly have succeeded, though it might have been accompanied by serious losses. When the thorn in the flank of Italy's line of communication across the Mediterranean had thus been eliminated, the occupation of Egypt would only have been a question of time, bringing with it incalculable consequences for the outcome of the war.

The responsibility for losing this opportunity rests, in my opinion, on the Italian General Staff and, still more, upon the German High Command which, by refusing to supply the necessary fuel for our warships and aircraft, "again displayed its underestimation of sea power in the general conduct of the war and in particular of the importance of the Mediterranean in the general picture of the entire conflict". (From the report of Admiral Weichold, a German liaison officer attached to the Italian Supreme Naval Command, submitted to the Anglo-Americans after the war.)

The great victory at Alexandria was therefore only partially exploited: the British were given time to draw naval and air reinforcements to the Mediterranean to such an extent that a few months later the situation was again reversed, to our disadvantage; it continued to deteriorate until the final collapse, of which the withdrawal from North Africa in May 1943 was the obvious proof.

But how great the danger which threatened the enemy was, and how near we were, after the blow delivered at Alexandria, to achieving decisive victory, was indicated, more clearly than by anyone else, by the man who, being in charge of the conduct of the war on the other side, realized it most fully: Winston Churchill. In a speech before a secret session of the House of Commons on the 23rd of April, 1942, after announcing the loss of the *Ark Royal*, the *Barham*, the *Repulse* and the *Prince of Wales*, he continued as follows:

A further sinister stroke was to come. On the early morning of December 19 half a dozen Italians in unusual diving suits were captured floundering about in the harbour of Alexandria. Extreme precautions have been taken for some time past against the varieties of human torpedo or one-man submarine entering our harbours. Not only are nets and other obstructions used but underwater charges are exploded at frequent irregular intervals in the fairway. None the less these men had penetrated the harbour. Four hours later explosions occurred in the bottoms of the *Valiant* and the *Queen Elizabeth*, produced by limpet bombs fixed with extraordinary courage and ingenuity, the effect of which was to blow large holes in the bottoms of both ships and to flood several compartments, thus putting them both out of action for many months. One ship will soon be ready again, the other is still in the floating dock at Alexandria, a constant target for enemy air attack. Thus we no longer had any battle squadron in the Mediterranean. *Barham* had gone and now *Valiant* and *Queen Elizabeth* were completely out of action. Both these ships floated on an even keel, they looked all right from the air. The enemy were for some time unaware of the success of their attack,* and it is only now that I feel it possible to make this disclosure to the House even in the strictness of a Secret Session. The Italian fleet still contains four or five battleships, several times repaired, of the new *Littorio* or of the modernized class. The sea defence of the Nile valley had to be confided to our submarine and destroyer flotillas, with a few cruisers, and of course to shore based Air forces. For this reason it was necessary to transfer a part of our shore based torpedo-carrying aircraft from the south and east coasts of England, where they were soon to be needed, to the north African shore . . .

The decoration, that of the Military Order of Savoy, which was conferred upon me, on the King's own initiative, after the Alexandria operations, was accompanied by the following citation:

Commanding officer of a submarine detailed to the Tenth Light

* This assertion is disproved by the Italian war Bulletins quoted above. (Author's note.)

Flotilla for special assault craft operations, he had already successfully carried out three daring and difficult undertakings; he studied and prepared, with great technical competence and shrewdness, the plan of a fourth operation, for forcing a further enemy base. He took his submarine close in to the heavily fortified harbour, facing with cool determination the risks incurred from the defence measures and vigilance of the enemy, in order to put the assault craft in the best possible position for forcing the enemy base. He then launched the assault craft in an action which achieved a brilliant success, leading as it did to the infliction of serious damage upon two enemy battleships.

THE FLYING TIGERS
Claire L. Chennault

The legendary Flying Tigers squadron – more properly the American Volunteer Group of the Chinese Nationalist Airforce – were the brainchild of Claire Chennault, a former USAAF pilot who had become the air adviser to the Chinese government of Chiang Kai Chek. Chennault's appointment in 1937 had virtually coincided with the Japanese invasion of China, to which the CNAF had only been able to put up a token resistance. Eventually, though, Chennault persuaded the Chinese government to bolster its airforce by buying 100 Curtiss Tomahawk fighters (P-40s) from the US, while he himself – with President Roosevelt's permission – recruited volunteer pilots for it from the US airforces. By spring 1941, 109 pilots from the US Marine Corps, the US Navy, the USAAF and civilian flying clubs had joined the American Volunteer Group (AWG).

Training lasted until December 1941, in which month the AWG flew its first missions against the Japanese. By now the USA itself was at war with Japan, but the Tigers retained their volunteer status until the summer of 1942, when they were reorganized as the 23rd Fighter Group of the USAAF. In seven months of fighting, the pilots of the AWG, in their shark-mouthed P-40s, had shot down 297 Japanese aircraft for the loss of 80 planes over the skies of China and Burma.

Below is Colonel Claire L. Chennault's personal account of the first AWG sorties against the Japanese, December 1941.

M Y WORST FEARS in thirty years of flying and nearly a decade of combat came during the first weeks after the attack on Pearl Harbor over the possibility of getting caught on the ground by a Japanese air assault on the A.V.G. at Toungoo. This fear had been gnawing at me ever since mid-October when the volunteer group began to take shape as a combat unit and I ordered the first aerial reconnaissance over the Japanese-built airfields in Thailand. I knew the Japanese were well informed on the condition of my group. I also knew they would have scant regard for the neutrality of Burma if they considered the A.V.G. a real menace to their activities in China. After Pearl Harbor I considered a Japanese attack on Toungoo a certainty. My only thought was to meet it with my planes in the air. During my long fight against the Japanese I constantly strove to put myself in the place of the enemy air commanders and diagnose their probable tactics. Generally my experience proved I allotted them too much credit.

Nearly half the A.V.G. men at Toungoo were Navy men and many of them had served at Pearl Harbor. I too had my own memories of Hawaii in the days when the 19th Fighter Squadron, which I commanded, was based on Ford Island as part of the air defenses of Pearl Harbor. In 1925 we experienced one of the Japanese attack scares that periodically swept the islands. It proved to be a baseless rumor. However, for three weeks I had the 19th Fighter Squadron warming up their planes in the dark of early morning. We took off before the first streaks of dawn to rendezvous over Oahu at 10,000 feet where it was already day. We patrolled the approaches to Pearl Harbor until long after sunrise hit the ground. There were no orders from my superiors to stand this alert, and our squadron took a lot of ribbing for the performance. I knew, as does every Regular Army officer, that the first responsibility of a unit commander – whether he heads an infantry platoon or an air force – is to take measures to ensure his own unit against tactical surprise by the enemy. The transition from peace to war comes hard for civilians, but for professional soldiers there is no excuse. If I had been caught with my planes on the ground, as were the Air Corps commanders in the Philippines and in Hawaii, I could never again have looked my fellow officers squarely in the eye.

The lightness with which this cardinal military sin was excused by the American high command when committed by Regular Army officers has always seemed to me one of the more shocking aspects of the war. Americans have been prone to excuse the failings of their military leaders partly because of the glow of final victory and partly because they still lack all the facts from which to form an honest and accurate appraisal – facts that have been carefully withheld from the public under the guise of censorship allegedly necessary to military security. It is high time the American people made it their business to find out more about why the men they paid for twenty years to provide for the national defense were so pitifully unprepared for the catastrophe that nearly engulfed us all. The penalty for the failure to do so will be a new and even more disastrous Pearl Harbor.

The Japanese attack on Hawaii confronted me with an abrupt change in plans. Although my fighter squadrons at Toungoo were ready for action, other phases of the project were in a more precarious state. Except for the P-40 tires sent by General MacArthur and Admiral Hart from the Philippines, we had no spares so vitally needed to keep the planes repaired after combat. Hudson bombers for the Second American Volunteer Group were parked on Lockheed's airport at Burbank, California. They were immediately taken over by the Air Corps, and we heard no more of them until they arrived in China for the Chinese Air Force in the late summer of 1942. A sizeable group of bomber crews already at sea on their way to Burma were diverted to Australia and inducted into the U.S. Army. First shipment of replacement fighter pilots met the same fate.

Events of December 7 and 8 made it clear that the fighter group was the only salvage from all the elaborate plans that had been so painstakingly woven in Washington. Had I known then that for over a year this fighter group would be the only effective Allied air force to oppose the Japanese on the Asiatic mainland I probably would not have entered the combat with such high hopes.

It was immediately evident that both ends of the Burma Road would have to be defended from heavy air assaults since the wrecking of Rangoon, the port of entry, and Kunming, the main division point in China, by air attack would offer a relatively cheap and effective means of tightening the Japanese fingers on China's throat without draining the far-flung enemy offensives in the southern Pacific. Rangoon was the only funnel through which supplies could still come to China. Kunming was the vital valve in China that controlled distribution of supplies to the Chinese armies in the field.

From the beginning there was dissension among the new Allies. The Generalissimo offered the British six divisions of his best troops and all of his heavy motorized artillery for the defense of Burma. The British spurned the offer, and Chiang's troops sat idle in Yunnan until March 1942 when the fall of Rangoon finally convinced the British they needed help. The British however showed no such reluctance over the American Volunteer Group of the Chinese Air Force. They pressed hard for transfer of the entire group to Rangoon to operate under R.A.F. command.

I opposed this transfer just as stubbornly as the British refused the help of Chinese ground troops. Early in the fall I conferred with Group Captain Manning over the aerial defense of Rangoon. He then had no warning net and only a single runway at Mingaladon, ten miles from Rangoon, on which to base his fighters. I suggested he build some dispersal fields to the west of Rangoon and fill in the gap between the new fields and the Thailand border with a network of air spotters' posts linked by special telephone and radio. With those facilities our fighters would have been able to meet the enemy over Rangoon with plenty of warning and altitude and be securely protected on the ground at fields beyond the Japs' range. I had learned early in this long game against the Japanese that it is suicide to fight air battles without adequate warning of the enemy's attacks and a main base out of his range. Manning, however, regarded his single runway within Japanese range as adequate and placed a reliance on his combination of radar and long-distance phone that was never borne out by experience. Manning had also committed the R.A.F. under his command to combat tactics that I regarded as suicidal. By serving under his command, I would have lost my own authority over the group and forced my pilots to accept his stupid orders. All during the period we were negotiating for transfer of all or a part of the A.V.G. to Rangoon, Manning refused to allow me to enter his fighter-control room or become familiar with any of the facilities that we were supposed to use jointly in the air defense of Rangoon.

We finally worked out an agreement, satisfactory to both the Generalissimo and the British, whereby one squadron of the A.V.G. would assist the R.A.F. in the defense of Rangoon with the other two squadrons to be stationed at Kunming, the China end of the Burma Road, where we had adequate warning net and dispersal fields. The Rangoon squadron remained under my direct command subject only to operational control by the senior R.A.F. officer in Burma. In this way the American pilots remained free to use their own tactics while coming under strategic direction of the R.A.F. Manning agreed to provide housing, transportation, food, and communications for the American squadron at Rangoon. This he failed to do.

The day after Pearl Harbor (December 9 by our calendar) we had half a dozen false alerts. With each new clang of the brass warning bell, Tom Trumble, my secretary, grabbed his rifle and tin hat and dashed for the slit trenches while I slung on my binoculars and trotted to the control tower. On December 10 Thailand "surrendered" to the Japanese, and enemy troops, ships, and planes poured into Bangkok to establish a base for the assault on Burma and Malaya. I sent Erik Shilling on a photo-reconnaissance mission over Bangkok in a special stripped-down P-40 equipped with an R.A.F. aerial camera. This improvised photo plane was about 18 miles per hour faster and could climb 3,000 feet higher than the average P-40, but it was completely outclassed by the speedy Japanese high-altitude photo planes that continued to do their work unmolested over Asia until the first Lockheed Lightnings (P-38) arrived in China in the summer of 1943. Escorted by Ed Rector of Marshal, North Carolina, and Bert Christman of Fort Collins, Colorado, in regular P-40s, Shilling photographed the docks and airfields of Bangkok from 26,000 feet.

When I saw his pictures, I exploded. Docks along the Menam River were jammed with enemy transports disgorging troops and supplies. Don Maung airdrome outside the city was packed with Japanese aircraft, parked wing tip to wing tip and awaiting dispersal to the chain of advanced bases closer to the Burma border. A dozen bombers could have wrecked the Japanese air offensive in twenty minutes.

This was but one of the many times during the war when a kingdom was lost for want of a few planes.

The Third A.V.G. Squadron commanded by Arvid Olson, of Hollywood, California, moved to Mingaladon airdrome on December 12 to join the R.A.F. in the defense of Rangoon. At Toungoo we encouraged every possible movement rumor about the rest of the group to confuse the Burmese spies while we tied up our loose ends preparatory to establishing a new base at Kunming. There were still twenty-five pilots not sufficiently trained to be turned loose in combat and a dozen P-40s under repair at Toungoo, but when the radio crackled from Kunming that the Japanese were bombing the city on December 18, it was apparent that the time to move had come.

The group was so organized that everything essential to immediate combat operations could be airborne. Permanent base personnel and supplies left Toungoo by truck convoy up the Burma Road. Three C.N.A.C. transports swooped down on Toungoo on the afternoon of the eighteenth and whisked me, my combat staff, and the oxygen, ammunition, and spare parts we needed for fighting to Kunming before dawn the next day.

The First and Second Squadrons flew from Toungoo to Kunming on the afternoon of the eighteenth with a refueling stop at Lashio. At Toungoo the First Squadron circled on patrol covering the Second Squadron's take-off, and at Kunming the roles were reversed as the Second stayed in the air until the First Squadron had landed, refueled, and was ready for combat again at Kunming.

By dawn on the nineteenth we had thirty-four P-40s ready to fight at Kunming with a fighter-control headquarters hooked into the Yunnan warning net and the Chinese code rooms that were monitoring Japanese operational radio frequencies and decoding enemy messages. For the first time since mid-October I breathed easier.

It was this kind of lightning mobility that was necessary to realize the full potential of airpower. To achieve it meant that I would always have to operate on a skeletonized basis with airmen doubling in ground duties and a few key men doing the work of an entire staff. It meant that I could never afford the excess staff personnel required by more orthodox military organizations.

It was this ability to shift my combat operations six hundred and fifty miles in an afternoon and a thousand miles in twenty-four hours that kept the Japanese off balance for four bloody years and prevented them from landing a counterpunch with their numerically superior strength that might easily have put my always meager forces out of business.

We had little strain on our patience for the first pay-off on these tactics. December 19 passed quietly with three P-40 reconnaissance patrols over southern Yunnan but no sign of life from the enemy. At 9:45 A.M. on the twentieth my special phone from the Chinese code room rang. It was Colonel Wong Shu Ming, commander of the Chinese Fifth Air Force and Chinese chief of staff for the A.V.G. His message said, "Ten Japanese bombers crossed the Yunnan border at Laokay heading northwest."

From then on the battle unfolded over Yunnan as it had done a hundred times before in my head. Reports filtered in from the Yunnan net as the enemy bombers penetrated deeper into China.

"Heavy engine noise at station X-10."

"Unknowns overhead at station P-8."

"Noise of many above clouds at station C-23."

Position reports recorded on our fighter-control board added up to a course designed to bring the enemy bombers to about fifty miles east of Kunming, from which point they would probably begin the circling and feinting tactics designed to confuse the warning net before their final dash to the target.

I ordered the Second Squadron to make the interception. Jack Newkirk, of Scarsdale, New York, led one four-plane element in search of the bombers while Jim Howard, of St. Louis, son of former medical missionaries in China, led another four-plane formation on defensive patrol above Kunming. Sixteen planes of the First Squadron commanded by Robert Sandell, of San Antonio, Texas, were held in reserve in the stand-by area west of Kunming, ready to join the fray at the decisive moment.

I fired a red flare sending the Second and First Squadrons into the air and drove with my executive officer, Harvey Greenlaw, and interpreter, Colonel Hsu, to the great timbered clay pyramid looming above the grassy mounds of a Chinese graveyard on a gentle slope overlooking the field. This was our combat-operations shelter with a duplicate set of radio and phone communications. Inside the dark, dank interior we studied the plotting board by the light of matches held by Greenlaw while Hsu took phone reports from the Chinese net. Outside, the winter air of the Kunming plateau was crisp and clear. Scattered puffball clouds floated lazily above the city at 10,000 feet. Weather reports to the south indicated a solid overcast brushing the mountain peaks.

This was the decisive moment I had been awaiting for more than four years – American pilots in American fighter planes aided by a Chinese ground warning net about to tackle a formation of the Imperial Japanese Air Force, which was then sweeping the Pacific skies victorious everywhere. I felt that the fate of China was riding in the P-40 cockpits through the wintery sky over Yunnan. I yearned heartily to be ten years younger and crouched in a cockpit instead of a dugout, tasting the stale rubber of an oxygen mask and peering ahead into limitless space through the cherry-red rings of a gunsight.

Suddenly voices broke through the crackling radio static.

"There they are."

"No, no, they can't be Japs."

"Look at those red balls."

"Let's get 'em."

Then maddening silence. I ordered Sandell's reserve squadron to dive to Iliang about thirty miles southeast of Kunming along the Japs' line of probable approach. There was nothing more on the radio. The Chinese net reported the bombers had reversed course and were heading back toward Indo-China. Sounds of gunfire were heard, and the heavy fall of Japanese bombs in the mountains near Iliang was reported. There was nothing to do but return to the field and wait.

Chinese were already streaming back to the city from their refuge among the grave mounds, incredulous that no bombs had fallen. Howard's patrol over Kunming came down. They had seen nothing. Newkirk's flight returned, sheepish and chagrined over a bad case of buck fever on their first contact with the enemy. They had sighted the Jap formation of ten gray twin-engined bombers about thirty miles southeast of Kunming, but for a few incredulous seconds could hardly believe the bombers were really Japs. The bombers jettisoned their bombs, put their noses down for speed, and wheeled back toward Indo-China. By the time Newkirk's flight recovered and opened fire, the bombers had too big a lead – too big that is for everybody except Ed Rector. The last the other pilots saw of Rector he was still chasing the Japs at full throttle.

Finally Sandell's squadron came straggling in. From the whistling of the wind in their open gun barrels and the slow rolls as they buzzed the field, we knew they had been in a fight. They had sighted the Jap formation in full retreat over Iliang about thirty miles southeast of Kunming, scuttling along on top of a solid overcast with Rector still in pursuit.

As the P-40s dived to attack, everybody went a little crazy with excitement. All the lessons of Toungoo were forgotten. There was no teamwork – only a wild melee in which all pilots agreed that only sheer luck kept P-40s from shooting each other. Pilots tried wild 90-degree deflection shots and other crazy tactics in the 130-mile running fight that followed. Fritz Wolf of Shawano, Wisconsin, shot down two bombers and then cursed his armorer because his guns jammed.

When he landed and inspected the guns, he found they were merely empty. When the P-40s broke off three Jap bombers had gone down in flames and the remainder were smoking in varying degrees. Ed Rector was the only A.V.G. casualty. His long chase left him short of gas, forcing him to crash-land his P-40 in a rice paddy east of Kumming with minor injuries.

Back at the field most of the pilots were too excited to speak coherently.

"Well, boys," I told the excited pilots, "it was a good job but not good enough. Next time get them all."

I herded them into the operations shack for an hour before

I let them eat lunch. We went over the fight in minute detail pointing out their mistakes and advising them on how to get all the bombers next time. Not until the spring of 1945 did I learn how close Sandell's flight had come to getting all the Japs in that first fight of the A.V.G.

Lewis Bishop of De Kalb Junction, New York, an A.V.G. pilot shot down five months after the Iliang battle and taken prisoner in Indo-China, met the Japanese pilot who led the raid. The Jap said his crew had been the sole survivors of the mission. Nine of the ten bombers had failed to return.

Bishop was a prisoner of the enemy for three years. He finally escaped by jumping from a moving train in North China while being transferred from Shanghai to Manchuria. He reached me in Kunming early in 1945 to write the final footnote to the A.V.G.'s first fight.

Japanese airmen never again tried to bomb Kunming while the A.V.G. defended it. For many months afterward they sniffed about the edges of the Yunnan warning net and dropped a few bombs near the border but never ventured near Kunming. Our border patrols shot down a half dozen of these half-hearted raiders, and by the spring of 1942 we were on the offensive carrying the war deep into Indo-China with dive-bombing and strafing missions. The Japs waited until sixteen months after their first defeat to launch another mission against Kunming in the spring of 1943, when they knew I was in Washington attending the Trident Conferences of the British-American Combined Chiefs of Staff. Then they brought thirty fighters to protect their bombers.

Although the A.V.G. was blooded over China, it was the air battles over Rangoon that stamped the hallmark on its fame as the Flying Tigers. The cold statistics for the ten weeks the A.V.G. served at Rangoon show its strength varied between twenty and five serviceable P-40s. This tiny force met a total of a thousand-odd Japanese aircraft over southern Burma and Thailand. In 31 encounters they destroyed 217 enemy planes and probably destroyed 43. Our losses in combat were four pilots killed in the air, one killed while strafing, and one taken prisoner. Sixteen P-40s were destroyed. During the same period the R.A.F., fighting side by side with the A.V.G., destroyed 74 enemy planes, probably destroyed 33, with a loss of 22 Buffaloes and Hurricanes.

Winston Churchill, then prime minister of the United Kingdom, added his eloquence to these statistics, cabling the Governor of Burma, "The victories of these Americans over the rice paddies of Burma are comparable in character if not in scope with those won by the R.A.F. over the hop fields of Kent in the Battle of Britain."

Air Vice Marshal D. F. Stevenson, who replaced Manning in January 1942, noted that while the ratio of British to German planes in the Battle of Britain had been 1 to 4, the ratio of Anglo-American fighters to Japanese planes over Rangoon was 1 to from 4 to 14.

The Japanese began their aerial assault on Rangoon with a strength of 150 fighters and bombers based on a few fields in southern Thailand. In Burma, the Allies could muster only 16 P-40s of the A.V.G., 20 Buffaloes of the R.A.F., some ancient British Lysanders of the India Air Force, and a few Tiger Moth training planes. As I anticipated, the radar-phone combination of the R.A.F. warning system failed to provide adequate warning. Many times the only warning my pilots received was a hurried phone call, "Bombers overhead," or the noise and dust of the R.A.F. Buffaloes scrambling for an alert. Numerous A.V.G. interceptions were made only after the enemy finished bombing and was leaving the target due to the inadequate warning. When the R.A.F. indicated that its only attempts to bolster the warning system consisted of providing advanced ground troops with heliographs to flash warning messages, I fought vigorously to withdraw the A.V.G. from what I considered an unnecessarily exposed position. Only the heavy pressure of the Anglo-American Combined Chiefs of Staff and the Generalissimo prevented me from doing so.

Shortly before the Rangoon battles began, the A.V.G. suffered its final blow from William D. Pawley. The contract between Pawley and the Chinese government provided that I could call on Pawley's Central Aircraft Manufacturing Company for technical personnel, tools, and materials for repairing damaged P-40s of the A.V.G. At a conference with

General Chow, chief of the Chinese Aeronautical Commission, in September it was agreed that all A.V.G. repair work west of the Salween River would be handled by CAMCO's Loi-Wing plant, located in Yunnan just across the Burma border, while the Chinese Air Force repair shop in Kunming would do all servicing east of the Salween.

As damaged planes began to pile up during training at Toungoo, I made repeated requests to Pawley for men and materials from his Loi-Wing plant to repair them. A few CAMCO men were sent to Toungoo but it was decided to do only emergency work there and to ship badly damaged planes over the Burma railroad to Lashio and thence by truck to the Loi-Wing factory. A number of P-40s were shipped to Loi-Wing, but after they arrived, little work was done on them.

CAMCO was engaged in the assembly of Curtiss-Wright Model 21 fighters and some trainers, which Pawley had already sold to the Chinese government. Pawley claimed that repairing A.V.G. planes interfered with his assembly program. I argued that repair of proven combat planes for experienced pilots rated higher priority than the assembly of trainers and experimental fighters. We also disagreed over the need for an A.V.G. squadron to be stationed at Loi-Wing for the protection of his factory. At that time the possibility of enemy air action against Loi-Wing was too remote to be considered seriously.

In mid-December Pawley issued an order to his American employees at Loi-Wing, forbidding them to touch an A.V.G. plane, and followed this with a radio to me that, as of January 1, CAMCO would do no more repair work on A.V.G. P-40s. I replied that Pawley's inability to do this work was regretted, but we would manage without him.

Loss of the CAMCO repair base was a serious blow to the group since we were already fighting over Rangoon. I took the matter to the Generalissimo in Chungking. He ordered the Chinese manager of CAMCO, Colonel Chen, to continue repairing A.V.G. planes. Chen did an excellent job for us until the plant was burned and abandoned in the face of the Japanese advance into Yunnan. The Chinese government acquired Pawley's interest in CAMCO, and he flew off to India where he had already begun construction of another aircraft plant.

I have always suspected that Pawley, like the Japanese, thoroughly believed the British and American intelligence reports that the A.V.G. would not last three weeks in combat. At any rate on the occasions when he had a chance to provide the A.V.G. with badly needed assistance, Pawley exhibited what I considered a remarkable lack of co-operation. It was only after the A.V.G.'s combat record had made the organization world famous that Pawley made strenuous efforts to have himself identified with it, even to the extent of attempting to secure an honorary membership of the Flying Tigers Incorporated, the only authentic postwar organization of former A.V.G. men, by offering a ten-thousand-dollar contribution to the corporation's funds. His offer was flatly rejected by the membership, who apparently felt that a few repaired P-40s during the dark days of 1941–42 would have been more valuable to them than a postwar check. After a succession of wartime manufacturing ventures, Pawley embarked on a diplomatic career as ambassador to Peru and Brazil. No doubt he found the Medal for Merit awarded him for "organizing the Flying Tigers" useful in his new work.

Two days before Christmas the Japanese shot their first aerial bolt against Rangoon with 54 bombers escorted by 20 fighters. The low fighter-bomber ratio indicated that the Japanese were confident·and expected little trouble from the Allied air defense. There was no warning at Mingaladon. The Third Squadron was casually ordered to clear the field. While still climbing they were informed by R.A.F. fighter control, "Enemy approaching from the east."

The Japanese had finished bombing and were on their way home before the A.V.G. sighted the formation. Jap fighters were diving on the city, strafing the crowds of civilians who jammed the streets to watch the raid. One bomber formation hit Mingaladon Field, and the other laid their eggs along the docks. In the brief fight that followed, the Americans shot down six Japanese planes and lost two of their own pilots – Neil Martin of Texarkana, Arkansas, riddled by a quartet of

Jap fighters, and Henry Gilbert of Bremerton, Washington, blown up by the top-turret fire of the bomber formations. The R.A.F. failed to make contact.

This raid put the torch of panic to Rangoon. Those who were rich enough to do so fled for their lives to India. Native Burmese rioted, looted, and began potting stray Britons. All the native cooks and servants fled from Mingaladon, leaving the A.V.G. without a mess. For two days they lived mainly on stale bread and canned beer, of which there seemed to be an ample stock.

On a cloudless Christmas day with the temperature at 115 degrees in the sun the Japanese came back to finish off Rangoon. They figured 60 bombers and 30 fighters would be ample for the job. This time 12 P-40s were waiting at altitude and sailed into the Japanese formations as they droned toward the city. "Like rowboats attacking the Spanish Armada," one observer on the ground described the attack. The R.A.F. put 16 Buffaloes into the fray later.

"It was like shooting ducks," Squadron Leader Olson radioed me at Kunming. "We got 15 bombers and 9 fighters. Could put entire Jap force out of commission with whole group here."

A.V.G. losses were 2 planes. Both pilots bailed out safely. The R.A.F. got 7 Jap planes and lost 9 Buffaloes and 6 pilots.

William Pawley happened to be in Rangoon that memorable Christmas and apparently suffered a slight change of heart in his attitude toward the A.V.G. He loaded a truck full of food and drink in Rangoon and drove it to Mingaladon to present the Third Squadron with Christmas dinner. Under the shade of banyan trees around the airport rim, with the smoke of burning Japanese wrecks still rising from the jungles beyond, the Third Squadron squatted to a dinner of ham and chicken liberally lubricated by beer and Scotch. The rest of the group, eight hundred miles to the north on the frosty Kunming plateau, dined on Yunnan duck and rice wine.

After the Christmas battle, the Third Squadron had only 11 serviceable P-40s left. Olson radioed for help, and I sent the Second Squadron, led by Newkirk, to relieve him. By the first week in January the transfer was completed, and the pattern of the Japanese effort against Rangoon became apparent.

While they gathered strength for another mass daylight assault, the Japanese sent night bombers to harass Rangoon, slipping in singly all night long to gain maximum nuisance value. A.V.G. efforts to halt them were unsuccessful, but the R.A.F. bagged several. Meanwhile the A.V.G. took the offensive, prowling the enemy fields in Thailand to smash their planes on the ground. Newkirk and "Tex" Hill led many of these early strafing attacks on the Jap airfields.

While the A.V.G. P-40s fought to keep the port of Rangoon open, our ground crews were working like beavers on the docks loading truck convoys with lend-lease equipment for shipment up the Burma Road to China. It was during this period, with the hot breath of the Japanese blowing on our necks, that the Burma Road first delivered twenty thousand tons a month to China. These supplies, trucked out of Burma before the fall of Rangoon, enabled the A.V.G. to continue operations in China long after every land line of communication with that unhappy land had been severed by the enemy. Every type of A.V.G. nonflying personnel, including our chaplain, Paul Frillman, of Maywood, Illinois, sweated like coolies on the Rangoon docks during those hectic weeks.

By the last week in January the Japanese were ready for another knockout attempt on Rangoon. From January 23 to 28 six major attacks of up to one hundred planes each rolled over the Burmese port. It was a tribute to the Anglo-American fighter pilots that the Japanese formations had switched to a three-to-one ratio of fighters protecting small bomber formations.

On January 23 and 24 the Japanese tried to floor the A.V.G. with a series of one-two punches. They led with a fighter sweep designed to get the Allied fighters into the air and use up their fuel. Then a second wave was scheduled to deliver the knockout punch while the A.V.G. and R.A.F. were on the ground refueling. It was a good plan but it didn't work. A.V.G. ground crews were too fast on refueling and rearming the P-40s and had them ready to fight again before the second wave of Japs appeared. By January 28 the Japs were sending over only large fighter formations, and the score for this offensive stood at 50 Jap planes destroyed against a loss of 2 A.V.G. pilots and 10 R.A.F. pilots killed.

Newkirk radioed Kunming, "The more hardships, work, and fighting the men have to do the higher our morale goes. Squadron spirit really strong now."

However strong the Second Squadron's spirit, they were down to ten P-40s, so I sent Bob Sandell and his First Squadron to take up the burden at Rangoon. The Japanese ground offensive into Burma had begun to roll during the last weeks in January, and it was evident that the British had neither the men, equipment, nor leadership to stop it.

Before I left the United States in the summer of 1941 I asked a few friends in Louisiana to watch the newspapers and send me any clippings about the A.V.G. Now I was being swamped with clippings from stateside newspapers, and my men were astonished to find themselves world famous as the Flying Tigers. The insignia we made famous was by no means original with the A.V.G. Our pilots copied the shark-tooth design on their P-40s' noses from a colored illustration in the *India Illustrated* Weekly depicting an R.A.F. squadron in the Libyan desert with shark-nosed P-40s. Even before that the German Air Force painted shark's teeth on some of its Messerschmitt 210 fighters. With the pointed nose of a liquid-cooled engine it was an apt and fearsome design. How the term Flying Tigers was derived from the shark-nosed P-40s I never will know. At any rate we were somewhat surprised to find ourselves billed under that name. It was not until just before the A.V.G. was disbanded that we had any kind of group insignia. At the request of China Defense Supplies in Washington, Roy Williams of the Walt Disney organization in Hollywood designed our insignia consisting of a winged tiger flying through a large V for victory.

Although the Flying Tiger victories made ready front-page copy for an Allied world rocked by a series of shattering defeats, I noticed too much tendency to attribute our success to sheer derring-do or some mystical quality and not enough on the solid facts on which our triumphs were really based. Whatever its later shortcomings, the Curtiss-Wright P-40 was an excellent fighter for the battles over Rangoon, all of which were fought below 20,000 feet. At those altitudes the P-40 was better than a Hurricane and at its best against the Japanese Army Nates and Navy Model Zeros. The two .50-caliber machine guns gave the P-40 a heavy, fast-firing gun that neither the British nor Japs could match. Pilot armor saved many a P-40 pilot's life, and the heavy rugged construction, though a disadvantage in maneuverability, was certainly an advantage in field maintenance and putting damaged planes back into battle. P-40s could be repaired after damage that would have made a Japanese plane a total loss.

The ground crews were a vital factor that most newspaper correspondents on the spot overlooked. It was the speed with which the ground crews repaired, refueled, and rearmed the P-40s that kept the A.V.G. from being floored by the Japanese one-two punches. The ground crews displayed ingenuity and energy in repairing battle-damaged P-40s that I have seldom seen equaled and never excelled. Their performance at Rangoon was in many ways symbolic, for in all the long years of the war to come, it was American maintenance that was one of the keystones in our eventual arch of triumph. Until the very end of the Rangoon holocaust our ground crews managed to keep a minimum of 10 P-40s ready to fight every day. In contrast the R.A.F. commander, Air Vice Marshal Stevenson, complained of his maintenance men who allowed a squadron of 30 Hurricanes arriving in January to slump to 11 planes fit for combat by mid-February and only 6 by March. I had never favored liquid-cooled engines for combat planes but the Allison engines in our P-40s certainly did more than the manufacturer claimed for them.

Our leadership at Rangoon was also superior. All of the squadron leaders who saw action there – Olson; Sandell and Newkirk before they were killed; "Tex" Hill of Hunt, Texas; and Bob Neale, of Seattle, Washington, were leaders of the highest quality. It was no accident that Hill and Olson became full colonels and commanded Army Air Forces fighter groups in combat or that the A.A.F. offered a lieutenant colonelcy to Bob Neale, who entered the A.V.G. as a Navy ensign.

Above all it was the kind of teamwork that is so typically American, wherein there is plenty of scope for individual brilliance but everybody contributes toward a common goal. You can see it on an autumn Saturday afternoon in a top-notch football team. It will take the same kind of well-co-ordinated teamwork to operate a guided-missile or push-button group in the next war or to pull us through the perils of peace.

In January my annual attack of chronic bronchitis laid me low in Kunming, and a projected trip to Rangoon had to be canceled. I alternated between brief spells in my airfield office and longer sieges in my sickbed at the University of Kunming where the A.V.G. was quartered. A radio was installed near my bed, so I could listen to the radio chatter of my pilots during their fights over Rangoon. It was over this radio that I heard of the Japanese attack on Toungoo, February 4. They struck at 6 A.M. There was no warning. All personnel were asleep. The operations building and a hangar were destroyed by direct hits; three P-40s still under repair were wrecked; and half a dozen R.A.F. Blenheims burned. That might all too easily have been the fate of the entire A.V.G. eight weeks earlier.

After the fall of Singapore in mid-February, the Japanese transferred the crack air units that blasted the R.A.F. out of the Malayan air to Thailand to join the assault on Rangoon. These reinforcements boosted enemy plane strength available to attack Rangoon to four hundred planes. Before the month's end, they were hammering at the city with two hundred planes a day.

It was during this period that a handful of battered P-40s flown by Bob Neale's First Squadron pilots wrote the final lurid chapter in the A.V.G. history of Rangoon. Neale had become First Squadron leader after the death of Bob Sandell, who died flight-testing a repaired P-40 over Mingaladon. Since the fall of Rangoon was already looming, Neale no longer retained damaged planes at Mingaladon but had them flown or shipped north by rail. About this time I also ordered Neale to cease all strafing and bomber-escort missions due to the worn condition of the P-40 engines, which were long overdue for overhaul. The fact that shark-nosed planes were observed flying north and were no longer seen over Thailand airdromes or accompanying R.A.F. bombers gave rise to rumors that the A.V.G. had left Rangoon. Neale radioed me for orders regarding the actual evacuation. I replied, "Expend equipment. Conserve personnel utmost. Retire with last bottle oxygen."

Neale took me literally. With 9 P-40s he waited for the final Japanese daylight assaults with their crack units from Singapore. R.A.F. strength had dwindled too. All the Buffaloes had been lost in combat or accidents. Thirty Hurricane reinforcements had shrunk to a dozen serviceable planes. New reinforcements of 18 Hurricanes and Spitfires being ferried from Calcutta to Rangoon cracked up in the Chin Hills with a loss of 11 pilots. When the Japanese began their final aerial assault on February 26, there were only 15 Allied fighters to meet the attack by 166 enemy planes. They fought off three raids on the twenty-fifth with the A.V.G. bagging 24 Jap planes. The next day was even worse, with 200 enemy planes over Rangoon. The A.V.G., now reduced to 6 P40s, bagged 18 Jap fighters to bring their two-day total to 43 enemy aircraft without loss to themselves.

In those two days of almost constant air fighting Neale's detachment turned in one of the epic fighter performances of all time. With the best of equipment it would have been a brilliant victory, but under the conditions Neale and his eight pilots fought, it was an incredible feat. The report of Fritz Wolf, who left Rangoon just before the final battles began, describes those conditions well.

Planes at Rangoon are almost unflyable. Tires are chewed up and baked hard. They blow out continually. We are short on them, and battery plates are thin. When we recharge them, they wear out within a day. There is no Prestone oil coolant in Rangoon. British destroyed the battery-charging and oxygen-storage depots without any advance warning to us so we could stock up. We are completely out of auxiliary gear shifts and they are wearing out in the planes every day.

Fresh food of any kind is completely lacking. We are living out of cans. Water is hard to get. Most of the city water supply has been cut off.

Dust on the field fouls up the P-40 engines considerably. It clogs carburetion so much that it is dangerous to increase manifold pressure when the engine quits cold. Entire carburetion systems are cleaned on the ground, but they are as bad as ever after a single day's operations. This tendency of engines to quit makes it hard to dogfight or strafe. Of the eight planes that took off for an air raid two days ago, only five got off the ground.

Conditions in Rangoon are getting dangerous. Authorities have released criminals, lunatics, and lepers to fend for themselves. Natives have broken into unguarded liquor stocks and are in a dangerous state. There are continual knifings and killings. Three British were killed near the docks a few nights ago. Stores are all closed. At least twenty-five blocks of the city are burning furiously. All fire trucks were sent up the Prome Road to Mandalay several weeks ago.

Our only contact with British intelligence was a visit from one officer about ten days ago. There seems to be little co-operation between the R.A.F. and British Army and less between the R.A.F. and us. It seems certain that the Japanese have crossed the Sittang River (only eighty miles from Rangoon), but we have had no word on it.

On the night of February 27 the R.A.F. removed the radar set from Rangoon without previous notice to the A.V.G. For Neale that was the last straw. The next morning he sent four of his remaining six P-40s to cover the route of the last A.V.G. truck convoy to leave Rangoon. He and his wingman, R. T. Smith, later an A.A.F. fighter group commander, stayed to make a final search for an A.V.G. pilot who had bailed out over the jungle some days before. Neale ripped out his own radio and enlarged the baggage compartment to hold a stretcher case if the pilot turned up injured. Neale and Smith sweated out February 28 waiting for news of the lost pilot, Edward Liebolt. The next day the Japanese cut the Prome Road, last land line of retreat from Rangoon. Neale and Smith jammed two cases of whisky into Neale's baggage

compartment and took off for Magwe, two hundred miles
to the north. Two days later the Japanese Army entered
Rangoon.

The battle of southern Burma was over.

SAINT NAZAIRE COMMANDOS
Adolphe Lepotier

*The assault by British Army Commandos on the port of Saint Nazaire,
on the occupied Atlantic coast of France, is widely considered to be
the greatest seaborne raid of World War II. The port, which lies
at the mouth of the Loire, had been a major target for the British
from the time of the German occupation. Not only did it contain
the largest dry-dock in the world – thus the only one which could
facilitate the gigantic German battleships* Tirpitz, Scharnhorst *and*
Gneisenau *– it was also an important U-boat base in the Battle of
the Atlantic.*

*A major target, but not an easy one. Saint Nazaire was outside
the range of most RAF bombers, and was heavily defended by
the 28 heavy guns of the German 280 Naval Atlantic Battalion,
plus a battery of railway-mounted 240 mm guns at La Baule,
seven miles inland. The port also bristled with anti-aircraft artillery, and was serviced by 6000 German personnel. Moreover, the
dry-dock itself – which had to be destroyed for any raid to be
considered successful – had an outer caisson (wall) of steel some
35 feet thick.*

*In the Commandos' raid on Saint Nazaire they were accompanied
by the Royal Navy escort destroyers* Athelstone *and* Tynedale, *16
motor launches, a motor torpedo boat (MTB74) and a motor gun
boat (MGB314). To break the caisson of the* Normandie *dock,
an old destoyer, HMS* Campbeltown, *was packed with four and
a quarter tons of high explosive on a time-delay pencil fuse, to be
delivered by head-on ramming. This account of Operation Chariot
is by the French admiral and military historian, Adolphe Lapotier.
It begins with the British flotilla approaching the French coast on
the night of 27 March 1942.*

T HE HOURS PASSED and night drew nearer. The occupied coast was no longer far away, and the enemy had not yet given any sign of life. For the men whose nerves were keyed up this seemed incredible, and their morale rose proportionately. The *Tynedale* had obviously been quite right about her submarine.*

As a last precaution, the course of the formation was maintained in the direction of La Pallice until nightfall, so that should an enemy plane appear it could still be mistaken about the destination of this unusual task force.

"Nevertheless," said Ryder, "when night fell we all felt immensely relieved."

At 20.00 hours, seventy miles south-west of St. Nazaire, *Atherstone* slipped M.G.B. 314. Ryder, Newman and their small staff got into the small boat, which got under way to accompanying cheers from the crew.

"Don't forget I've been a good father to you," signalled *Atherstone*.

The *Campbeltown* also slipped the M.T.B. 74 which, after a few cavortings, took her place in the queue.

During this time the remaining M.L.s took up their position in the assault formation, with M.G.B. 314 ahead. Behind her came the *Campbeltown*, and astern and on the flanks the leading motor-boats of the two columns.

The *Tynedale* and *Atherstone* took up their positions provisionally about a mile apart to increase their chances of finding the submarine H.M.S. *Sturgeon*, which had taken up a position by day forty miles south-west of St. Nazaire to act as marker. It had to show a discreet light, directed south-west.

"M.L. 341 signals damage to her engine," reported Pike, the skilful signalman of M.G.B. 314.

"Tell her to transfer her Commandos to one of the M.L.s astern."

The M.L. 446 took them off and struggled to rejoin the column, leaving M.L. 341 to her own devices.

---

* It was learned later that this submarine was not sunk and signalled effectively that it had been attacked by two destroyers sailing on a south-westerly course.

"Light ahead."

This small light on the water could only be the discreet lamp of the *Sturgeon*. A few minutes later the M.G.B. sighted the submarine. They were close enough to thank him by megaphone. They had reached point Z of the plan. Here the escorting destroyers had to patrol, while waiting for the return of the survivors from the raid. They vanished in the darkness, while the small wooden boats and the doomed destroyer advanced alone into the semi-circle of enemy guns of all calibres.

The lights of various fishing-boats appeared on both bows. Ryder thought this was proof that the enemy had not got wind of the attack. This encounter also seemed to him a piece of luck, for the enemy radar would find it difficult to distinguish the suspicious echoes among all the normal ones given by the fishing-boats of a type and volume similar to those of the M.T.B.s.

Towards midnight they saw gun flashes in the distance, in the direction of St. Nazaire. As they approached nearer, they could make out the classic pattern of flak; searchlight beams, the firework display of shells and luminous tracers crossing each other in the sky. This evidence of the presence of friendly aircraft at the promised hour was very comforting.

As they approached the Châtelier Buoy they began to make out the coast to port. The *Campbeltown* received the order to set course at 50° and to guide the formation, for in order to use her rudimentary radar, whose transmitting and reception beam was set fore and aft, the M.G.B. would be obliged to manœuvre constantly while taking the bearings. At the same time, however, she zigzagged to take soundings in front of the columns.

On the fluorescent radar screen the luminous teeth of the "pipes" appeared and disappeared, according to the evolution of the boat, each time it set its course on some protruding object. A very much larger "pipe" appeared when it headed to port. Their course allowed them to pinpoint this obstacle, and at 01.25 hours they could distinguish the big Morées Tower, 400 yards away to the north.

After thirty-three hours of navigation, out of sight of land, the British ships had arrived exactly at their fixed point, despite changes of course and the variable currents met with on the way. Their meeting with *Sturgeon* was another example of the precision of this navigation.

This was the moment when the excitement reached its climax. They were nearing the target. It seemed more and more improbable that the Germans realized eighteen enemy ships were entering a roadstead where they had concentrated every conceivable weapon of lookout, detection and defence.

They wondered if this indifference were merely a ruse and whether they intended to let them come close in before crushing them at one blow.

For the *Campbeltown* there was an additional worry. Was there enough water for her to pass over the Mindin sand bank?

Suddenly all the men on the bridge looked at each other anxiously. By a vibration of the hull beneath their feet, which could deceive no sailor, they realised that the destroyer had touched bottom.

Would she get across?

They bent anxiously over the side to gauge the slowing down of the wake. Their speed seemed constant.

Another jolt. Another anxious moment. They had made it!

Their mates in the M.L.s did not know that a few inches less water and the *Campbeltown* would have been stopped for good a few hundred yards from the goal, even before the enemy had intervened.

But could the Germans wait much longer?

Nerves were keyed up to breaking-point, waiting for what would happen from one minute to the next.

What form would it take?

At that moment the sky was entirely covered by low cloud, through which the moonlight hardly trickled. White wisps of mist floated past from time to time.

On board the M.G.B. they could already make out the dark lines of the outer harbour, just as twenty-four years before

the men on the *Vindictive* had seen the Zeebrugge mole a few
seconds before the battle began.

Suddenly the narrow beam of a searchlight from the bank lit
up the roadstead. The strip of light fell astern of the flotilla.

For a few seconds, while several hundred men held breath,
it moved slowly and drew near to the rear motor-boats. A
moment before it reached them it went out.

Was it possible that once more the enemy had let slip the
opportunity of discovering the attackers?

They did not have to wait long for the answer. Less than
a minute later all the searchlights of the two banks went on
simultaneously, focused on the roadstead, which was suddenly
lit up as bright as day.

Despite the dark, dull paint of the hulls, all the boats were
visible at once by the silver foam of their wakes. It reminded
one of the appearance of the Moors in the Quadalquivir at
Seville, described by Corneille:

> *La flotte qu'on craignait, dans le grand fleuve entrée,*
> *Croît surprendre la ville et piller la contrée.*
> *Les Maures vont descendre et le flux et la nuit*
> *Dans une heure à nos murs les amènent sans bruit.*
>
> . . .
>
> *L'onde s'enfle dessous et d'un commun effort*
> *Les Maures et la mer montent jusques au port . . .*

But it was no more a question of one hour, as in the poem.
In ten minutes the *Campbeltown* would have reached the target
unless she suffered some major damage.

Each of the commanding officers ordered: "Full speed
ahead!"

They had to start at once now, trying to delay the enemy
from opening fire.

Since there was no longer any question of concealing the
approach of the ships, they must try and fox the defences by
trying to deceive them about their nationality. It was with
this in view that the *Campbeltown* had been given the shape
of a German destroyer of the identical class of those signalled
that very day at sea off St. Nazaire. International law forbids

hiding under an enemy flag at the moment of opening fire, but the British hoisted White Ensigns, tattered and blackened by smoke and spray – flags which a yeoman of signals would have considered unserviceable, even for stormy weather.

The little signal searchlight of a coastal battery spelt out its recognition letters in morse. The British ignored them. Leading Yeoman Pike, of the M.G.B., replied at first by illegible flashes; and to another searchlight at the entrance to the harbour, which questioned in turn, he transmitted the letters which the battery had given. A few shots were fired sporadically over their bows.

This was the moment to play the last card.

"Go ahead, Pike."

Pike, who knew how to transmit in German, signalled to his unknown interrogator: "Wait." Then he gave the indication, known to the English, of a German destroyer, followed by a long message in German, preceded by the word "Urgent": "Two vessels damaged in the course of an engagement with the enemy, request entrance to the port immediately." He finished by the signal which meant: "I still have something else to transmit."

He was about to send a message to his other interrogator, when the light batteries of the port opened fire more strongly, although still hesitatingly. Taking his most powerful Aldis lamp, Pike slowly flashed the letters of the international signal code, which meant: "I am a friend – you are mistaken."

The firing ceased again.

In another six minutes the *Campbeltown* would have reached the lock-gate. Her chances improved considerably with each second gained. The British knew that on the quays there were light cannon and machine-guns, and 40-mm. guns on Mindin Point. The heavy coastal batteries could not fire so near the port. It would therefore need a really unlucky shot to stop the destroyer now.

At last the Germans understood what was up. The storm broke loose. The only thing to do was to reply as best they could, and the leaping curves of the multi-coloured tracers crossed each other between the banks and the ships with their powerful wakes.

At that moment the M.G.B. passed a German armed trawler anchored just opposite the southern entrance. She gave it a few bursts from her pompom, and all the British ships astern followed suit as they passed the unfortunate vessel. As she dominated the M.L.s by her height, the German batteries in turn, taking her for a target, finished by sinking her.

The battle was an unequal one between the British crews, in the open, lit up by searchlights on the deck of their wooden M.L.s loaded with petrol, and the German artillery comfortably installed behind the concrete walls of their pill-boxes, hidden in the shadow of the quays and the buildings. However, the accurate fire from the sea slowed down the fire on land. It must also be mentioned that as they approached the Vieille Entrée the ships could concentrate their fire on the batteries surrounding it, while the other German coastal defences could no longer intervene.

On the bridge of the *Campbeltown* Beattie knew that on the promptness of his judgment and of his reflexes in these last moments depended the success of the main operation. Spitting clouds of smoke, the destroyer was now making nineteen knots. Each change of course had to be given in a split second. He could only make out indistinctly the details of the port in the blinding glare of the searchlights, hampered by the tracers, some of which burst on board and ricochetted in stars on the armour plating of the bridge. He suddenly noticed that his ship was heading for the end of the Vieux Môle.

"Starboard 10. Midships."

"Port 20."

Then he had to swing almost 60° to approach the gate, bows on.

The destroyer drew near. Thank God – it was in perfect alignment.

Instinctively everyone crouched. With an appalling ripping of metal, a huge spray of sparks and flames spurted from the bows. The shock was less violent than had been expected. In the engine-room they wondered whether they had really hit.

The plan had reckoned on the ramming taking place at

01.30 hours. It was 01.34 hours. The ship had penetrated almost to the opposite face of the lock-gate; in other words, to a depth of about thirty-three feet. All the forward bulkheads, torn to pieces, were firmly attached by their debris to those of the aperture. The upper part of the stern rose about six feet above the gate.

Immediately the eighty Commandos unrolled their rope ladders and climbed down from both sides onto the improvised quay. They ran off to their targets, covered by the destroyer's 20-mm., while, by the light of their torches, the special squad ran down into the holds to set the scuttling fuses.

On a level with the Vieux Môle, the M.G.B. had veered seawards to leave the *Campbeltown* a free run. She continued to reply to the fire from the light guns posted on both sides of the Vieille Entrée.

Ryder had been relieved to hear the destroyer's crash, punctuated by the spray of sparks, and to see the Commandos climbing down onto the improvised quayside.

The M.L.s of the starboard column had to land their assault troops at the stone stairs to the right of the Vieille Entrée and the jetty of the Mindin Ferry to the left of this same entrance, from the river side.

Unfortunately M.L. 192, which was leading this column, was the first to be hit by a shell, which set her on fire. Lieutenant-Commander Stevens, R.N.V.R., Flotilla Leader in Command, veered to port through the neighbouring column and managed to beach on the shallows south of the Vieux Môle.

Blinded and disturbed by this accident, the captains of M.L. 262 and 267, who were behind, missed the Vieille Entrée and had to make a complete circle in the roadstead before spotting their position again.

The next, M.L. 268, turned at the right moment to her landing point, but before reaching it was set on fire by a shell.

M.L. 156, the fifth in this column, was badly hit at the beginning of the action. More than half her crew and Commandos were out of the battle. The wheel was out of action.

It had to turn off and try to get astern of the last boat still under way.

The last boat in this column, M.L. 177 refused to be discouraged by the lot of those in front and managed to disembark her Commandos at the ferry jetty. At the same moment the M.G.B. put Colonel Newman and his staff ashore at the stairs opposite. When the M.L. 177 drew astern to leave her landing point Ryder gave it orders by megaphone to go alongside the *Campbeltown* and take off the survivors of the crew. In the meanwhile the M.G.B. made off and came alongside the stairs once more, near the lock-gate, its bows towards the Loire.

The M.T.B. 74, which approached, was hailed and stayed with the M.G.B. to await instructions. After their detour the M.L.s 262 and 267 managed to disembark their troops on the south bank of the Vieille Entrée, but they were so violently repulsed that they had to re-embark and retire beneath heavy fire.

The troops in the boats of the port column had to be disembarked at the stone stairs on the north side of the Vieux Môle.

Their main task was to take possession of the old port, which consisted of a small islet, bounded by the Loire, the St. Nazaire basin and the Vieille and Nouvelle Entrées. In order to do this they had to blow up the locks and the swing bridges connecting the islet and the mainland. The crews landed from the *Campbeltown* and the M.G.B. on the Penhoët islet, bounded by the lock and the St. Nazaire basin, had to join up with the others across the Vieille Entrée swivel bridge, which would be later destroyed, so that the general re-embarkation on the Vieux Môle would not be disturbed.

The M.L. 447, the leading ship of this column, approached the Vieux Môle to port, but was set on fire before she arrived.

The M.L. 457 which followed did not hesitate to attempt the same manœuvre and managed to land her troops. Manœuvring to return to the stairs, the enemy concentrated their fire on it and set it on fire.

Passing between the two flaming boats, the M.L. 307 made her way along the mole. She was machine-gunned at point-blank range in enfilade and grenades were hurled at her from the wall. Her fire killed several Germans on the jetty, but she had suffered several casualties, and after beaching had to set off again to attack the batteries and searchlights at Mindin.

Blinded by the searchlights, the flames and the smoke from the burning ships, Lieutenant Horlock overshot the mole. He brought his ship back to the boarding point, but came up against even stronger opposition, which forced him to turn back. Henderson, the last in the line, found himself in the same difficulties.

We have seen that M.L. 446 took on board the passengers from M.L. 341, which broke down before entering the Loire. Arriving in turn near the Vieux Môle, Lieutenant Falconer saw that the majority of his Commandos were already out of the battle. After a consultation with their N.C.O.s, he gave up the attempt at landing.

To sum up. Of all the M.L.s of the port column only M.L. 457 managed to land her troops. By an additional piece of bad luck, she was carrying a demolition group, badly equipped to fight an advance-guard action at a particularly well-defended point.

There remained the M.L.s armed with torpedoes. The M.L. 270 was hit in the stern as she was trying to silence the guns at the Vieille Entrée. She had to pull away. The M.L. 160 brought the valuable support of her fire to this zone and then returned to the Vieille Entrée, where she fired her torpedoes at a ship anchored in the outer harbour, without being able to observe the results of her fire. Lieutenant Boyd then went to the rescue of the burning boats near the Vieux Môle. He fished out three men and made a stern manœuvre to come alongside the only part of the M.L. 447 which was not yet ablaze. Surrounded by flames and smoke, he managed to embark eight soldiers, six of whom were wounded, four sailors, and, finally, in accordance with the rules of the sea, Lieutenant Platt, who completed the first day of his first command in this unforgettable manner.

The M.L. 298 fired on the batteries to the east of the lock
and then on those on the Vieux Mole. Crossing a sheet of
burning petrol, she caught fire. Becoming a concentrated
target for the enemy, she blew up with all aboard.

On board the M.G.B., stuck against the north quay of the
Vieille Entrée, Ryder did not know what had happened. The
blinding searchlights pin-pointed target after target. Bursts of
tracers, sparkling with gold, flame colour or silver, made the
water spout on the glassy surface of the river. Tall flames and
heavy black smoke rising from the boats transformed them
into living torches, and a sheet of blazing petrol spread all
around them. How could anyone follow the action of the
various boats in these conditions? Moreover, his aerial had
been shot away at the beginning of the battle. When the
M.G.B. drew alongside the stairs for the second time he saw
a large part of the *Campbeltown* crew arrive, carrying their
wounded, but among them there was no officer capable of
telling him the exact situation of the ship. He decided to go
and see for himself. Pike followed at his heels to serve as a
bodyguard, brandishing a broken bayonet he had found in a
corner.

Hardly had the two men taken a few steps than a sentry
barred their passage with a very determined air. The naval
chief of the raid hastily reassured him and gave the naval password, which in actual fact was his own name – "Ryder".

The destroyer was in the exact position desired. She seemed
abandoned. While the two men took shelter from bullets
behind the wall of a small building, the stern was shaken by
the explosion of the scuttling charges and slowly sank. There
was nothing to be done except to return to his M.G.B.

At that moment they heard dull explosions coming from
the pump-house and the manœuvring cabin of the lock-gate.
The Commandos had carried out their missions.

For Ryder, the immediate problem was the re-embarkation
at the Vieux Môle. He made his way there with his boat.

Also, it remained to utilize the torpedo mines of M.T.B.
74, since the *Campbeltown* had fulfilled her mission. They were
fired against the outer gate of the Vieille Entrée lock. They hit

it full in the middle and sank silently against it, as had been foreseen. After this manœuvre, the M.T.B. came alongside the M.G.B. and took aboard nine survivors from the destroyer.

"Return to England at full speed," ordered Ryder.

With her forty knots, this M.T.B. was the one with the greatest chances of coming undamaged out of this inferno.

As soon as the M.G.B. came out of the Vieille Entrée Ryder was unpleasantly surprised to find that the Vieux Môle was still stoutly defended by the enemy. The hulks of the burning M.L.s bore witness to the bitterness of the struggle. At that moment an M.L., making a new attempt, was caught in the violent fire from a concrete blockhouse on the extremity of the mole. The roofs of the neighbouring sheds were bristling with machine-guns, which added their deadly fire to that coming from the pill-box. Beneath this hail the M.L. was pierced by incendiary bullets and retired in turn, burning fiercely.

Before the M.G.B. could bring any support, another M.L. entered the slaughter. It was immediately hit and its burning petrol spread out over the black waters of the river.

Savage, the gun-layer of the M.G.B.'s pompom, directed his fire at the embrasure of the blockhouse, which momentarily ceased fire.

"Try and knock out the machine-guns on the roofs," said Curtiss.

This was very difficult, because they were situated slightly to the rear. The shots went too high and were lost, without leaving any traces, and those which were too short crashed against the walls, without effect. The M.G.B., on the contrary, lit up by the searchlights, was a magnificent target. So much so, in fact, that the 40-mm. guns from Mindin were able to fire on her across the estuary and threw up sprays of water nearer and nearer round the boat.

The blockhouse on the mole woke up again and was once more silenced by Savage's accurate firing, but unfortunately the gunner was hit by a shell and killed at his gun. It was an irreparable loss at a crucial moment.

Ryder ordered Curtiss to return to the Vieille Entrée.

There the battle was raging furiously. The quays and roofs were lit up for a moment with flashes from new guns.

Some Germans climbing aboard the *Campbeltown* succeeded in getting one of the oerlikons in action and began to enfilade the entrance.

One could no longer recognize friends and foes.

The battle became more and more unequal. The Germans could multiply indefinitely the guns firing on the estuary which could not be reached from the river, while the boats, which formed ideal targets, were nearly all out of action. Both points of possible re-embarkation seemed to be in the hands of the enemy. As far as his eyes could see along the estuary, Ryder was met with the spectacle of blazing or sinking M.L.s. Among the fifty men crowding on the M.G.B., the number of wounded grew from minute to minute.

A quick decision had to be made. A smoke-float was thrown into the water. After a brief consultation it seemed obvious that the moment had come when the only hope of saving the survivors of the M.G.B. was to put out to sea at full speed. The rudder and the engines still seemed intact. At any moment one of these vital parts might be hit.

With death in his heart when he thought of his abandoned comrades ashore, Ryder ordered: "Full speed ahead, course south-west."

At twenty-four knots, the M.G.B. leapt forward among the hulks, which were now sinking, and the sheets of flaming petrol. The wake which she threw upon each side of her keel attracted the cross-beams of the searchlights and the dangerous tracers which thrashed the water around her.

What had happened ashore?

The motto of the Commandos – "Quick in and quick out" – was particularly applicable at St. Nazaire, since it was estimated that the garrison numbered about ten thousand men – sailors, infantry, gunners, flak, Todt workers, etc.

In actual fact Me Grimaud, who at the time was attached to the Mayor of St. Nazaire, told me that more than a hundred thousand Germans were in the region around the Loire estuary from Pornichet Point to St. Gildas.

Newman had split his forces into small groups, with orders to carry out in the minimum of time the exact tasks for which the men had been so carefully trained. The disadvantage of this procedure was that for each group which failed to land some mission would not be carried out. In actual fact it was precisely the groups entrusted with the task of capturing and holding the re-embarkation point which could not carry out their mission.

But could one operate any differently in the short time available?

Furthermore, on such a long crossing, each M.L. could only carry fifteen men in addition to its own crew. This meant splitting up the Commando; and the troop which was the main formation of these special forces, comprising sixty-five men, was broken.

Each team had studied, down to the smallest detail, the model of St. Nazaire harbour, reconstructed from the R.A.F. reconnaissance photos. On this model all the quays, sheds goods yards, sluices, bridges, cranes, railway lines, trenches and pill-boxes were built to scale and in their actual aspects.

The Commandos in the *Campbeltown* were split into five groups of between ten to twenty men each.

Assault groups were ordered to capture the flak emplacements on either side of the lock-gate. The first group was then to destroy the oil reservoirs and to prevent the arrival of enemy reinforcements from this direction. The second had to make a bridgehead on the north side of the Vieille Entrée to collect all the *Campbeltown* groups once they had carried out their tasks.

Two demolition groups had to blow up the pumping station and the machinery of the north and south caisson gates. The fifth group, composed of Major Copland, second in command to Newman, and eight other men, was to supervise the assault from *Campbeltown* and the re-embarkation at Vieux Môle.

After the ramming, Lieutenant Roderick, at the head of the east assault group, captured the light batteries between the lock-gate and the Loire. He then went on to the mounds which covered the oil reservoirs. A hundred yards farther on he ran up against stiff opposition from German reinforcements, which greatly outnumbered his own group. As there was no possibility of pushing on farther, he held the enemy until the moment he took a spray of tracers for the signal to retire, and fought his way back towards the Vieille Entrée.

Captain Roy and his men landed at the same time on the Penhoët islet, quickly took the positions adjoining the quay. It now remained for him to put out of action the machine-guns on the terraced roof of the pumping station. The big cube-shaped building stood close beside the lockgate.

"Follow me," ordered Roy; and like Indians on the warpath, his men went forward in silence, skirting the west wall.

The attention of the German gunners was obviously concentrated on the southern side, towards the roadstead. At the foot of the north wall everything was quiet. "Attach the ladders to the edge of the roof."

Light ribbons of rope ladder were unrolled like serpents and, after a few attempts, hung down from the wall.

"All together, up you go!"

In the excitement, and deafened by the noise of their own firing, the German gunners did not see the smeared faces with their flat steel helmets suddenly emerge over the parapet of the roof. In an instant they were put out of action by a few unexpected tommy-gun bursts. Climbing down from their terrace, Roy and his men proceeded to hold the bridgehead, as arranged, in front of the bridge crossing the Vieille Entrée.

While they were attacking the roof, the sabotage squad had forced an entrance into the building.

The huge iron door was locked.

"Give me the gun cotton," called Lieutenant Chant.

In a flash the explosive was in place; retreat, crash, lock broken.

"Come on! Look out – it's a vertical descent."

He rushed down the iron ladder which led to the turbines, forty feet below.

"You know your jobs. You take the switchboards, you the valves down there at the bottom to the left. You get on with the electric motors and we'll look after the transformers."

"Everything O.K.? Have you checked everything? Well, get out quick."

Almost simultaneously the explosions shook the ground. Chant immediately went back to inspect the damage.

"Not a bad job," he said to his men. "I hope they'll enjoy it when they return. Set the transformer oil on fire. It won't do any harm."

At the same moment the team at the control post of the southern lock-gate blew up the machinery.

For their part, Lieutenant Etches and seventeen men ran off towards the north of the lock. They placed their charges along the gate in such a way as to scuttle it and to prevent it being manœuvred. The northern control post was completely destroyed and set on fire.

In this way all the teams from the *Campbeltown* carried out their missions with conscientious rapidity.

On landing from the M.G.B., Colonel Newman, his adjutant Captain Day and the six other men of his staff made their way towards the building situated south of the Vieille Entrée bridge, where it had been planned to make a temporary headquarters.

They ran into a German sentry, who, under the threat of a tommy-gun, declared that the building in question was occupied by a German headquarters.

"Go and tell them to come out with their hands up," Newman told him.

The man disappeared. No one came out, but a boat in the basin opened fire on them. Very opportunely, they were reinforced by Haynes' group – the only one which was able to land from M.L. 177 on the Mindin Ferry pontoon near the Vieille Entrée. The rest of the troops which were to have brought the material, and in particular the special flares with thirty-five red and green stars intended for the re-embarkation signal, could not get ashore from M.L. 267.

They had to act quickly. The German destroyers anchored in the basin now added their fire to that of the machine-guns mounted on the roof of the submarine pen. While Haynes replied with his 2-in. mortar, the German headquarters was cleared with grenades and taken over by the Commandos.

The M.L. 192, leader of the starboard column, hit at

the start, was steered by the Flotilla Leader, Lieutenant-Commander Stevens, towards the shallows south of the Vieux Môle. On board were Captain Burn and fourteen men charged to capture the two flak nests on the extreme north of the Penhoët islet, near the swivel bridge separating the two basins.

After being landed between the outer harbour and the Vieux Môle, Burn and the survivors of his group managed to cross the St. Nazaire islet as far as the Vieille Entrée. After this they followed the west quay of the Penhoët islet to their objective, which they found unoccupied. The installations were burnt.

Swiftly, after operating on the Penhoët islet, all the groups retired to headquarters and reported to Newman that their tasks had been carried out. Major Copland came back with his group and discussed with his chief the possibilities of re-embarkation.

The moment had come to retire to the Roy bridgehead, south of the Vieille Entrée. In default of the flares which had been arranged a runner was sent. Corporal Harrington rushed over the bridge, which was swept by fire from the destroyers and from the submarine base, and returned with Roy's group.

So far everything had gone well ashore, but what would be the reaction of these men when they learnt that all hope of re-embarkation had to be abandoned?

The only group landed on the Vieux Môle was Captain Pritchard's demolition squad, which had to blow up the swing-bridge and the southern lock-gate of the Nouvelle Entrée.

As soon as they were ashore these men came under violent simultaneous fire from the mole pill-box, the roof of a nearby shed and the very tall building near the submarine pen, from where the Germans were able to enfilade the street that crossed the old port on a level with the mole. While they were seeking shelter in vain behind some railway trucks several of them fell, including Captain Pritchard. They were joined by the covering group of five men under Lieutenant Watson, who had landed from the same M.L.

They decided to make their way to the swing-bridge by skirting a shed to reach the basin quay, but as soon as they tried to round the corner of this building they were caught once more in a converging fire from the destroyers and the machine-guns of the submarine pen. Time was slipping by. They had to get it over. Watson decided to make an attempt at all costs to reach the Nouvelle Entrée in a succession of rushes.

"Everyone set?"

At that moment a man rushed towards them, shouting an order. It was a runner from headquarters, giving the order for a general assembly at the Vieux Môle.

Very disappointed at the thought of not having carried out their mission, they assembled near an old building fifty yards west of the mole.

It was here that the real tragedy awaited these men.

Not a single M.L. lay alongside, and as far as the eye could see over the roadstead, hulks were still burning, surrounded by sheets of burning petrol.

All hope of being re-embarked had to be abandoned. Newman immediately called Copland and Day for a discussion behind a railway truck and told them of his intention to force a passage through the town. He would let the men split up in the country, so that they could try and make their way back to England through Spain, or any other way they chose.

These men, armed against all physical and moral ordeals, were by no means downcast at the tragedy of their situation. They had long been prepared for the worst eventualities. This was one of those which always have to be envisaged in such forays.

"We knew," said one of them, "that unless there was a surprise at the last moment we had little chance of ever being re-embarked."

Newman was perfectly cool and even made a few jokes.

"What a magnificent moonlight night. A night for lovers, eh?"

After telling them that they could now fend for themselves and try and get back to England, he added, with almost cockney humour, "Perhaps the smartest of you boys will be able to paddle home in your rubber boots. What do you think?"

Major Copland organised a defence round a line of railway trucks, which served as a temporary shelter. The machine-guns from the rooftops began to concentrate their fire in this direction.

An enemy group advanced, shouting, "*Heil Hitler*." Newman held his fire until the Jerries were twelve yards away. They were all mown down by bursts of tommy-gun fire, but gradually the enemy pressed home his advantage. The firing increased in intensity. Hand grenades were thrown over the trucks.

There was not a moment to be lost.

Swiftly Newman and Copland split the men up into groups of twenty, which were to try, independently, to make their way through the town. To get out of the "islands" some had to cross the iron turn-table of the railway track at the Nouvelle Entrée. The others would take the swivel-bridge between the Penhoët and the St. Nazaire basins.

The groups led by Newman, Copland and Day dashed towards the turn-table, lit up brightly by the moon and sprayed by wicked fire from the destroyers and the rooftops. Advancing in short rushes, the men crossed the bridge, while the bullets spattered or burst against the metal plates, and entered the main street facing them. Some German motor-cyclists riding towards them were wiped out immediately.

A little farther on they noticed a stationary car with all its lights on. They sensed a trap.

"So much the worse," said Major Copland. "I'll have a try. It's really too good an opportunity."

He tried in vain to start the car.

"Pity," he said. "It would have been an elegant way of going for a ride in the country. I don't think we'd better look and see what's wrong with the engine." Newman's idea was to get out of the main streets as soon as possible and go through the gardens of the houses in an attempt to reach the country. The best way of doing this was to split up into small groups of two or three men.

A Canadian who managed to get back to England a few

months later hid with a comrade in a courtyard. He knocked on the door, and as soon as it was opened he said: "Where's the back door?" Without further explanation, the two men forced their way through the house and found themselves in a garden, at the back of which was a pile of logs, which allowed them to leap the wall into a second garden. Dawn would soon replace the sinking moon. It was impossible to reach the country in broad daylight. They had to find some place to hide. After crossing some more gardens, they noticed a cellar window at the foot of a wall, at ground level. They slipped inside and spent the whole day in this cramped hiding-place between the floorboards and the soil.

They were too uncomfortable to be able to sleep, and they could hear all the comings and goings of the occupants just over their heads. They heard gunshots, tommy-gun bursts, and thought that some of their comrades must be waging their last battle. Between eleven o'clock and midday a tremendous explosion shook the earth. They looked at each other and said, with one accord: "That's the good old *Campbeltown*."

Towards midnight the two men climbed out of their hole and were at last able to stretch their aching limbs. They leapt over the garden wall and found themselves in a deserted street.

Still that bloody full moon. They made for the country by the stars and skirted close to the walls. They passed in front of a house, from which they heard the sound of German songs. The temptation of bursting in the door and emptying their tommy-gun magazines was very great, but common sense took the upper hand, and they went on their way. Eventually the town lay behind them.

Another group entered a cul-de-sac, and just as they turned back found their passage barred by some Germans. The British forced a passage and then, as dawn was near, they took refuge under the floor of a bomb-damaged house. The seriously wounded men were left lying not far from an enemy post, and those who were still fit decided to leave their hiding-place in twos at half-hour intervals during the following night.

Shortly before midday they, too, heard the violent explosion

and interpreted it, without hesitation, as their comrades had
done. During the evening a German patrol entered the ruins.
One of the men bent over the yawning hole.

In the darkness the Commandos were watching his movements with their fingers on the triggers of their tommy-guns.

The German stood up and uttered a few words which the
British, to their great relief, interpreted as meaning: "There's
no one there." He walked away with the rest of the patrol.

From 21.00 hours onwards the Commandos came out in
pairs at half-hour intervals, to take their chance. One of them
who was too seriously wounded shook his mates by the hand
and said that he would give himself up as a prisoner.

Many more men remained with Colonel Newman. They
went from street to street, diving into alleys to avoid enemy
trucks, which were firing in all directions. They, too, realized
that they could not reach the open country before daylight.
Their ammunition was practically exhausted. Many of the
men were urgently in need of attention. Among them was
Lieutenant Etches, who had led the demolition squad at the
northern lock-gate. He was wounded at the beginning of the
action on board the *Campbeltown* and, after carrying out his
mission at the other end of the lock, had fought until this
moment to remain with his chief.

Newman led them to a cellar which he had discovered by
chance. The wounded men were bandaged. The remaining
rations and ammunition were checked and redistributed to
give the unwounded men a chance of getting away the following night. Suddenly they heard the sound of hurrying
footsteps and orders shouted in German. In a flash the house
was surrounded by a substantial force.

"Come out with your hands up or else we'll bomb you
out!"

The situation was hopeless. They had to carry out the
order.

Of the men we saw leave the harbour only five escaped
capture and returned to England.

Newman wondered if the speed of the German reaction had
not been due to a previous warning.

The delay in opening fire on the flotilla showed without a doubt that its arrival had been a surprise, but all the military and auxiliary German organizations had been on the alert for an hour since the air raid.

The German anti-aircraft measures included the alert of all detection apparatus, of all searchlights, quick-firing guns, patrols for the maintenance of order, first-aid teams and fire fighters, both on land and on board the warships anchored in the basins.

As soon as the approach of the amphibian task force was discovered, all these measures were immediately directed against it. Even more so, since the British planes, numbering about a hundred, which had flown over the town had not dropped their bombs because they did not consider visibility good enough to find their target accurately.

In actual fact this air raid did more harm than good. Instead of diverting the defence, it merely put it on the alert.

The M.G.B. sped away like a thoroughbred when given its head. The water, more crushed than torn beneath the bows well out of the water, and threshed by the screws, burst behind them in a broad, long, silver wake, which bubbled furiously.

"That's fine and dandy – they're still firing at the smoke-screen."

In their haste to finish off this last surviving boat the German gunners had not seen it leave the cloud of smoke thrown off by the smoke-float, and continued to aim on the latter.

The estuary was too well lit by the moon and the search-lights for the broad, increasing wake not to draw the attention of the other batteries. One after the other they went into action, but, misjudging the wake and the speed of the craft, they fired at its stern.

"M.L. on the port bow."

It was a survivor which the M.G.B. would quickly outstrip. It would have been useless to wait, as they could have afforded it no protection.

"Give her a smoke-screen when we draw level," said Ryder; "that's all we can do to help her get out of the jam."

At this speed the M.G.B. would soon be out of range of the quick-firing flak guns. Gordon Holman, the only war correspondent with the party, looked after the wounded. The few other unwounded men helped in this task, and Curtiss took the wheel himself to allow the topman to give a hand to his comrades.

"That's a big fellow."

A red flash burst on the dark coast, followed by a growl of thunder. A few seconds and tall "poplar trees" rose from the water some way ahead.

"Straddled by the first salvo, eh? Those fellows must have some good layers who can gauge the speed of their target."

"What an honour for our cockleshell!"

The sprays of water raised by the salvos were still in the air when the M.G.B. reached them, and Curtiss was obliged to manœuvre between them so as not to wreck his boat. These zigzags might confuse the layers.

The seconds passed. Already the extremities of the searchlight beams merged with the unreal lunar light, and yet the big shells, with the same regularity, kept planting an avenue of poplar trees on either side of the small craft. It was obvious that the Germans were following all the movements of their little quarry with radar.

At last the rhythm of the flashes, punctuated by the sound of the bursts, died down and ceased, without the batteries having been able to sink this small fugitive.

Their respite was short-lived.

"Motor launch on the starboard bow. Another one we've probably caught up with."

A sudden familiar dry crackle in the petrol tank punctuated the shots which came from the unknown craft. It was a German E-boat.

"Are we going up in flames?"

The seconds seemed like centuries, while Curtiss took avoiding action to give the enemy the slip. With this movement, the forward gun, the only one still able to fire, was masked by the superstructure. As soon as it became clear, the skipper bore down on the German to return his fire.

To the great relief of the British, luck was on their side once more. Their petrol did not catch fire and, on the contrary, after the first bursts from the oerlikon, bright flames spurted on board the enemy vessel, which was left to its fate.

"Another M.L. ahead."

This time they were not going to mistake her nationality. She gave her recognition signals. It was M.L. 270, still steering with the handwheel. As they were now out of range of the shore batteries, Ryder reduced speed to twelve knots to sail in company with her. He set course for point Y, thirty miles south-west of St. Nazaire, the first rendezvous planned for the homeward journey.

The sea was still calm and extraordinarily phosphorescent. Hosts of silver spangles glittered in the wakes. Towards 04.25 hours a bright gleam, which they wrongly interpreted as the explosion on the *Campbeltown*, appeared in the direction of St. Nazaire, and a few minutes later the two craft arrived at point Y.

"Nothing in sight."

The spot was too unhealthy for the two little vessels to hang about at that moment.

"Let's be on our way," said Ryder.

An hour later they noticed to the north the usual exchanges of tracer shells. They would only know later what was going on in that direction.

An hour passed and then another exchange of gunfire, this time much nearer. Shots of greater calibre and no tracers, but the flashes to be seen in the east. Ships with that type of gun must be at least destroyer class.

"Perhaps they're the five famous Jerries we were warned of."

There was nothing to be done but to carry on out to sea, for it would soon be dawn. The officers scanned the horizon around them with their binoculars as its circle grew larger.

Something to stern. It was an M.L. Another to port about a mile away. They gave their recognition signals. The former was the M.L. 156 and the latter the M.L. 446, both of which, as we have already seen, had to give up landing their troops on account of the heavy losses suffered during the approach. The M.G.B. turned about to pick up the M.L. 156.

"Destroyers in sight."

"Are they Jerry's or ours?"

There were two of them searching on the exact itinerary of their homeward course. No mistake this time – they were the *Atherstone* and the *Tynedale*.

The former arrived swiftly alongside the M.L. 156. It was high time, for she was shipping water fast and the survivors were in a state of extreme exhaustion. Fortunately the state of the sea allowed them to be taken aboard the destroyer. Letting the M.L. sink, the latter came alongside the M.G.B.

On board Ryder's craft the dawn revealed a heartbreaking sight. The bridge was covered with wounded men, huddled in all the corners, and blood was running all over the deck. The hull and superstructures – particularly in the bows – had been pierced by small shells, including the last salvo from the E-boat, which had hit a petrol tank.

Despite the calm sea, it was not easy to hoist the wounded men aboard the *Atherstone*. They managed it somehow. In the meanwhile the *Tynedale* had taken aboard the survivors of the M.L.s 270 and 446.

This operation took about half an hour, during which time there was every fear of an irruption by the five German destroyers, for Ryder, as he boarded the *Atherstone*, learned that the battle he had seen to the east was an exchange of shots between the two British destroyers and the Germans in question.

Lieutenant-Commander Jenks told him what had happened.

"We had to patrol parallel to the shore on either side of point Y to await your return. We had to avoid at all costs revealing our presence before the start of your action, for fear of arousing the suspicion of the enemy as to the true reason for this unusual incursion off St. Nazaire.

"We knew that your chances of getting back to England depended to a large extent on our skill in being there in a place to help you at the time of the rendezvous. The signal from Pompey made us fear that we might meet the five German destroyers, a force at least double our own.

"Moreover, we knew how things had gone at St. Nazaire. We spent a very anxious night. After half-past two we received departure signals in succession from M.L.s 177, 160, 307 and 443. That was all.

"Towards half-past four, when we were in the neighbourhood of point Y, I noticed three groups of M.L.s heading for the open sea.

"Those at least have got through, I thought. An hour later, as dawn was about to break, we put five miles between us to scour the return route and come to the assistance of strugglers.

"Dawn broke and the horizon grew larger from minute to minute.

"And then we saw them. Not our M.L.s, but the enemy destroyers.

"All five of them in line ahead to port, with the characteristic silhouette of the *Moewe* class, which we copied so well on the *Campbeltown*.

"We had to lure them away from the M.L.s somehow, so sailed southwards and the *Tynedale* tried to join me at top speed. The enemy followed our movements and opened.

"For ten minutes it concentrated its fire on the *Tynedale*, which replied energetically. She was hit twice, but registered a hit on the third German destroyer of the line. We broke off action and put out a smoke-screen. Despite his evident superiority in numbers, the enemy did not give chase."

In his report the officer in command of the German flotilla tried to explain this lack of fighting spirit by damages to his engines, which, he said, reduced the speed of his flotilla to eighteen knots.

What happened to the other M.L.s?

In addition to the group found by the destroyers at dawn, the M.L.s 443, 307, 160 and 306 also managed to reach the open sea.

After the setback at the attempted approach to the Mindin ferry pontoon the M.L. 267 made off on fire and had to be

abandoned by the survivors. The M.L. 177, which managed
to disembark Haynes' troop at this point, approached the
stern of the *Campbeltown*. She embarked the part of her crew
which did not join the M.G.B. at the north stairs on land,
including Lieut.-Commander Beattie and his officers. As soon
as this operation was completed she set a course for the open
sea at fifteen knots. Would she manage to come undamaged
through this infernal circle with her precious crew? Somehow
she did. She weaved among the vicious little sprays from the
flak and sped farther out to sea, minute by minute. Another
few seconds and she would be out of range.

A ripping of wood and spurts of flames dashed this last hope
to the ground. The fire spread rapidly. They had to abandon
ship. The wounded men were put in carley floats, to which
the more or less unwounded clung. For four hours these men
were buffeted in the cold water, lit up by the sinister gleams
of the burning hull. In the early morning a German trawler
spotted them and picked them up. Several of them died from
exhaustion.

Beattie was among the survivors. A few months later
the German military commandant of his oflag ordered a
ceremonial parade and solemnly read out the citation of
the V.C. which had been awarded to him as a tribute to
the crew of the *Campbeltown*.

The M.L. 298 suffered a similar fate after completing at
least a mile of the return journey. As for the famous M.T.B.
74, which with her thirty knots seemed to have the best
chance of not being hit, once out at sea her skipper exposed
her courageously to danger, by trying to rescue the crew of
one of the burning M.L.s. By stopping, she made an easy
target for the enemy and was set on fire in turn, a victim of
his chivalrous comradeship.

Let us return to the last M.L. of the port column. Her
skipper, Lieutenant Henderson, tried in vain to land his
passengers at the Vieux Môle. At two o'clock, with only
one oerlikon in action and many of his men wounded, he
had to give up his attempt unless he wished to share the
fate of all the craft which came under the reinforced fire

from the pill-boxes and the neighbouring roofs. He had
to retire.

"Full speed ahead. Drop a smoke-float."

Pursued by sprays of flak, the M.L. 306, making eighteen
knots, miraculously escaped any fatal hits. The big batteries,
busy no doubt with the M.G.B., neglected her and she was
soon out of range.

The worst seemed to be over. They were already forty-five
miles away from the rat-trap. It was half-past five. It would
soon be dawn, and in daylight there would be more chance
of joining up with their friends.

"Hell! What are those shapes I can make out on the port
bow? They're too tall for M.L.s. They must be at least
destroyers, and there are too many of them to be ours."

"Stop!"

They had to endeavour not to be seen until they could
identify the suspicious craft. For a small M.L. at night, the
first thing to do was to eliminate the revealing wake. Perhaps
in these conditions they could escape the enemy spotters and
pass for one of those many fishing-boats they had passed the
night before in these waters. It was dark enough to hope they
would not be noticed.

The unknown ships passed a hundred yards away from the
M.L. At that distance they could make out the silhouettes of
the German *Moewes*.

Moments of great anxiety. They passed. They were already
far away. There was no sign to show that they had spotted
the M.L.

"On our way."

The engines started. The screws sent a cloud of phosphorescent bubbles to the surface. Did this betray them
or had the enemy already spotted them? At that moment
the rear destroyer's searchlight lit them up and the flotilla turned about with the obvious intention of attacking them.

To these five heavily armed hunters the harmless laggard
only seemed worthy of a little buckshot. The macabre dance
of the tracers which they thought they had left behind
began again.

Henderson replied with the only gun in action and the enemy was so close that the Commandos fired bursts of their Bren-guns.

Continuing his manœuvre, the leading destroyer got into position to ram its fragile adversary.

"Full speed ahead! Hard to starboard! Hard to port!"

With these movements, the M.L. 306 avoided the bows of the German and followed him round.

This game of cat-and-mouse could not go on. The hunters grew impatient. As buckshot was not enough, let's try a dose of shells.

Profiting by a moment when the M.L. was fifty yards away, the destroyer trained her guns on her. A 4-in. shell carried away the bridge, with the skipper. The surviving officers were seriously wounded.

The enemy drew alongside the immobilized M.L. and in bad English ordered the survivors to surrender. As they had no more means of continuing this unequal struggle, the survivors climbed aboard the enemy ship.

"Aircraft due east."

The rescue over, the British destroyers and the three M.L.s still afloat got under way.

The suspicious plane grew larger and the noise of its engines louder. It was a Heinkel III. The gun crews were at action stations, but after a reconnaissance at a respectful distance the plane took as its target the M.L. 156, which had been abandoned to stern. After an abortive attempt it registered a direct hit, thus completing the task the *Tynedale* had intended to carry out later – to prevent her falling into the hands of the enemy.

The Heinkel would obviously report the British squadron and they would now be subjected to constant air attack throughout the day.

"Aircraft to the north." The game went on.

But they had a surprise. The first Beaufighter from Coastal Command came to their rescue.

It arrived at the right time. The other plane from the east would find his answer in his own element. It was a Junkers

88. All the spectators below followed the opening moves of this strange combat with the keenest interest.

What was happening? The Beaufighter was behaving in the strangest manner. It looked as though it were going to ram the Ju.

That was it. The two machines collided and their entangled debris crashed into the sea. The *Tynedale* searched in vain for survivors.

"Bearing 315 degrees. Two unidentified ships."

"Identify them."

Reply: "H.M.S. *Cleveland* and *Brocklesby*." The two reinforcing destroyers announced the day before by Plymouth. Better late than never.

Signal from the *Cleveland*: "I am taking over. Stop. Have just met three M.L.s on their way to England."

Commander Sayer, the senior officer of the ships present, took over command, to Ryder's great relief. Exhausted by the responsibilities of that terrible night, he could now relax.

The M.L.s were the 160, 307 and 443, which, as we saw, got away from St. Nazaire.

The new commander immediately had grave decisions to take. The fine weather from the east, which had held so far, was rapidly changing. The normal west wind had sprung up and was increasing in strength. The sea, which had been calm a few moments before, began to rock the M.L.s and to slow them down more and more. They began to ship water through all the holes received in the battle. Many of the seriously wounded would not survive unless they received quick attention in hospital.

The slowing down was even more disturbing, since they were still only sixty miles from the enemy coast and without air cover, after the Beaufighter crashed. Low clouds scudding from north-west to south-east offered magnificent cover for attacking aircraft. The latter had no intention of relinquishing their prey and attacks continued throughout the morning, but so far without damage to the ships. During one of these attacks, the *Brocklesby* shot down a Ju. 88, but the luck could easily change.

All this time the Aldis lamps were repeatedly in action.
Sayer kept asking the M.L. skippers: "What is the state of
your craft?"

"We're shipping a lot of water – we shall be obliged to
reduce speed even more. If the sea increases we shall have
to heave to."

To heave to, of course, meant to abandon the convoy and to
lay head on to the waves on the spot. There was no question of
going to these extremes, particularly in view of the dilapidated
state in which the M.L.s were at the moment. The captain had
to take his decision. Before the operation became impossible
he must get the crews on board the destroyers and scuttle
the M.L.s.

Very intelligently Commander Sayer sent the signal: "Prepare to abandon ship and scuttle."

The operation was carried out early in the afternoon. It
was high time. Fortunately there were only fit men on board,
for they had profited by the calm before dawn to evacuate
the wounded. It was with sinking hearts, as every sailor can
understand, that the skippers saw the small craft, to which
their destinies had been bound during the battle, disappear
beneath the waves.

After this painful but necessary surgical operation the four
destroyers could increase their speed to twenty-five knots and
deploy in an effort to find the three other M.L.s they had met
that morning.

That evening the *Cleveland* picked up a message from them.
Commander Sayer ordered the *Atherstone* and the *Tynedale* to
make for Plymouth at full speed and to disembark the wounded
as quickly as possible. The *Cleveland* and the *Brocklesby* tried in
vain to get into contact again with the three M.L.s.

The latter, under the command of Lieutenant Platt, a
survivor of M.L. 447, and the senior officer of the party,
continued with their crossing unescorted. They beat off enemy
aircraft with their oerlikons.

The first attacker, a Heinkel III, was shot down and crashed
into the sea. A big Blohm and Voss, despising these frail
adversaries, ventured too near, was greeted by a firework
display, and after being hit broke off the engagement.

One of the most serious difficulties was their fuel consumption. If the sea delayed them any more they would be out of juice before arriving at the English coast.

At last they came in sight of land.

"Direct course for Falmouth."

To leeward of the Lizard the sea grew calmer. They arrived just in time, with barely a few gallons of petrol left in their tanks.

We remember that the M.L. 341, which had engine trouble at the entrance to the Loire, transferred her Commandos on board the M.L. 446. Having tried in vain to rejoin the expedition, she was obliged to turn for home. This was the fourth M.L. which managed to get home out of the eighteen which had embarked forty-eight hours earlier, full of faith and keenness, upon this memorable adventure.

And what of the people of St. Nazaire?

Woken up by the wail of the air-raid siren, some went down into their shelters; others, without leaving their rooms, tried to see the firework display in the sky through closed shutters during a strictly enforced blackout.

They heard the drone of a great number of planes grow louder and then fade away without it being accompanied by the terrible explosion of the bombs which such a noise usually heralded.

The searchlight beams broke on the low clouds, which the flak tracers pierced in their fury.

Silence followed, but the all-clear signal was not given.

Suddenly the crackle of small-arms fire started, hesitant at first and then suddenly unleashed and increasing in volume. An extraordinary thing, this time the trajectories did not rise to the sky. The searchlights and the fire of the German guns were trained on the roadstead.

The more inquisitive townsmen, whose windows looked out onto the sea-front, could see in the beams of the searchlights a group of ships, one of which, larger than the others, was a destroyer type. They were making at full speed towards the port.

"I had a close view of a fast ship making for the Place du

Basin," said M. Gordé, who had been smoking a cigarette on
his balcony in the rue Thiers.

"The British fire rained on the town, skimming the roofs
or bursting against the façades. Mc Grimaud, the Deputy
Mayor, told me that, not knowing what was happening in
the roadstead, he thought at once: 'The Boche are losing
their heads. Now they're machine-gunning the streets and
the houses'."

"They're firing low."

This was the news which spread from cellar to cellar
and naturally to the A.R.P. headquarters – rue de l'Hôtel
de Ville.

M. Compradon, the head of the A.R.P., took the receiver
off the telephone, which had just rung.

"Doctor Bizard here, Chief Warden of the Naval Prison.
British destroyers are making for the south entrance. We are
being heavily shelled."

"Don't talk rubbish."

The communication was interrupted. Runners arrived in
quick succession.

"They're fighting in the streets of Old St. Nazaire."

"The British troops are infiltrating the yards."

"The Boche can't get over it – they don't know where to
strike."

Mc Grimaud told me that, intrigued by this continued sound
of machine-gun fire and knowing nothing at his post in the fire
station, he telephoned to the Town Hall headquarters.

"What's going on?"

"There's a landing."

"Are you pulling my leg?"

Monsieur Lecornu, the Sub-Prefect, took out the A.R.P.
ambulances and tried to get them through the German
cordons. The soldiers cried, *"Zivilisten heraus."* When he
got to headquarters he phoned M. Deniaud, the Departmental A.R.P. Chief, and tried to convey indirectly the
sensational news.

At the moment of the air-raid alert the Germans who had
no action stations took shelter with their weapons. When

their officers realised the new form of attack which had been launched against them they had great difficulty in arming and regrouping their men into counter-attack detachments.

"A landing, a landing!" repeated the bewildered soldiers, without really knowing what was happening.

On the Boulevard Albert Ier, the Town Major von Trotha, who confirmed the news to M. Lecornu and gave him instructions what route to take with the ambulances, assembled his men, revolver in hand, and led them to the old town. Trucks loaded with German soldiers roared noisily through the streets in the direction of the harbour. Sentries were posted at every street corner.

Many of the French began to think that an attack from the sea, accompanied by an air raid, so far from the nearest Allied bases, could only be a major operation, designed perhaps to open the famous Second Front which had been so long discussed.

They were about to witness one of those historic moments – dangerous moments for unarmed witnesses, looked upon with suspicion by the occupying forces! Some of them who had managed to conceal a weapon decided to go down into the streets when the time came to lend a hand to the liberators.

Before dawn the noise of firing spread from the old harbour to the town and then ceased at daybreak. The German patrols continued to search the cellars and the houses, crying, "Tommies, Tommies." They evacuated the civilians and proceeded to carry out their usual perquisitions, firing at the least provocation. Mc Grimaud was nearly hit by a burst of machine-gun fire. A young A.R.P. worker was wounded outside the Town Hall. In all, three of the town folk were killed during the night.

It is impossible to portray the amazement of my compatriots when they saw the British in battle dress or Scots in their kilts appear in their houses or cellars. Seventeen of them descended into the shelter of the Caisse d'Epargne, asking for a plan of the town and for civilian clothes. Then they went to the Town Hall police station, where they were surrounded by overwhelming German forces. A police official intervened to avoid a general massacre and negotiated their surrender.

The cellar where Newman and about thirty of his men took refuge was just opposite the Kommandantur. This accounts for the swift descent of the Germans, who captured them in their shelter.

As day broke, from the Boulevard de L'Ocean could be seen the horrible sight of the estuary in flames, with the M.L.s burning like torches in the water. About 05.25 hours (4.25 British time) one of them exploded with a tremendous fracas, making the window-panes rattle. This was the explosion that the M.G.B. saw from out at sea and wrongly interpreted as being the *Campbeltown*.

In the town order was not restored until half-past eight. The event was eagerly commented. The first B.B.C. broadcast at 6.30 was laconic. "A raid has been carried out on St. Nazaire. All the objectives were reached. Further details will be given on the return of the expedition."

This left the stage clear for enemy propaganda. The first German communiqué read: "British forces tried to land in the bay of St. Nazaire. Caught by the fire of the shore batteries and the flak, they suffered considerable losses. The few elements who landed were immediately surrounded and wiped out. The majority of the naval units were sunk."

The second communiqué gave more details:

"An old American destroyer loaded with explosives, which was to have rammed the lock-gate, blew up without having reached the target. A destroyer, nine fast motor-boats and four motor torpedo launches were destroyed. In addition to his severe losses, the enemy left more than a hundred prisoners in our hands. No German war unit has been lost and no damage has been caused to the submarine base."

According to what the townspeople of St. Nazaire could see and hear, the German version appeared, alas, to be true. During Saturday morning, 28th March, with aching hearts, they saw trucks loaded with British prisoners, most of them wounded, on their way to the camps at La Baule. Access to the harbour yards was forbidden. Until ten o'clock sporadic firing could be heard in the town.

Shortly before midday a formidable explosion rocked the houses and broke all the windows in a large radius round the port. A heavy silence followed. The occupying forces were obviously flabbergasted. A few isolated shots rang out during the course of the following night.

In the morning of the 29th the workers and dockers who tried once more to reach their work in the port found that the Germans were completely disorganized. Having heard the B.B.C. story of the *Campbeltown*'s mission and the German-controlled radio proclaim that she blew up before reaching the target, the most inquisitive did their best to approach the lock from where the terrible explosion the night before seemed to have come. The disorganization of the German services allowed them to get there.

A hideous spectacle met their eyes. The quays near the outer lock-gate were literally piled with corpses. Others were floating in the lock, whose south gate seemed to have disappeared. Shreds of uniform allowed them to recognise the macabre remains of German soldiers of all ranks. Fatigue parties were fishing the bodies out of the water and piling them up. They spread sand on the more bloodstained spots.

Contrary to the normal military behaviour of the Germans, there seemed to be a lack of organization and efficiency. Judging it more prudent not to linger in the vicinity, the French dockers returned to their workshops or yards and questioned the German workers as to what had happened.

They learnt that the *Campbeltown* had approached the caisson-gate, right in the middle, and had rammed it, without making a total breach, which would have allowed the sea to invade the lock.

The German admiral Kellermann, the commandant of the base, went on board, accompanied by several officers and engineers, to study the wreck. He worked out the best means of rapidly disengaging it from the door and repairing the breach. Behind the cordons of troops some Germans tried to approach and take a look at the enemy destroyer. After sizing up the position, the German admiral left, but several officers remained on board to make further investigations.

We shall probably never know if those experts discovered the famous bomb bay. One thing is certain: the fuses do not appear to have functioned, since it was shortly before midday, after a delay corresponding to that of the explosive pencils introduced into every third depth charge on entering the roadstead, which produced the explosion.

The effect of igniting about four tons of powerful explosive in such conditions is difficult to imagine in all its sinister horror. From information obtained later by the British it was discovered that sixty officers and three hundred and twenty private soldiers were killed by this explosion. The caisson-gate was subjected to such pressure that it literally crumpled at the point of ramming. Its ends protruded from their hinges in the quayside and the swift entrance of the sea forced it inside and thrust it up against the west wall.

Under the effect of this cataclysm, which forecasts what the explosion of an atomic bomb would be like in an outer port, the lock was suddenly invaded by the sea. Two huge cargo ships which were in dry dock were instantaneously lifted up like straws and flung against the northern door, causing great damage to it. But strange as it may seem, they themselves remained afloat without sustaining any major damage. The scuttled stern of the *Campbeltown* was flung to the end of the lock. The pumping station, already sabotaged by the Commandos, was destroyed. In this way the main goal of the raid – putting the great lock of St. Nazaire out of service for a long time – was a complete success, but the British only learned of this later.

AFTERWORD

Of the 619 officers and men of the Royal Navy and British Army Commandos (mostly drawn from No. 2 Commando) who went up the Loire on that fateful day in March 1942, 159 were killed, 200 wounded and captured. It was an action marked by extraordinary bravery: no less than five Victoria Crosses were awarded to the St. Nazaire raiders. The citations were careful to express gratitude not only to the individuals concerned, but to the services they were from. Those awarded the VC were Lieutenant Commander S. H. Beattie, the captain of the Campbeltown, *Lieutenant-Colonel C. Newman, Commander R.E.D. Ryder, Able Seaman W. Savage and Sergeant*

T. F. Durrant. The latter was awarded the VC posthumously for attempting to defend his Motor Launch against the German destroyer Jaguar *whilst severely wounded. The award was recommended by a German officer who witnessed Durrant's bravery.*

ASSAULT INTO HELL
E. B. Sledge

Eugene Sledge served as a mortarman with the 1st Marine Division of the United States Marine Corps in the Pacific during WWII. He took part in the invasion of the Japanese-held island of Peleliu – a little known but uncommonly bloody battle – in September 1944, and later in the invasion of Okinawa. His memoir of that time, With the Old Breed, *is one of the finest to emerge from the Second World War. In the following pages from the book, he describes the 1st Marine Division's assault on Ngesebus, a small island off Peleliu.*

The 1st Marine Division occupies a place of special honour in the history of the United States Marine Corp, being the sole Marine Division to have had units fight in all America's major wars in the twentieth century: its Fifth Regiment fought at Belleau Wood in 1918 (so ferociously that the Germans nicknamed its members Teufelhunden, *or "devil dogs"); during WWII, the 1st Marine Division fought at Guadalcanal and Cape Gloucester, as well as Peleliu and Okinawa; it was the only Marine division to fight in Korea and, along with the 3rd and 5th Marine Divisions, it fought in Vietnam.*

EARLY THE NEXT morning our battalion made a successful assault on a small hill on the narrow neck of northern Peleliu. Because of its isolated position, it lacked the mutual support from surrounding caves that made most of the ridges on the island impregnable.

At this time the rest of the regiment was getting a lot of enemy fire from Ngesebus Island. The word was that several days earlier the Japanese had slipped reinforcements by barge down to Peleliu from the larger islands to the north; some of the barges had been shot up and sunk by the navy, but

several hundred enemy troops got ashore. It was a real blow
to our morale to hear this.

"Sounds just like Guadalcanal," said a veteran. "About the
time we think we got the bastards boxed in, the damn Nips
bring in reinforcements, and it'll go on and on."

"Yeah," said another, "and once them slant-eyed bastards
get in these caves around here, it'll be hell to pay."

On 27 September army troops took over our positions. We
moved northward.

"Our battalion is ordered to hit the beach on Ngesebus
Island tomorrow," an officer told us.

I shuddered as I recalled the beachhead we had made on
15 September. The battalion moved into an area near the
northern peninsula and dug in for the night in a quiet area.
It was sandy, open, and had some shattered, drooping palms.
We didn't know what to expect on Ngesebus. I prayed the
landing wouldn't be a repeat of the holocaust of D day.

Early in the morning of 28 September (D + 3) we squared
away our gear and stood by to board the amtracs that would
take us across the 500–700 yards of shallow reef to Ngesebus.

"We'll probably get another battle star for this beachhead,"
said a man enthusiastically.

"No we won't," answered another. "It's still just part of
the Peleliu operation."

"The hell you say; it's still another beachhead," the first
man responded.

"I don't make the regulations, ole buddy, but you check
with the gunny, and I'll betcha I'm right." Several mumbled
comments came out about how stingy the high command
was in authorizing battle stars, which were little enough
compensation for combat duty.

We boarded the tractors and tried to suppress our fear.
Ships were firing on Ngesebus, and we saw Marine F4U
Corsair fighter planes approaching from the Peleliu airfield
to the south. "We gonna have lots of support for this one,"
an NCO said.

Our amtracs moved to the water's edge and waited for H
hour as the thunderous prelanding naval gunfire bombardment covered the little island in smoke, flame, and dust. The

Corsairs from Marine Fighter Squadron (VMF) 114 peeled off
and began bombing and strafing the beach. The engines of the
beautiful blue gull-winged planes roared, whined, and strained
as they dove and pulled out. They plastered the beach with
machine guns, bombs, and rockets. The effect was awesome
as dirt, sand, and debris spewed into the air.

Our Marine pilots outdid themselves, and we cheered,
yelled, waved, and raised our clenched fists to indicate our
approval. Never during the war did I see fighter pilots take
such risks by not pulling out of their dives until the very last
instant. We were certain, more than once, that a pilot was
pulling out too late and would crash. But, expert flyers that
they were, they gave that beach a brutal pounding without
mishap to plane or pilot. We talked about their spectacular
flying even after the war ended.

Out to sea on our left, with a cruiser, destroyers, and other
ships firing support, was a huge battleship. Someone said
it was the USS *Mississippi*, but I never knew for sure. She
ranked with the Corsairs in the mass of destruction she hurled
at Ngesebus. The huge shells rumbled like freight cars – as
the men always used to describe the sound of projectiles from
full-sized battleships' 16-inch guns.

At H hour our tractor driver revved up his engine. We
moved into the water and started the assault. My heart
pounded in my throat. Would my luck hold out? "The
Lord is my shepherd," I prayed quietly and squeezed my
carbine stock.

To our relief we received no fire as we approached the
island. When my amtrac lurched to a stop well up on the
beach, the tailgate went down with a bump, and we scrambled
out. With its usual din and thunder the bombardment moved
inland ahead of us. Some Company K Marines on the beach
were already firing into pillboxes and bunkers and dropping
in grenades. With several other men, I headed inland a short
distance. But as we got to the edge of the airstrip, we had to
dive for cover. A Nambu (Japanese light machine gun) had
cut loose on us.

A buddy and I huddled behind a coral rock as the machine-
gun slugs zipped viciously overhead. He was on my right.

Because the rock was small, we pressed shoulder to shoulder, hugging it for protection. Suddenly there was a sickening crack like someone snapping a large stick.

My friend screamed, "Oh God, I'm hit!" and lurched over onto his right side. He grabbed his left elbow with his right hand, groaning and grimacing with pain as he trashed around kicking up dust.

A bypassed sniper had seen us behind the rock and shot him. The bullet hit him in the left arm, which was pressed tightly against my right arm as we sought cover from the machine gun out front. The Nambu was firing a bit high, but there was no doubt the sniper had his sights right on us. We were between a rock and a hard place. I dragged him around the rock out of sight of the sniper as the Nambu bullets whizzed overhead.

I yelled, "Corpsman!" and Ken (Doc) Caswell, the mortar section corpsman, crawled over, opening his pouch to get at his first aid supplies as he came. Another man also came over to see if he could help. While I cut away the bloody dungaree sleeve from the injured arm with my kabar, Doc began to tend the wound. As he knelt over his patient, the other Marine placed his kabar under the injured man's pack strap and gave a violent upward jerk to cut away the shoulder pack. The razor-sharp blade sliced through the thick web pack strap as though it were a piece of string. But before the Marine could arrest its upward motion, the knife cut Doc in the face to the bone.

Doc recoiled in pain from the impact of the knife thrust. Blood flowed down his face from the nasty gash to the left of his nose. He regained his balance immediately and returned to his work on the smashed arm as though nothing had happened. The clumsy Marine cursed himself for his blunder as I asked Doc what I could do to help him. Despite considerable pain, Doc kept at his work. In a quiet, calm voice he told me to get a battle dressing out of his pouch and press it firmly against his face to stop the bleeding while he finished work on the wounded arm. Such was the selfless dedication of the navy hospital corpsmen who served in Marine infantry units. It was little wonder that

we held them in such high esteem. (Doc later got his face
tended and was back with the mortar section in a matter of
a few hours.)

While I did as Doc directed, I yelled at two Marines coming
our way and pointed toward the sniper. They took off quickly
toward the beach and hailed a tank. By the time a stretcher
team came up and took my wounded friend, the two men
trotted by, waved, and one said, "We got the bastard; he
ain't gonna shoot nobody else."

The Nambu had ceased firing, and an NCO signaled us
forward. Before moving out, I looked toward the beach and
saw the walking wounded wading back toward Peleliu.

After we moved farther inland, we received orders to set
up the mortars on the inland side of a Japanese pillbox
and prepare to fire on the enemy to our company's front.
We asked Company K's gunnery sergeant, Gy. Sgt. W. R.
Saunders, if he knew of any enemy troops in the bunker. It
appeared undamaged. He said some of the men had thrown
grenades through the ventilators, and he was sure there were
no live enemy inside.

Snafu and I began to set up our mortar about five feet from
the bunker. Number One mortar was about five yards to our
left. Cpl. R. V. Burgin was getting the sound-powered phone
hooked up to receive fire orders from Sgt. Johnny Marmet,
who was observing.

I heard something behind me in the pillbox. Japanese were
talking in low, excited voices. Metal rattled against an iron
grating. I grabbed my carbine and yelled, "Burgin, there're
Nips in that pillbox."

All the men readied their weapons as Burgin came over
to have a look, kidding me with, "Shucks, Sledgehammer,
you're crackin' up." He looked into the ventilator port directly
behind me. It was rather small, approximately six inches by
eight inches, and covered with iron bars about a half inch
apart. What he saw brought forth a stream of curses in his
best Texas style against all Nippon. He stuck his carbine
muzzle through the bars, fired two quick shots, and yelled,
"I got 'em right in the face."

The Japanese inside the pillbox began jabbering loudly.

Burgin was gritting his teeth and calling the enemy SOBs while he fired more shots through the opening.

Every man in the mortar section was ready for trouble as soon as Burgin fired the first shot. It came in the form of a grenade tossed out of the end entrance to my left. It looked as big as a football to me. I yelled "Grenade!" and dove behind the sand breastwork protecting the entrance at the end of the pillbox. The sand bank was about four feet high and L-shaped to protect the entrance from fire from the front and flanks. The grenade exploded, but no one was hit.

The Japanese tossed out several more grenades without causing us injury, because we were hugging the deck. Most of the men crawled around to the front of the pillbox and crouched close to it between the firing ports, so the enemy inside couldn't fire at them. John Redifer and Vincent Santos jumped on top. Things got quiet.

I was nearest the door, and Burgin yelled to me, "Look in and see what's in there, Sledgehammer."

Being trained to take orders without question, I raised my head above the sand bank and peered into the door of the bunker. It nearly cost me my life. Not more than six feet from me crouched a Japanese machine gunner. His eyes were black dots in a tan, impassive face topped with the familiar mushroom helmet. The muzzle of his light machine gun stared at me like a gigantic third eye.

Fortunately for me, I reacted first. Not having time to get my carbine into firing position, I jerked my head down so fast my helmet almost flew off. A split second later he fired a burst of six or eight rounds. The bullets tore a furrow through the bank just above my head and showered sand on me. My ears rang from the muzzle blast and my heart seemed to be in my throat choking me. I knew damned well I had to be dead! He just couldn't have missed me at that range.

A million thoughts raced through my terrified mind: of how my folks had nearly lost their youngest, of what a stupid thing I had done to look directly into a pillbox full of Japanese without even having my carbine at the ready, and of just how much I hated the enemy anyway. Many a Marine veteran had already lost his life on Peleliu for making less of a mistake than I had just made.

Burgin yelled and asked if I were all right. A hoarse squawk was all the answer I could muster, but his voice brought me to my senses. I crawled around to the front, then up on top of the bunker before the enemy machine gunner could have another try at me.

Redifer yelled, "They've got an automatic weapon in there." Snafu disagreed, and a spirited argument ensued. Redifer pointed out that there surely was an automatic weapon in there and that I should know, because it came close to blowing off my head. But Snafu was adamant. Like much of what I experienced in combat, this exchange was unreal. Here we were: twelve Marines with a bull by the tail in the form of a well-built concrete pillbox containing an unknown number of Japanese with no friendly troops near us and Snafu and Redifer – veterans – in a violent argument.

Burgin shouted, "Knock it off," and they shut up.

Redifer and I lay prone on top of the bunker, just above the door. We knew we had to get the Japanese while they were bottled up, or they would come out at us with knives and bayonets, a thought none of us relished. Redifer and I were close enough to the door to place grenades down the opening and move back before they exploded. But the Japanese invariably tossed them back at us before the explosion. I had an irrepressible urge to do just that. Brief as our face-to-face meeting had been, I had quickly developed a feeling of strong personal hate for that machine gunner who had nearly blasted my head off my shoulders. My terror subsided into a cold, homicidal rage and a vengeful desire to get even.

Redifer and I gingerly peeped down over the door. The machine gunner wasn't visible, but we looked at three long Arisaka rifle barrels with bayonets fixed. Those bayonets seemed ten feet long to me. Their owners were jabbering excitedly, apparently planning to rush out. Redifer acted quickly. He held his carbine by the barrel and used the butt to knock down the rifles. The Japanese jerked their weapons back into the bunker with much chattering.

Behind us, Santos yelled that he had located a ventilator

pipe without a cover. He began dropping grenades into it. Each one exploded in the pillbox beneath us with a muffled *bam*. When he had used all of his, Redifer and I handed him our grenades while we kept watch at the door.

After Santos had dropped in several, we stood up and began to discuss with Burgin and the others the possibility that anyone could still be alive inside. (We didn't know at the time that the inside was subdivided by concrete baffles for extra protection.) We got our answer when two grenades were tossed out. Luckily for the men with Burgin, the grenades were thrown out the back. Santos and I shouted a warning and hit the deck on the sand on top of the pillbox, but Redifer merely raised his arm over his face. He took several fragments in the forearm but wasn't wounded seriously.

Burgin yelled, "Let's get the hell outa here and get a tank to help us knock this damn thing out." He ordered us to pull back to some craters about forty yards from the pillbox. We sent a runner to the beach to bring up a flamethrower and an amtrac armed with a 75mm gun.

As we jumped into the crater, three Japanese soldiers ran out of the pillbox door past the sand bank and headed for a thicket. Each carried his bayoneted rifle in his right hand and held up his pants with his left hand. This action so amazed me that I stared in disbelief and didn't fire my carbine. I wasn't afraid, as I had been under shell fire, just filled with wild excitement. My buddies were more effective than I and cut down the enemy with a hail of bullets. They congratulated each other while I chided myself for being more curious about strange Japanese customs than with being combat effective.

The amtrac rattling toward us by this time was certainly a welcome sight. As it pulled into position, several more Japanese raced from the pillbox in a tight group. Some held their bayoneted rifles in both hands, but some of them carried their rifles in one hand and held up their pants with the other. I had overcome my initial surprise and joined the others and the amtrac machine gun in firing away at them. They tumbled onto the hot coral in a forlorn tangle of bare legs, falling rifles, and rolling helmets. We felt no pity for them but exulted over their fate. We had been shot at and shelled too much and had lost too many friends to have compassion for the enemy when we had him cornered.

The amtrac took up a position on a line even with us. Its commander, a sergeant, consulted Burgin. Then the turret gunner fired three armor-piercing 75mm shells at the side of the pillbox. Each time our ears rang with the familiar *wham – bam* as the report of the gun was followed quickly by the explosion of the shell on a target at close range. The third shell tore a hole entirely through the pillbox. Fragments kicked up dust around our abandoned packs and mortars on the other side. On the side nearest us, the hole was about four feet in diameter. Burgin yelled to the tankers to cease firing lest our equipment be damaged.

Someone remarked that if fragments hadn't killed those inside, the concussion surely had. But even before the dust settled, I saw a Japanese soldier appear at the blasted opening. He was grim determination personified as he drew back his arm to throw a grenade at us.

My carbine was already up. When he appeared, I lined up my sights on his chest and began squeezing off shots. As the first bullet hit him, his face contorted in agony. His knees buckled. The grenade slipped from his grasp. All the men near me, including the amtrac machine gunner, had seen him and began firing. The soldier collapsed in the fusilade, and the grenade went off at his feet.

Even in the midst of these fast-moving events, I looked down at my carbine with sober reflection. I had just killed a man at close range. That I had seen clearly the pain on his face when my bullets hit him came as a jolt. It suddenly made the war a very personal affair. The expression on that man's face filled me with shame and then disgust for the war and all the misery it was causing.

My combat experience thus far made me realize that such sentiments for an enemy soldier were the maudlin meditations of a fool. Look at me, a member of the 5th Marine Regiment – one of the oldest, finest, and toughest regiments in the Marine Corps – feeling ashamed because I had shot a damned foe before he could throw a grenade at me! I felt like a fool and was thankful my buddies couldn't read my thoughts.

Burgin's order to us to continue firing into the opening interrupted my musings. We kept up a steady fire into the pillbox to keep the Japanese pinned down while the flamethrower came up, carried by Corporal Womack from Mississippi. He was a brave, good-natured guy and popular with the troops, but he was one of the fiercest looking Marines I ever saw. He was big and husky with a fiery red beard well powdered with white coral dust. He reminded me of some wild Viking. I was glad we were on the same side.

Stooped under the heavy tanks on his back, Womack approached the pillbox with his assistant just out of the line of our fire. When they got about fifteen yards from the target, we ceased firing. The assistant reached up and turned a valve on the flamethrower. Womack then aimed the nozzle at the opening made by the 75mm gun. He pressed the trigger. With a *whoooooooosh* the flame leaped at the opening. Some muffled screams, then all quiet.

Even the stoic Japanese couldn't suppress the agony of death by fire and suffocation. But they were no more likely to surrender to us than we would have been to them had we ever been confronted with the possibility of surrender. In fighting the Japanese, surrender was not one of our options.

Amid our shouts of appreciation, Womack and his buddy started back to battalion headquarters to await the summons to break another deadlock somewhere on the battlefield – or lose their lives trying. The job of flamethrower gunner was probably the least desirable of any open to a Marine infantryman. Carrying tanks with about seventy pounds of flammable jellied gasoline through enemy fire over rugged terrain in hot weather to squirt flames into the mouth of a cave or pillbox was an assignment that few survived but all carried out with magnificent courage.

We left the craters and approached the pillbox cautiously. Burgin ordered some of the men to cover it while the rest of us looked over the fallen Japanese to be sure none was still alive; wounded Japanese invariably exploded grenades when approached, if possible, killing their enemies along with themselves. All of them were dead. The pillbox was out of action thanks to the flamethrower and the amtrac. There

were seven enemy dead inside and ten outside. Our packs
and mortars were only slightly damaged by the fire from the
amtrac's 75mm gun.

Of the twelve Marine mortarmen, our only casualties were
Redifer and Leslie Porter, who had taken some grenade
fragments. They weren't hurt seriously. Our luck in the
whole affair had been incredible. If the enemy had surprised
us and rushed us, we might have been in a bad fix.

During this lull the men stripped the packs and pockets of
the enemy dead for souvenirs. This was a gruesome business,
but Marines executed it in a most methodical manner. Helmet
headbands were checked for flags, packs and pockets were
emptied, and gold teeth were extracted. Sabers, pistols, and
hari-kari knives were highly prized and carefully cared for until
they could be sent to the folks back home or sold to some pilot
or sailor for a fat price. Rifles and other larger weapons usually
were rendered useless and thrown aside. They were too heavy
to carry in addition to our own equipment. They would be
picked up later as fine souvenirs by the rear-echelon troops.
The men in the rifle companies had a lot of fun joking about
the hair-raising stories these people, who had never seen a live
Japanese or been shot at, would probably tell after the war.

The men gloated over, compared, and often swapped their
prizes. It was a brutal, ghastly ritual the likes of which
have occurred since ancient times on battlefields where the
antagonists have possessed a profound mutual hatred. It was
uncivilized, as is all war, and was carried out with that
particular savagery that characterized the struggle between
the Marines and the Japanese. It wasn't simply souvenir
hunting or looting the enemy dead; it was more like Indian
warriors taking scalps.

While I was removing a bayonet and scabbard from a
dead Japanese, I noticed a Marine near me. He wasn't in
our mortar section but had happened by and wanted to get
in on the spoils. He came up to me dragging what I assumed
to be a corpse. But the Japanese wasn't dead. He had been
wounded severely in the back and couldn't move his arms;
otherwise he would have resisted to his last breath.

The Japanese's mouth glowed with huge gold-crowned

teeth, and his captor wanted them. He put the point of his kabar on the base of a tooth and hit the handle with the palm of his hand. Because the Japanese was kicking his feet and thrashing about, the knife point glanced off the tooth and sank deeply into the victim's mouth. The Marine cursed him and with a slash cut his cheeks open to each ear. He put his foot on the sufferer's lower jaw and tried again. Blood poured out of the soldier's mouth. He made a gurgling noise and thrashed wildly. I shouted, "Put the man out of his misery." All I got for an answer was a cussing out. Another Marine ran up, put a bullet in the enemy soldier's brain, and ended his agony. The scavenger grumbled and continued extracting his prizes undisturbed.

Such was the incredible cruelty that decent men could commit when reduced to a brutish existence in their fight for survival amid the violent death, terror, tension, fatigue, and filth that was the infantryman's war. Our code of conduct toward the enemy differed drastically from that prevailing back at the division CP.

The struggle for survival went on day after weary day, night after terrifying night. One remembers vividly the landings and the beachheads and the details of the first two or three days and nights of a campaign; after that, time lost all meaning. A lull of hours or days seemed but a fleeting instant of heaven-sent tranquility. Lying in a foxhole sweating out an enemy artillery or mortar barrage or waiting to dash across open ground under machine-gun or artillery fire defied any concept of time.

To the noncombatants and those on the periphery of action, the war meant only boredom or occasional excitement; but to those who entered the meat grinder itself, the war was a nether world of horror from which escape seemed less and less likely as casualties mounted and the fighting dragged on and on. Time had no meaning; life had no meaning. The fierce struggle for survival in the abyss of Peleliu eroded the veneer of civilization and made savages of us all. We existed in an environment totally incomprehensible to men behind the lines – service troops and civilians.

*   *   *

A trip inside the pillbox by Redifer and Burgin solved the mystery of how some of the occupants had survived the grenades and shell bursts. (Burgin shot a soldier inside who was feigning death.) Concrete walls partitioned the bunker into compartments connected by small openings. Three or four enemy soldiers occupied each compartment which had its own firing ports to the outside. Each would have had to be put out of action individually had we not had the help of Womack and his flamethrower.

When our gunny came by and saw the results of our encounter with the pillbox he had thought was empty, he looked sheepish. He gazed in amazement at the enemy dead scattered around. We really razzed him about it – or rather, we gave him the nearest thing approaching the razz that we Marine privates dared hand out to the austere personage of Gy. Sergeant Saunders. I have thought often that Burgin should have been decorated for the fine leadership he exhibited in coordinating and directing the knockout of the pillbox. I'm sure men have been decorated for less.

We set up our two mortars in a large crater near the now knocked-out pillbox and registered in the guns for the night. The ammo carriers dug into the softer coral around the edge of the crater. An amtrac brought up rations and a unit of fire for the company. The wind began to blow briskly, and it got cloudy and heavily overcast. As darkness settled, heavy clouds scudded across the sky. The scene reminded me of hurricane weather on the Gulf Coast back home.

Not far behind us, the heat of the fire burning in the pillbox exploded Japanese grenades and small-arms ammunition. All night occasional shifts of wind blew the nauseating smell of burning flesh our way. The rain fell in torrents, and the wind blew hard. Ships fired star shells to illuminate the battlefield for our battalion. But as soon as the parachute of a star shell opened, the wind swept it swiftly along like some invisible hand snatching away a candle. In the few hundred yards they still held at the northern end of the island, the enemy was fairly quiet.

The next morning, again with the help of tanks and amtracs, our battalion took most of the remainder of Ngesebus. Our casualties were remarkably low for the number of Japanese we killed.* In midafternoon we learned that an army unit would relieve us shortly and complete the job on the northern end of Ngesebus.

* Official accounts vary somewhat as to the actual casualty figures for Ngesebus. However the Marines suffered about 15 killed and 33 wounded, while the Japanese lost 470 killed and captured. Company K suffered the largest portion of the casualties in 3/5 by losing 8 killed and 24 wounded. This undoubtedly resulted from the presence of a ridge and caves on Ngesebus in our sector.

THE TWILIGHT OF THE GODS
Jules Roy

The Vietnamese hamlet of Dien Bien Phu was the graveyard of the French Foreign Legion, but also the site of its most heroic stand in modern times. In 1953 the French Army High Command in Vietnam (then a French colony) decided to garrison the hamlet in order to prevent Viet Ming excursions into neighbouring Laos. The problem with Dien Bien Phu, unseen by the High Command, was that it lay in the middle of a natural geographical bowl, surrounded by a ring of small hills. On these hills were placed eight French strongpoints (allegedly named after the mistresses of the garrison commander, Colonel de Castries). But if ever the French were to lose control of the strongpoints, they would lose strategic control of the valley.

At 1700 on 13 March 1954, 37,500 men from the cream of the nationalist-Communist Viet Minh attacked the outlying strongpoints at Dien Bien Phu. The onslaught was stunning, not least because the Viet Minh, under Vo Nguyen Giap's generalship, had managed to bring heavy guns into the area undetected. The first French outpost, Beatrice, fell on 14 March, Gabrielle on the following day. Thereafter Giap could pound the garrison in the valley with impunity.

Against all the odds the garrison held out until the 7th May. The remaining outposts were only surrendered after days of bloody, often hand to hand, combat. The brunt of the fighting was borne by just 3000 Legionaires – out of a total French force of 10,500 – from the 13th Legion Half-Brigade, the 1st Foreign Legion Parachute Battalion, and the 2nd and 3rd Foreign Legion Infantry Regiments. Alongside them was another elite French force, the 6th Colonial Parachute Battalion, led by the legendary Major Marcel Bigeard.

The account of the last day of the French stand below is from Jules Roy's The Battle of Dien Bien Phu, *one of the greatest pieces*

*of twentieth century war reportage. The battle cost the lives of 1500
Legionaires. It was also the de facto end of French rule in Vietnam.*

THE NIGHT OF MAY 6–7, 1954

AT ISABELLE, ALL the 105-mm. guns but one had been
destroyed. On Éliane, where a terrible storm of shells had
just broken, Major Botella heard Langlais calling Bréchignac
on the radio.

"Young Pierre calling Brèche, Young Pierre calling Brèche,
who is that deluge meant for?"

"Brèche calling Young Pierre; it's for Éliane 2."

The shelling moved to Éliane 3, then to Éliane 4, while
the guns on former Éliane 1 and Mont Fictif opened fire.
Langlais sent three tanks still capable of movement over to
the left bank, at the foot of the peaks.

At 1815, hard on the heels of their last salvo, the Viets,
wearing gauze masks, hurled themselves against Éliane 2.
Using radio communication between its companies and battalion command posts for the first time, the 98th Regiment
was in position in front of the peaks of Éliane 4.

Botella replied with his mortars and his recoilless guns.
The Viets got as far as his command post but were driven
back by Vietnamese troops, who, when they had good officers
and NCOs, fought as fiercely as their brothers on the other
side, just as North Koreans and South Koreans had fought
one another. One of their officers, Captain Phan van Phu,
saw his company reduced to thirty men.

At 2100 hours, signals orderly Tran ngoc Duoï of the
People's Army went into action with his unit. In the white
light of the flares which had taken the place of the moon in
its first quarter, he could make out the movements of the
counterattacks. In spite of shell splinters in his head and right
leg, he refused to allow himself to be evacuated, sheltered a
wounded platoon commander and went on carrying out his
orders with a limp. When a dynamiter was killed, he took
his charge, placed it, lighted it and went back to his mission.
The Viet troops were cut to pieces by the mortars, but the
following waves covered them and went on.

On Éliane 2, which was held by two companies of the
1st Battalion, Parachute Chasseurs, under Captain Pouget,
a Viet jumped in front of Sergeant Chabrier, pointed an
automatic pistol at him and shouted, "Give yourself up.
You're done for – " then fell back dead. At 2300 hours a
great silence suddenly descended on the position, and Pouget
said to himself, "Perhaps they're going to let us have a bit of
peace?" But then, like the spray of a huge black wave breaking
almost noiselessly against a jetty, the earth was hurled high
into the air by the thousands of pounds of explosive in the
Viet mine, and fell with a thunderous din on the roofs of
the shelters and into the trenches. The crater which opened
under the defenders' feet and buried them still exists. The
vegetation has not returned to it, but the rains fill it in a little
every season.

The shock troops, who had been waiting for the signal
of the explosion to go into action, felt the earth rumble
and hurled themselves screaming at the shattered position.
Section Leader Dang phi Thuong, under the orders of the
commander of No. 7 Platoon of the 3rd Company of the 98th
Regiment, advanced rapidly through the hail of bullets from
automatic weapons toward the smashed blockhouses, but
found his way barred by the fire from Sergeant Chabrier's
platoon, which mowed the attackers down and toppled them
into the muddy crater which the mine had opened. "What a
sight for sore eyes!" cried one of the machine gunners. But
the weapons ended up by jamming, the stocks of ammunition
by running out, and the swarm of Viets overran the position.
The 12.7-mm. machine gun on the tank "Bazeilles" was the
last to fall silent.

At midnight, the five Dakotas which were to drop the last
company of reinforcements asked, in the interests of their
safety, that no more flares be sent up. Langlais and Bigeard
hesitated. Even if it was dark, how could the pilots make out
the tiny dropping zone in the midst of all the fires of the battle?
Wouldn't the Viets take advantage of the darkness to resume
the attack? Near the door of the Dakota, the pockets of his
battle dress stuffed with whisky for General de Castries and
brandy for Langlais, and worried in case he should break his

bottles when he landed, Captain Faussurier waited for the
green lamp to light up. Finally Bigeard queried Lieutenant
Le Page on the radio.

"The flares must come first," Le Page replied unhesi-
tatingly.

Langlais ordered the planes to turn back, and the men of
the 1st Battalion, Parachute Chasseurs, returned to Hanoï,
sick at heart. In the shelter of the camp headquarters where
Geneviève de Galard was sleeping, sheltered under a table,
on a mattress of parachutes, Bigeard felt a certain comfort
at the thought that the sacrifice of that company had been
avoided; a hundred men could no longer alter the course
of events. Calls for help were jamming the lines to the
artillery and the radio links with the strong points. As for
the enemy radio receivers, they resounded with shouts of
victory.

With one of his radio operators killed and the other hit
by a bullet in the stomach, Pouget had stopped answering
calls from the main position. He had been given up for dead
and no more calls had been sent out to him. At four in the
morning, he operated his transmitter himself and got through
to Major Vadot.

"I've reoccupied all of Éliane 2, but I've only thirty-five
men left. If we're to hold out, you've got to send me the
reinforcements you promised. Otherwise it'll all be over."

"Where do you expect me to find them?" Vadot answered
calmly. "Be reasonable. You know the situation as well as I
do. Not another man, not another shell, my friend. You're a
para. You're there to get yourself killed."

On the wavelength of the Éliane command network the
Viets played the record of the "Song of the Partisans," and
now and then their waiting voices took up the refrain:

> Friend, can you hear the black flight of the crows
> In the plain? . . .

"The swine," muttered Pouget, "the swine."

At Éliane, Botella had fifty mortar shells left and a few cases
of grenades. The loudspeakers of Bigeard's radio receivers

vibrated: "Dédé calling Bruno, the ammunition's running out."

"Brèche calling Bruno, we're nearly finished."

On all the hills, the strong points changed hands several times within a few hours: The enemy hurled himself at any breach he made, then fell back in disorder. Dead and wounded dropped to the ground. On the west face, Claudine 5 was overrun, near a tank which could not fire any more.

Sitting out in the open near his radio set, Pouget watched the 120-mm. mortar shells pounding Éliane 4 where Botella was holding out. The ground was cracking open. Pouget saw some Viets running along the crest of Éliane 4, lit up by the flares dropped by the planes. Down below, Dienbienphu was burning and fireworks were spurting from the shell stores. Now and then a few stars appeared through the clouds which filled the darkness.

At 0410, before his eyes, along the whole front of Éliane 2, the Viets stood up without firing. Pouget heard them shouting: "Di di, di di! Forward, forward!"

The survivors of Éliane 2 had one machine-gun charger and one grenade left. Pouget ordered the sole remaining lieutenant and those men who could still walk to return to the main position, and, falling back from one hole to the next, found himself reunited with them at the foot of the peak, in a trench full of corpses which they piled up to protect themselves.

Another shrieking tidal wave surged from the ground and broke over the 5th Battalion, Vietnamese Paratroops, covering Captain Phu; but a handful of Legionnaires and paratroops counterattacked again, recaptured some lost trenches, pushed aside the dead and dying to place their machine guns in position, and brought their fire to bear on the shadows in the flat helmets. Officers who were not yet twenty became company commanders or died when, like Second Lieutenant Phung, they called for mortar fire to be directed on them. Of the 6th Battalion, Colonial Paratroops, twenty men remained alive around Major Thomas. Sergeants gathered survivors together and rushed into the attack. Who would be victor or vanquished when this night came to an end? To help the men hanging onto the last peaks, Langlais withdrew some platoons from battalions in the center and threw them into the action among the burning eastern peaks. Everywhere men stumbled over shattered bodies. In the light of the flares which the wind carried toward the mountains, faces ran with sweat and with thick black ink. On Éliane 2, where since four in the morning nobody had answered Bréchignac's calls, the groaning of the wounded filled the dawn. Behind the eastern crests, the sky was turning golden.

MAY 7, 1954
On Éliane 10, at the foot of the peaks, day was breaking. The enemy was advancing everywhere, searching the shelters. Besieged in a block-house, Lieutenant Le Page managed to escape with a couple of men. The miracle was that Éliane 4 was still alive, that Bréchignac and Botella were still in command, calling for help. But what help could they be given? Lemeunier went into Langlais's shelter; he had gathered together a few Legionnaires and was ready to fight his way to the west.

"Not to the west," said Langlais. "To Éliane 4 where they're still holding out."

Langlais emerged from his shelter into the brutal light of summer. In the sky, Dakotas were dropping supplies. In all the trenches leading to the hospital, pitiful files of men trampled on corpses gradually being buried by the mud. Wounded men nobody could attend to any more were left where they lay. Turned loose by the Viets, who had told them, "Go back to your people and tell them we are coming," some battalion medical officers got through to Grauwin with the half-naked cripples who had returned to the fight a few days before.

On the other side of the river and the shattered ammunition dump swarmed the hundreds of men who had taken refuge weeks before in holes in the river banks in order to avoid the fighting, and whom Langlais compared to the crabs on tropical coasts. Dregs of humanity, deserters – Langlais could not find words sufficiently contemptuous for them. He could have mown them down with machine-gun fire or crushed them with a few 105-mm. salvos, but he turned away in disgust. Like Bigeard now, he was beyond all that. Like Béatrice, Gabrielle, Anne-Marie, Huguette and Dominique, Éliane had a new lover . . .

Under the bursts of automatic-pistol fire, Pouget had felt the corpses he was sheltering behind tremble. A grenade exploded near his helmet, stunning him. As in a nightmare, he heard a little nasal voice saying, "You are a prisoner of the Democratic People's Army of Vietnam. You are wounded. We shall take care of you. Can you walk?"

He looked up at his victor in the gauze mask.

"And my comrades?"

"We shall attend to them. Their wounds will be dressed. The medical orderlies are coming."

Pouget got laboriously to his feet. It was all over for him. He was stripped to the waist, with no weapons or marks of rank, hairy and haggard. Somebody helped him to walk. His radio operator leaned on his shoulder.

> Friend, can you hear the muffled cry of the country
> Being loaded with chains?

He was no longer strong enough even to hum the tune the Viets had been broadcasting all night. Defeated, he refused to resign himself. At the end of the suffering and humiliation that awaited him and were already escorting him, he knew that he was going to find the great explanation and salvation.

Suddenly the artillery in the east opened fire again and the shells started falling once more. Long, deep, whistling notes pierced the general din. Hope suddenly mingled with amazement. Captain Capeyron, Sergeant Sammarco, Corporal Hoinant and a great many others, surprised to see the first salvos fall between the positions, turned toward the west. Voices cried, "It's Crèvecoeur!" Faces revealed a joy which did not yet dare express itself freely, but which would burst forth a torrent ready to turn against the course of fate and carry everything with it. Yes, it must be the Crèvecoeur column, which the radiotelegraphers had been claiming to be in touch with for days and which they had said was approaching, which was swooping down from the mountains into the valley with an apocalyptic din. Men did not know whether to shriek or weep for joy. They were already hoisting themselves out of their holes when the range lengthened, reached the command posts and crushed the innocents getting ready to meet their saviors. They were expecting Crèvecoeur, but what they heard was the thunder of Stalin's organs.

Three men dressed in mud, haggard, their faces black with stubble and smoke, staggered up and collapsed on the ground. Bigeard bent over one of them and took his hand. Was he crying? It no longer mattered at this moment when everything had been surpassed, when the grandeur of the ordeal made them giddy, when words were no use except to those witnessing from afar the death agony of Dienbienphu. Bigeard, who had never been known to utter a cry of commiseration, simply said over and over again, "Poor Le Page . . ."

He was weeping for a whole body of knights massacred in vain because a general had flung his army into the enemy's trap, giving in to the bluster of those who had urged him to throw himself into the wolf's jaws. Among those who would be cited among the dead and the prisoners, how many names represented the flower of that army, sacrificed turn and turn about, for centuries past, for great causes and solemn idiocies! Bigeard had a vague suspicion that the disaster taking place had achieved nothing but a crucifixion, of which countless former high commissioners, secretaries of state or prime ministers were already washing their hands with affected delicacy. Obsessed by the idea of the coolie's pole on his shoulder, he could not yet imagine what was waiting for him. Who could tell? The diplomats were gathered together at Geneva; everything might be arranged at the last moment. He did not know that the men by whose fault battles are lost are not those whom they kill. Without suspecting it, it was himself that Bigeard discovered beneath the masks of clay and blood drying on his lieutenants' faces.

"Stop shelling . . ." Bréchignac had just asked Bigeard to spare Éliane 4 a bombardment that would kill off the wounded when he received a report from Botella that any further resistance was impossible. Botella then called Bigeard.

"Dédé calling Bruno, Dédé calling Bruno . . ."

It was the same metallic voice which used to announce, "Objective reached." Bigeard pressed the transmitter switch. "Bruno here."

"Dédé calling Bruno. It's all over. They're at the command post. Goodbye. Tell Young Pierre that we liked him."

A click. A curter voice: "I'm blowing up the radio. Hip hip hooray . . ."

It was nine o'clock. On the heights surrounding Éliane 4, in the rice fields in the ravines, swarmed a host of little armed men, dressed in coarse green cloth, with sandals cut out of tires on their feet, helmets of interlaced bamboo decorated with the ruby of a red star on their heads, and gauze masks over their faces, who came running out of their hiding places in the forests and mountains. They reached the crests of Éliane in a huge roar which was carried along in waves by gusts of wind as they arrived on the summits. Spreading out over the sides and ridges of the Élianes, they uttered shouts of triumph and raised their weapons in a victorious gesture at sight of the yellow curves of the river and the plowed fields of the entrenched camp. On the double crest of Éliane 4, they could be seen jumping over the ruined trenches, crossing the tangled barbed-wire defenses, and stepping over piles of corpses lying on top of one another in the macabre reconciliation of death, or stretched out on their backs, their arms open, their faces eaten by flies, their mouths still full of a last groan, men fallen from their crosses, nailed to the pulverized ground among the wretched wooden supports of the shelters, or swimming in the slimy mud.

In the face of this swarm of human insects sprung up from all sides, the artillery of the entrenched camp, nearly out of ammunition and gun crews, remained silent. It had three hundred 105-mm. shells left and ten 120-mm. Fighters dived out of the sky, dropped bombs, fired their machine guns and spread disorder for a moment, but the swarm gradually resumed its advance when the planes disappeared after the ten minutes at their disposal. Botella decided

to stay at his command post, but ordered Second Lieutenant Makowiak to rejoin the main position with a few
uninjured men and a few wounded who could still walk.
Soon afterward, the Viets surrounded him and took him
into their lines. Section Commander Dang phi Thuong,
second-in-command of Platoon No. 7 of the 98th Regiment, returning the action to give Élaine the *coup de grâce*,
saw him go by, surrounded by guards, bare-headed and
balding, on his way to the first regrouping center where
he would find Bréchignac and Pouget, mute with misery.
At Opéra, Bizard was holding out and getting ready to
launch a counterattack against the Élianes, but Langlais
incorporated him into the defense system of the main position.

Capeyron, who was searching near Éliane 2 for some men
from his company who had gone up there during the night,
was hit by some grenade splinters which slashed his left wrist
and groin like a razor.

At ten o'clock, from his office in the citadel at Hanoï, Cogny
called Castries. The storms moving over the whole region
crackled in the receivers. The conversation, which might be
the last contact with the entrenched camp, was recorded in
the radio room.

"Good morning, my friend," said Cogny. "What resources
have you got left?"

Castries's voice was clear, slow, deliberate; a little shrill, as
it always was on the telephone. Now and then, he searched
for a word, corrected himself, repeated himself. Cogny punctuated his remarks with muffled words of acquiescence.

"The 6th Battalion, Colonial Paratroops, the 2nd Battalion,
1st Parachute Chasseurs, and what was left of the Algerian
Rifles."

"Yes."

"In any case, there's nothing to be done but write the whole
bunch off."

"Yes."

"Right . . . At the moment, that's what's left, but greatly
reduced of course, because we took, we drew on everything

there was on the western perimeter in an attempt to hold out in the east . . ."

"Yes."

"What's left is about two companies from the two BEPs put together . . ."

"Yes."

". . . three companies of Moroccan Rifles, but which are no use at all, you realize, no use at all, which are completely demoralized . . ."

"Yes."

". . . two companies of the 8th Assault . . ."

"Yes."

". . . three companies of BT2s, but that's only to be expected because it's always that way, it's the Moroccan Rifles and the BT2s that have the most men left because they don't fight."

"Of course."

"Right, and out of the 1st Battalion, out of the 1st Battalion, Foreign Infantry, there're about two companies left, and about two companies of the 1st Battalion, 13th Demibrigade. It's . . . they are companies of seventy or eighty men."

"Yes. I see."

"Well, there you are . . . We're defending every foot of ground."

"Yes."

"We're defending every foot of ground, and I consider that the most we can do . . ."

Static suddenly interrupted the transmission.

"Hello, hello," Cogny repeated.

"Hello, can you hear me, General?"

". . . that the most you can do?"

". . . is to halt the enemy on the Nam Youm. Right?"

"Yes."

"And even then we would have to hold the bank, because otherwise we wouldn't have any water."

"Yes, of course."

"Right, So, well, that's what I suggest we try, I'll try to bring that off, ah, I've just taken, I've just seen Langlais, we're in agreement about that. And then, damn it all, I'll try, I'll try, conditions permitting, to get as many men as possible out toward the south."

"Good. That'll be by night, I suppose?"

"What's that?"

"By night?"

"Yes, General, by night of course."

"Of course. Yes."

"And I . . . I need your permission to do that."

"All right, fellow."

"You give me permission?"

"I give you permission."

"Anyway, I'll hold out, I'll try to hold out here as long as possible, with what is left."

Castries paused for a while, then intimated that he had nothing more to say.

"General?"

"Yes, all right."

"That's it . . ."

"From the ammunition point of view, have you . . . is there anything to be recovered?" Cogny asked very quickly.

"Ammunition. That's more serious, we haven't any."

"There isn't anything that . . ."

"We don't have any, you see. There are still a few 105-mm. shells, but . . ."

A sentence in the transcript is undecipherable. Castries may have referred to 155-mm. shells, for all those guns were unserviceable.

". . . they aren't any use here."

". . . for the moment. And as for the 120-mm., the 120-mm. shells . . ."

"Yes."

"I still have, I must still have, between 100 and 150."

"Yes."

"Which are all over the place, you see."

"Yes, of course." Cogny repeated.

"Which are all over the place. We can't . . . it's practically impossible to collect them. Obviously the more you send, the better, eh?"

"Yes."

"So we'll hold out, we'll hold out as long as possible."

"I think the best thing," said Cogny, talking fast, "would be for the Air Force to put in a big effort today to bring the Viets to a halt."

"Yes, General. The Air Force must keep up its support, eh? Nonstop, nonstop. Yes, and about the Viets, I'll put you in the picture as to how they stand."

"Yes."

"In the east the Viets have thrown in everything they've still got."

"Yes."

"Including two regiments of the 308th Division."

"Really? Yes."

"You see? On the western perimeter at the moment there isn't anything, there can't be anything but the 36th Regiment."

"The 36th, yes, I think so too."

"Just the 36th Regiment, eh? The 102nd Regiment . . ."
Suddenly he was cut off.

"Hello, hello," Cogny repeated in a panting voice while the technicians tried to re-establish contact.

"Can you hear me?" Castries continued.

"The 102nd Regiment, you were saying?"

"Yes, General."

"The 102nd Regiment?"

"Just that they've been thrown in on the eastern perimeter . . ."

"Yes."

". . . the 102nd Regiment and the 88th Regiment."

"That's it."

"You see? Plus what . . . plus what remained of the 312th . . ."

"That's it. Yes."

". . . and now the 316th."

"Yes."

"You see?"

"They've thrown everything in on the eastern perimeter," said Cogny.

"But you see, as I foresaw, the 308th, as I think I've already mentioned, escapes me, you see, as usual."

"Yes, that's it . . . Good, well, what about the withdrawal to the south?" asked Cogny. "How do you envisage it? Toward Isabelle or a scattered movement?"

"Well, General, in any case, in any case they'll have to pass south of Isabelle, won't they?"

"Yes, that's right."

"But I'll give orders, I'll give orders to Isabelle, too, to try, to try to pull out, if they can."

"Yes. Right. Well, keep me in the picture so that we can give you the maximum air support for that operation."

"Why, of course, General."

"There you are, my friend."

"And then, why, damn it all, I'll keep here, well, the units that don't want to go on it . . ."

"That's it, yes."

". . . the, how shall I put it, the wounded of course, but a lot of them are already in the enemy's hands, because there were some in the strong points, Éliane 4 and because . . . and Éliane 10."

"Yes, of course."

"You see? And I'll keep all that under my command."

"Yes, fellow."

"There you are."

"Good-bye, fellow."

"I may telephone you again before . . . before the end."

"There now, good-bye, Castries, old fellow."

"Good-bye, General."

"Good-bye, fellow."

Castries put down the receiver. Two hundred miles away, Cogny did not look at the officers standing silently around him. Sweat was running down his forehead. Hanoï lay crushed under the heat of the storm which refused to break.

At midday, Bigeard went to see General de Castries.

"It's all over," he told him. "If you agree, I'll get out of here at nightfall with my men. But we've got to make the Viets think that we're still holding out, and to do that the artillery, mortars and automatic weapons have got to keep on firing. Leave a good man here – Trancart, for instance."

"No," replied Castries. "I won't give that job to anybody.

I'll stay, Bruno, old fellow. Don't worry; we'll keep on firing all night. At daybreak we'll cut our losses."

At 1300 hours, Captain Capeyron took up position on Junon with fifty-four Legionnaires. Sergeant Sammarco, at whose feet a 75-mm. shell had landed without exploding, said to a pal, "If we get out of this alive, we'll get blind drunk for a fortnight." In readiness for the sortie, Sergeant Kubiak emptied the flasks of rum in the "Pacific" ration crates into his water bottle. Langlais, Bigeard and their staff officers had some hot soup. Together they studied the situation and summoned the battalion commanders who were going to take part in "Operation Bloodletting." Tourret, Guiraud and Clémençon were unanimous in the opinion that it was impossible. However slim the chances of success, for they were completely cut off, they would have to make the attempt, but the Viets occupied the whole of the left bank, except for the bridge which they were trying to capture, and, like broken-down horses on the point of collapse, paratroopers and Legionnaires were at the end of their tether. One of the two boxers had been knocked out.

At 1530, accompanied by Bigeard, Lemeunier and Vadot, Langlais went to see General de Castries. He did not know that a telegram sent from Dienbienphu at 1400 hours had fixed the cessation of hostilities for seven the next morning. At Isabelle, where there were still two thousand shells left for a solitary 105-mm. gun, Colonel Lalande had permission to attempt a sortie. Castries was free to decide Langlais's fate and that of the remaining officers and men. He said to Bigeard, "You're going to pay dearly for all this, Bruno. You ought to try to make a break for it with a few men."

Who could possibly pull off that sortie? Perfectly calm and self-assured, Castries agreed that within five miles all of them would be overcome by exhaustion. Castries dismissed the officers and remained alone with Langlais. Exactly what they said to each other has been forgotten. Between the remarks exchanged with Bigeard, or by radio with Cogny, everything has become confused. Besides, what can they add to what was? Even monks end up, under the influence of communal life, hating one another.

These two men so different in character and methods no longer had any grounds for dispute. Who bore the responsibility for the fall of Dienbienphu? Neither of the two. Outstripped by events, Castries had failed to react at the right moment, but he had not wanted this post for which he was completely unsuited. He had not deceived anybody; others had been mistaken about him. He had been honest enough to warn Navarre, "If it's a second Na San that you want, pick somebody else. I don't feel cut out for that." And he had lacked the necessary humility to see that he ought to be replaced. Cynical and frivolous as he was, was it his fault also that he didn't like Langlais and Langlais didn't like him? Was Langlais also to blame if, preoccupied with the patrols he had been ordered to organize every day, he had been unable to rehearse the counterattacks intended to recapture outposts which nobody expected to fall? To imagine that he should have demanded the necessary time and resources from Castries and Gaucher is to be wise after the event. It is necessary to go back in time, to breathe the atmosphere of optimism which reigned among the garrison, to hear the roar of Piroth's artillery when it fired its salvos into the mountains at the slightest alert. Who had had any premonition, at the time, of the disaster which had just occurred? As for his animosity toward Castries, that was only skin-deep. Langlais had made offensive remarks on several occasions about Castries's reluctance to leave his shelter, but if everybody paid homage to Langlais's spirit, who hadn't quarreled with him and suffered from his anger and bad temper?

"It's all over," said Castries. "We mustn't leave anything intact."

A brief access of emotion suddenly misted over Castries's eyes and froze Langlais's icy features. When Langlais saluted, Castries stepped forward with his hand outstretched, and Langlais, without saying a word, threw himself into his arms.

About 1600 hours, in the course of a radiotelephone conversation, Lieutenant Colonel de Séguins-Pazzis offered Colonel Lalande the choice between a pitched battle and an attempted sortie toward the south. Lalande was given no indication that the main position would not hold out until the following morning. He chose a sortie at nightfall, issued the orders prepared for that purpose, and sent out reconnaissance patrols toward the south, along both banks of the Nam Youm, to gauge the resistance the enemy was likely to offer. Since the direction of the sortie had been altered from the southwest to due south, there were no maps or guides available. Moreover, only one track seemed to be practicable, by way of Muong Nha, Ban Ta Mot and Ban Pha Nang, and Lalande had to change his plan.

On returning to his command post, Langlais gave orders for the destruction of all weapons, optical and signals equipment. Bigeard remained aloof from all this. The news spread at once that surrender was imminent. Sergeant Sammarco had the barrels of rifles and machine guns thrust into the ground for the last cartridges to be fired. With incendiary grenades they soldered the breeches of the 105-mm. guns or melted the mortars and the bazookas. The ammunition was thrown into the river. The engines of the tanks which were still in working order were raced without any oil. The chaplains gathered together their chalices and holy oils. Grauwin buried a few bottles of penicillin with markers to indicate their position.

The fighting began again and the Viet battalions gradually advanced toward the center, surrounding paratroop units which fell immediately. There was no longer any question of fighting. Already, on the left bank, white rags were being waved among the Moroccans and the river-bank population. Dressed in green, with motley scraps of parachute material in their helmets and their duck trousers rolled up to the knees, the Viets appeared from all sides, in a silent, overwhelming flood. The river was crossed at 1700 hours. Hearing his battalion commander utter an oath, Sergeant Kubiak turned toward Castries's command post over which a huge white flag was waving. It suddenly occurred to Captain Capeyron that he ought to burn the 3rd Company's flag. Bending over the fire which his Legionnaires had hurriedly lit, he had just seen the last letters of the word "Loyalty" embroidered on the silk eaten up by the flames when the Viets arrived. A Viet officer gave the order: "Hands up!"

Capeyron did not obey. Some Viets came up and kicked him

in the buttocks. Some Legionnaires broke ranks to intervene. Pale with humiliation, Capeyron restrained them.

"Don't move. It's too late."

In all the trenches on Éliane, the Viets began piling up the corpses from both sides and covering them with earth. On the summit of Éliane 2, they erected a sort of bamboo cenotaph, thirty feet high, which they decorated with white silk parachutes.

Algerians and Moroccans who had remained in hiding for days and nights on end came out into the open, waving rags and, naturally choosing the word which in all the armies of the world has always meant the end of fighting and the fraternization of former enemies, shouted, "Comrades!"

Company Commander Tho, entrusted with the task of establishing a clearing station, found the prisoners unusually docile; most of them stretched themselves as if they had been lying down for a long time and did breathing exercises. They were sent to the rear in groups of ten or so, without guards, simply being shown the way to the first collecting center. The head of the surgical block at Him Lam, Dr. Nguyen duong Quang, a pupil of Professor Tung, had tents made of parachute material put up to shelter the wounded, and started for the hospital.

"Here they come." These were the words you heard everywhere. In his shelter, Langlais hurriedly burnt his letters, his private notebook, the photographs of the woman he loved and even his red beret. He kissed Geneviève de Galard and gave her a message for his mother while his staff officers destroyed the command archives and the typewriters. He put on his old bush hat, which made him look like a melancholy sailor in a sou'wester. Why had he burnt his red beret when Bigeard had kept his? It was because he was afraid the Viets would use it as a trophy; unconsciously, he also wanted to spare what he held dearest in the way of military uniform the humiliation of defeat. Born for action, he suddenly found himself deprived of everything and at a loss as to what to do, whereas Bigeard, without decorations or marks of rank, but with his red beret pulled down over his head, was already preparing his escape; he rolled a nylon map of the highlands round his ankle and thought of hiding in a hole, under a pile of parachutes. Why shouldn't he succeed in escaping?

Little by little, the camp started swarming with activity, while clouds of smoke rose into the air and the ground shook with the explosions of material being blown up. Demoralized by the savagery of the fighting and by the bombardment which had gone on without stopping since the evening of May 1, thousands of haggard men, who had been drinking the yellow river water out of buckets since the purification plant had been destroyed, regained hope of surviving. Spontaneously, as if they had been slaves all their lives, they formed up in columns, knotted little squares of white material to the ends of sticks, and allowed themselves to be driven toward the northeast along the sides of Route 41 beneath the contemptuous gaze of the Legionnaires and the paratroopers. These were not the pictures of the disaster which would be taken a few days later by cameramen rushed to the spot to reconstruct, with docile North Africans disguised as paratroopers, the scenes the Vietminh had dreamed of. How many were there, at that moment, who preferred captivity to insolence? Ten thousand? And are we entitled to think that Dienbienphu would never have fallen if they had fought like the other two thousand who were preparing to force a way out?

The guns destroyed, the sandbags ripped open, the shelters in ruins, the burned-out trucks lying in puddles of yellow water – everything showed that the defeat was complete. Dirty parachutes covered the hills and the valley, hung on the river banks, clung to the parapets of the bridge and the barbed-wire entanglements like torn spiders' webs. There could no longer be any doubt about it: all was lost. Some, like Sergeant Sammarco, said to themselves, "It wasn't worth the trouble of killing so many people." Most remained silent. Corporal Hoinant, who had never seen anybody but his chief, Major Guiraud, could not understand anything any more. He had been told that it was essential to hold out until the Geneva Conference was over, and now they had just given in. As for hoping, he had abandoned all hope since he had been deceived with the assurance, repeated every day, that Crèvecoeur was on the way.

"Come out with your hands up . . ."

If the fortunes of war had gone the other way, Hoinant and Sammarco considered that the victory of the paratroops and the Legion would have been more harshly imposed on the defeated side. Neither of them had witnessed the humiliation inflicted on Captain Capeyron and, through him, on all the vanquished. They noted the correct behavior and lack of hatred of the Viets, who said to them, "The war is over." Perhaps. Commandos jumped down into the trenches, holding their noses because the smell was so atrocious, and ransacked the command posts in search of documents. Others, in token of their joy, threw grenades into the river, where they exploded with a muffled noise. Grauwin inspected the uniforms of his medical orderlies and distributed armlets on which red crosses had been painted with Mercurochrome.

"Whatever you do," Grauwin told his team, "don't leave my side."

In Hanoï, where he had heard Castries outline the situation to him once again, Cogny had the signal switched to the floor below, to General Bodet, whom Navarre had left on the spot to represent him and who wanted to bid Castries the official farewell, worthy of the Commander in Chief and his brilliant deputy.

Bastiani, Cogny's chief of staff, intervened.

"Wait a minute," he said to Cogny. "You didn't mention the question of the white flag."

Catapulted out of his seat by a terrible premonition, Cogny rushed downstairs and burst into Bodet's office just as Navarre's deputy, in his shrill little voice, was saying to Castries, "Good-bye, my friend. And all the very best. You've put up a good fight."

Cogny pushed him to one side and snatched the receiver from his hand. Navarre had never conceived the possibility that the white flag might be hoisted. In his directive of April 1, he had declared that under no circumstances was the idea of capitulation to be considered.

"Hello, hello, Castries? . . . Hello, Castries?"

"General?"

"Look, man, naturally you've got to call it quits. But one thing certain is that everything you've done so far is superb. You mustn't spoil it all now by hoisting the white flag. You're overwhelmed, but there must be no surrender, no white flag."

Did Castries suddenly realize the extent of his blunder? Probably nobody will ever know, and General de Castries and Séguins-Pazzis will take their secret to the grave. What is striking about the recording of this conversation – and the copies I have heard have been cut at precisely this point – is Castries's embarrassment after Cogny's injunction and the argument he uses to justify himself. To justify himself for what if not for having hoisted the white flag?

"Ah! Very good, General," Castries replied after a pause, in a heart-broken voice. "It was just that I wanted to protect the wounded."

"Yes, I know. Then protect them as best you can, letting your [. . .] act on their own [. . .] What you've done is too fine to be spoilt like that. You understand, don't you?"

"Very good, General."

"Well, good-bye, fellow, see you soon."

There was no "*Vive la France!*" as the commander of the entrenched camp was reported saying. Radio operator Mélien, who was putting the signal through from an office near Castries's, concluded for the benefit of his opposite number in Hanoï, "The Viets are a few yards away. We're going to blow up the transmitter. So long, fellow."

The white flag which Sergeant Kubiak had seen flying over Castries's command post while Bigeard and Langlais were getting ready in their shelters to receive the Viets was hurriedly taken down.

Cogny informed Madame de Castries of the fall of Dienbienphu and asked her to keep the news secret. In Cogny's anteroom Mr. Hedberg, a journalist on the *Expressen*, was waiting.

There was the sound of feet running over the roof of the shelter. When Platoon Commander Chu ta Thé's squad reached the superstructure of Castries's command post at a gallop, did it unfold and wave the red flag with the gold star that day, or was the scene reconstructed later? On the French side, nobody knows. The only flag that Sergeant Kubiak saw flying over Castries's command post was the white one. He stated this in writing, and the official periodical of the Foreign Legion published his story in its issue of April, 1963, without anyone protesting.

When the Viets entered the command post and pushed aside the door curtain, Castries was waiting for them standing, unarmed, his sleeves rolled up. He had changed his shirt and trousers and, as usual, was wearing his medal ribbons. The parachutist Sergeant Passerat de Silans, who belonged to Langlais's signals section, maintains that at the sight of the submachine guns aimed at him Castries cried, "Don't shoot me." This doesn't sound like Castries, who may have said, in an attempt to change the squad's threatening attitude, "You damn fools, you aren't going to shoot, are you?"

Grauwin glanced toward the sap and caught sight of Castries, pale under his red forage cap, a cigarette between his lips, dazzled by the sunlight. He was promptly driven away in a jeep to be questioned by the Viet Military Intelligence. Did Grauwin also see, as he would subsequently write, Langlais, with his frozen, unseeing face, and Bigeard, his head bent under his beret, swept away in a crowd of prisoners? Langlais and Bigeard had come out together, without putting their hands up, but at a different time from Castries, whom they would not see again for ten days. Grauwin, his heart pounding, went down to the hospital. A Viet soldier, his legs covered with mud, his belt hung with grenades, appeared and gestured toward the sap.

"Outside!"

In the operating theater, where Lieutenant Gindrey of the medical service was bending over a torn body, men lay groaning on stretchers, waiting their turn. Followed by Geneviève de Galard and his medical orderlies, Grauwin came out onto the terreplein, where some wounded men, who had just been put down near some rotting corpses, watched him go by like salvation disappearing from sight.

In the vicinity of the command post, the Viets called for Langlais, who went toward them.

"That's me."

He was surrounded and Bigeard followed him, walking
among his staff. The Viets also shouted, "Bigeard! . . . Where
is Bigeard?"

His hands thrust deep into his pockets, Bigeard went on
walking in the long column, anonymous and walled up in
a silence from which he would not emerge for days, ready
to seize the slightest opportunity to escape. They could look
for the wolf Bigeard themselves. He carried nothing on him,
not a single packet of cigarettes or tin of rations, while some
prisoners were bent under suitcases stuffed with food. His
faithful orderly, knowing what he was like, had taken a carton
of Lucky Strikes for him from Castries's command post. No
doubt Bigeard knew that he was down on the canvas, but he
was already getting to his feet. The fight wasn't over. Nothing
was over as long as life went on flowing through his veins.
This business was not simply an affair between the West and
the rebels, the Expeditionary Corps and the People's Army;
it was a scrap between the Viets and himself. How had these
little men, the youngest of whom looked like boys of fifteen
and who had always avoided battle for fear of meeting their
match, managed to win? How were fresh humiliations to be
avoided in the future? What lessons were to be learned from
this affair and from this army of ants which had fought on
empty bellies but with their heads full of the ideas and the
hope with which they had been crammed? These were the
questions which haunted him. He, too, had heard the "Song
of the Partisans" all night on the Viet wavelength. He felt
sick at heart.

For the moment, shutting out everything around him, his
shoulders hunched so as not to irritate anybody, he watched
through half-closed eyes for any relaxation of the guards'
supervision so he could escape into the mountains with a
few companions, as Second Lieutenant Makowiak would do,
reaching an outpost in Laos. From the generosity of the
People's Army, Bigeard expected nothing. Defeated, he would
suffer the lot of the defeated, without ever accepting it. "Poor
bastards." He kept repeating this insult to punish himself
and the simpletons who had thought they were bound to

win because their camp was stuffed with artillery and heavy machine guns and received supplies every day by air from Hanoï. Perhaps he remembered that at Agincourt, too, the French had despised the enemy and had prepared for battle with the same arrogant self-assurance. But above all else, there must be no tears such as he had seen on the faces of some of his comrades. Victory over the ants of the totalitarian regimes was won in other ways; as for the victory parade, led by a band through the streets of a capital, which some officers had vaguely dreamed of, once the Viets had been laid out in the barbed-wire entanglements, Bigeard laughed at the idea. Here it was, the victory planned by the staffs of the Expeditionary Corps and approved by the government. He did not know that in a few weeks the prisoners would be gathered together and made to march all day long, with bowed heads, in columns of eight, a procession of shame escorted by little men armed with automatic pistols, in front of the cameras of the Communist world; but when he was asked to take part in the reconstruction of the capture of the command post, he would reply, "I'd rather die." And the Viets would not insist.

If the Viets were calling for Bigeard everywhere, it was because they wanted to see at close quarters the wolf finally in captivity with the sheep. How could they recognize him with nothing to distinguish him from the men plodding like a procession of caterpillars toward the northeastern heights?

Under a sky suddenly empty of planes, the little group of doctors crossed the bridge. The last packages of the seventy tons which twenty-eight Dakotas had dropped during the morning were spread out; 105-mm. shells, food supplies, small arms, pharmaceutical products, canned milk, everything henceforth belonged to the victor. On the other bank the medical team was stopped and Grauwin was ordered to return to care for the wounded. Dr. Nguyen duong Quang had just inspected the hospital, which he had found far better equipped than his own; he had noted that the Vietminh soldiers were treated on an equal footing with the French. Touched by Grauwin's sadness, he had some coffee brought to him.

At 1755 a dispatch from Cogny asked Colonel Lalande at

Isabelle to tell him his plans for the coming night. Lalande was still unaware that the main position had fallen. He learned it only at 1830 from the decoding of a message and the sudden opening of a bombardment which blew up his ammunition dumps, cut his telephone wires and set fire to his dressing station. After which the Vietminh radio told him on his own wavelength, "It is useless to go on fighting. The rest of the garrison are prisoners. Give yourselves up."

About 2000 hours, guided by the Thais who had not yet dared to desert and wanted to disappear into the country, the 12th Company of the 3rd Foreign tried to escape along the right bank, following the curves of the river. Radio contact was poor and it was difficult to follow its progress. From the firing which broke out, it was possible to locate more or less accurately the points where it had met Viet resistance. A little later, the 11th Company set off between the track and the left bank. About 2100 hours, silence seemed to indicate that it had succeeded. One by one, in the total darkness, all the units followed, laboriously extricating themselves from the barbed-wire entanglements and the muddy trenches. The noise of fighting came from the south, where the 57th Regiment was barring the way with one battalion on each side of the Nam Youm. At 2300 hours, Captain Hien, who with a third battalion was blocking the junction of the Nam Youm and the Nam Noua, where Route 41 met the track from Laos, was ordered to return. An attack created disorder among the bulk of the units, cut them off, split them up and overwhelmed them. Soldiers of the People's Army and the Expeditionary Corps mingled with one another. Voices shouted, "Don't shoot. You will be well treated." Colonel Lalande then decided to try to hold out on the spot and ordered his units to return to Isabelle, where utter confusion reigned.

In Paris, it was nearly five o'clock. M. Joseph Laniel, the Prime Minister, mounted the tribune of the National Assembly to announce, in a voice which he tried to keep steady, the fall of Dienbienphu. All the deputies, except those on the Communist benches, rose to their feet. The stupor of defeat suddenly weighed upon the city, where the papers were publishing dispatches which had arrived out of order, mutilated by the Saigon censorship. A special edition of *France-Soir* carried a banner headline spread over eight columns: "DIENBIENPHU HAS FALLEN." *Le Monde* announced that the plane of Bao Dai, who had been accused for some days of delaying the evacuation of the wounded by his stay on the Côte d'Azur, had narrowly escaped an accident. The weather was fine that Friday afternoon, and the chestnut trees in the Bois de Boulogne and along the quays were in flower. The theaters and movie houses would be open that evening as usual.

About one o'clock in the morning of May 8, a small group of French-speaking Viets waving a white flag advanced toward the command post of Isabelle. "Let us pass," they told the soldiers who stopped them. "We want to see your commander, Colonel Lalande." Colonel Lalande agreed to see these envoys, who told him, "All further resistance is useless. Don't be stubborn." Lalande then gave orders for a cease-fire.

For Bigeard and Langlais the darkness was falling, whereas it seemed to Captain Hien as if a long night had come to an end. Everywhere the news of the victory spread like wildfire from village to village. Professor Tung, on his way toward the hospitals in the rear, had learned it at 2000 hours. Already people were shouting, "It's all right. We know." The entrenched camp looked like a huge flea market where the victors were dividing their booty of bars of soap, flashlights and canned foods. Lights were shining in the basin, where there was no longer any fear of air raids which would kill as many French as Viets. Yet planes continued to fly over the region, ready to drop flares or bombs on the poor stars in the valley.

General Navarre's former aide-de-camp was marching with ten thousand prisoners toward the Tonkin camps. The Viets had tied his hands behind his back because he had refused to answer their questions. Throughout the world, where Waterloo had created less of a sensation, the fall of Dienbienphu had caused utter amazement. It was one of the greatest defeats ever suffered by the West, heralding the collapse of the colonial empires and the end of a republic. The thunder of the event rumbles on.

PROJECT DELTA
Shelby L. Stanton

The US Army Special Forces – the Green Berets – was formed in 1952 to fight unconventional warfare in unconventional wars. Initially regarded with suspicion, if not hostility, by the US military hierarchy and government, the Green Berets were expanded in 1961 by President Kennedy, who believed that their counter-insurgency skills could play a vital part in defending US interests – in particular, in South East Asia, where the country was becoming embroiled in the Vietnamese War.

By 1963 some 1500 Green Berets from 5th Special Forces Group were in place in Vietnam. Highly trained in the arts of jungle combat, and equipped with specialist equipment (including the STABO rig, which allowed personnel to be lifted into a helicopter while still firing their weapons), the Special Forces were assigned to reconnaissance and sabotage work deep in communist-held territory.

As a refinement to their operations, the Special Forces in Vietnam set up Project Delta in 1964, a self-contained group designed to carry out the most dangerous missions against the Viet Cong and NVA. Run jointly by the US and South Vietnamese Special Forces, Delta was organized into 16 recon teams, each composed of two US Special Forces and four native peoples ("indigs"), mostly from the Nung tribe. Other Delta personnel were operated as "Roadrunners", indigs disguised as Viet Cong who infiltrated enemy routes and bases. The assault element of the project, used to "neutralize" enemy targets identified by the recon and Roadrunner teams, was a South Vietnamese Ranger Battalion, the 91st Airborne.

This account of the work of Special Forces Delta Project is from Green Berets at War *by Shelby L. Stanton, a former captain in US Army Special Forces.*

*   *   *

T HE FIRST INTELLIGENCE-GATHERING missions were
     costly, since these tasks placed a premium on mastering
difficult techniques, with little chance for error deep in Viet
Cong territory. During Operation MASHER in the first month
of 1966, the 1st Cavalry Division requested Project DELTA
reconnaissance assistance in the jungled An Lao Valley of
Binh Dinh Province. Major Charlie Beckwith's Detachment
B-52 left Nha Trang in C-123 aircraft and landed at Bong
Son on 26 January 1966. The schedule provided insufficient
preparation prior to the commitment of the recondo teams.
They were inserted into the operational area the very next
evening, despite marginal weather. Operation 2-66 in the An
Lao Valley was one of the worst disasters to befall Project
DELTA in the Vietnam War.

   Sfc. Henry A. Keating's Team Eskimo was composed of
five Special Forces sergeants. In a skirmish with Viet Cong
on the morning of 28 January. Staff Sergeant Dupuis suffered
a head wound from grenade shrapnel. The team climbed a
ridgeline overlooking the valley and radioed for extraction.
The helicopter spent two hours unsuccessfully searching for
the team in the drizzling rain. The aircraft returned after
refueling, spotted Keating's panel, and dropped rope ladders
to them in the high elephant grass.

   Team Capitol, a six-man American team under Sfc. Frank
R. Webber, Jr., scouted several trails on 28 January but was
spotted by woodcutters. Webber led his men to higher ground
where they spent the night. Heavy fog and rain hampered their
difficult trek through the tropical underbrush, which became
so thick at the base of a rock cliff that they were forced to
crawl on their hands and knees. At noon on 29 January, the
team reached a small clearing, assumed defensive positions,
and prepared to discuss its next move. Suddenly, Viet Cong
automatic rifle fire ripped through the foliage. Sfc. Jesse L.
Hancock was killed instantly and S. Sgt. George A. Hoagland
III collapsed on his back, mortally wounded. Both Webber
and Sfc. Marlin C. Cook were also wounded in this initial
volley of fire.

   The surrounding jungle was so dense that no one knew
where the firing was coming from. Cook had been hit in the

stomach and back. Although paralyzed from the waist down, he returned fire into the shrubbery. Webber's lower arm was shattered, but he also fired into the foliage as S. Sgt. Charles F. Hiner ran over to Cook's position, took the radio from his backpack, and frantically called for assistance. S. Sgt. Donald L. Dotson was shot through the chest and killed while trying to move across the clearing.

Hiner managed to contact an aircraft, and the team emergency was relayed to the forward air controller. After spotting Hiner's red smoke grenade, the control aircraft departed to guide two helicopter gunships to the team position. After some initial confusion in relocating the shattered team, the helicopters were overhead and responded to Hiner's desperate pleas to make gun-runs on his own perimeter. Hiner was wounded, but the VC fire became sporadic. Webber crawled back from the edge of the clearing and dragged Cook with him to the rock where Hiner was. Minutes later Cook was killed by helicopters strafing through the middle of the clearing.

Hiner and Webber were the only team members still alive, and they were both faint from loss of blood. Hiner kept passing out over the radio, but he regained consciousness in time to hear that Lieutenant Holland's reaction team was working its way to them and needed signal smoke. Ten minutes later the rescue group reached them. Rope ladders were used to lift the two wounded sergeants and four bodies out of the jungle.

The third team, Roadrunner, was led by Sfc. Marcus Huston. They exchanged gunfire with Viet Cong near a stream and were evading uphill on 28 January, when they came under fire for the second time. Staff Sgt. Frank N. Badolati was hit in the upper left arm with such force that the arm was nearly severed. Sfc. Cecil J. Hodgson's rifle was blasted out of his hands. The other sergeants opened fire and provided covering fire as the team ran from the area. Badolati begged the team to leave him and save themselves. A tourniquet was applied to his arm and morphine was administered four times during the retreat. The team paused to radio a distress call near a rock ledge and was inadvertently split up by renewed fighting.

Huston and Staff Sergeant McKeith took Badolati with them, although he protested, encouraging them to continue without him. Badolati realized that his comrades would stop if he did, so he kept moving through sheer willpower. Finally, his wounds forced him to halt, and he told Huston, "Save yourselves." Huston and McKeith placed Badolati among the boulders near a mountain stream, where they prepared for a final stand. Badolati died during the next two hours. They put his body at a fork in the stream and continued moving until dark. The next morning, Huston and McKeith's panel was sighted by an L-19 aircraft, and the forward air controller diverted an extraction helicopter to them.

The other element under M. Sgt. Wiley W. Gray was involved in another firefight before they could reach the emergency pickup point. Gray heard S. Sgt. Ronald T. Terry yell that he had been hit and turned around to see him holding his side with both hands. Within seconds Terry was shot again and killed. Gray could not find Hodgson (later declared missing in action). Suddenly helicopter gunships appeared overhead, strafing the area as part of the Huston-McKeith extraction. The confusion enabled Gray to escape, and later that afternoon he was able to signal rescue helicopters with his flare pistol.

Major Beckwith was wounded in his helicopter during the extractions and replaced. After Operation 2–66, Project DELTA was overhauled and conducted multiple reconnaissance missions across the Central Highlands throughout I and II CTZ. The next combat fatality did not occur until Operation 10–66 (9 August to 5 September 1966) while DELTA was under the operational control of the 196th Infantry Brigade in War Zone C. In that operation DELTA teams that had infiltrated from Song Be and Tay Ninh reconnoitered extensive trail networks entering the area from Cambodia. The Viet Cong were reluctant to engage the Special Forces, possibly from fear of airstrikes, but on the afternoon of 27 August, contact was lost with Team #2.

Maj. Robert E. Luttrell, commanding Detachment B-52, was aloft with the air relay pilot and spotted a red panel, smoke, and a signal mirror being flashed at them. Helicopters were dispatched to the scene, and medical Sgt. Timothy O'Connor dashed out under heavy fire to place seriously wounded patrol advisor Sgt. Johnny Varner in the pickup aircraft. O'Connor was wounded in the leg trying to reach Sgt. Eugene Moreau, who already appeared dead. An LLDB team member crawled into the helicopter from the other side, and they lifted off as automatic weapons fire cut across the landing zone. Shortly thereafter, another LLDB team member was spotted in the forest and taken out by McGuire rig. The 4th Company, 91st Airborne Ranger Battalion, arrived on the battlefield after dark and retrieved the bodies of Moreau and LLDB Corporal Mo. Although Operation 10–66 resulted in one Special Forces soldier killed and another four wounded, extensive DELTA-directed airstrike damage was inflicted on Viet Cong installations.

Project DELTA returned to War Zone C in Operation 12–66 during late September, after vainly searching for a downed F4 Phantom crew near Cam Ranh Bay. Airstrikes were used to silence several VC base facilities. On 15 October the unit was dispatched to Khe Sanh in Operation 13–66 and found an extensive storage area just south of the DMZ near the Laotian border. Aerial bombing caused large secondary explosions and intense munitions fires. During the second phase of the operation, a patrol was destroyed by the North Vietnamese on 2 December 1966. Sgt. Irby Dyer III was killed, and the LLDB survivors last saw S. Sgt. Russell P. Bott attending to the wounded patrol leader, Sfc. Willie E. Stark, whom he refused to abandon even though they were surrounded and outnumbered.

The next three operations (1–67 through 3–67) were cancelled by intensive training in Nha Trang. Project DELTA reentered the An Lao Valley under the 1st Cavalry Division in Operation 4–67. Commencing 4 March 1967, fifty-two reconnaissance missions verified slight Viet Cong presence, since bivouac and way stations had fallen into disuse and trail activity was light.

Project DELTA entered the A Shau Valley west of Hue on 10 April 1967 during Operation 5–67. Forty-eight patrols gained vast intelligence value at the cost of five wounded Special Forces members. The sweeps proved that the NVA were using the valley as a major infiltration corridor, had

linked Route 922 from Laos to other roads, and were using
vehicular convoys at night. DELTA elements directed hundreds of airstrikes into the area and substantially reduced the
North Vietnamese traffic.

The A Shau intrusion was also harrowing. On the afternoon
of 14 May, Staff Sergeant Gleason's Reconnaissance Team
#1 was being landed when the helicopter was blasted by
automatic weapons fire, causing it to lose all oil pressure.
The pilot crash-landed, and everyone formed a defensive
circle around the downed aircraft. One NVA machine gun
was silenced, and after dark another helicopter lifted out the
crewmen and three LLDB soldiers. Staff Sergeants Gleason
and Brierley remained with an LLDB soldier and were joined
by a DELTA sergeant who had voluntarily left the recovery
aircraft to make room for those taken out. A second helicopter
trying to reach them struck the trees with its rotor and crashed
only twenty yards away. The crew and another Special Forces
sergeant joined the first group. All personnel were extracted
under flarelight at 9:30 P.M., without further incident.

Operations SAMURAI I to III extended Maj. Charles
"Chuck" A. Allen's DELTA searches from the northern
stretches to the A Shau Valley into Happy Valley, west of Da
Nang, where further infiltration was discovered from 10 July
through the end of October 1967. Elements overran an NVA
aid station, capturing numerous documents and prisoners. In
the Happy Valley area DELTA ranger, roadrunner, and recon
forces fought a series of firefights with the *368B NVA Rocket
Regiment*, which had been bombarding the Da Nang area.

From 27 November 1967 to 28 January 1968, Major
Allen moved his unit into the Plei Trap Valley along the
Laotian border of II CTZ for Operations SULTAN I and
II. His teams confirmed that the *32d NVA Regiment* had
moved into the area following the battle of Dak To. Project
DELTA moved north again into the A Shau Valley for
Operations SAMURAI IV and V, which lasted from 3
March until 20 May 1968. General Westmoreland ordered
the unit to help interdict infiltration routes leading into
Hue. Despite unfavorable weather and the first real jump
in casualties, the Special Forces and LLDB rangers engaged

the North Vietnamese in a series of deliberate confrontations.

Operation ALAMO was conducted next in the III CTZ Song Be River area near Cambodia. Project DELTA was under control of the 5th ARVN Division. The lack of helicopters necessitated reducing the usual twelve reconnaissance teams operating at any one time to only six. Twenty-seven missions were conducted during a month of September patrolling that uncovered a large number of base sites, hospitals, ammunition stocks, and food caches. Project DELTA was responsible for the discovery of a number of high speed, bamboo-matted infiltration trails.

Project DELTA was displaced north on Operation WAR BONNET in the An Hoa vicinity but returned south to Binh Long Province in III CTZ during Operation ARES on 16 November 1968. Eighty-five missions identified a major rear service and supply area there. On 29 March 1969 the unit was flown back into I CTZ and placed under the control of the 101st Airborne Division (Airmobile). During Operations CASS PARK I and II, followed by TROJAN HORSE I and II, reconnaissance teams scoured the Vuong River Valley, An Hoa basin, and northwestern fringes of the country. Captured documents enabled the 3d Marine Division to gain additional appraisals of several regiments and battalions operating in its area.

During Operation CASS PARK II, Roadrunner Team #103 was infiltrated southwest of An Hoa on 17 June 1969. Two days later they spotted thirty NVA walking along a trail, followed by one 37mm antiaircraft gun that was being pulled by two water buffaloes. Reconnaissance Team #1A had spotted something much prettier the day before. Their final report stated:

181515H Vic[inity] coord[inates] Z0085002, tm [team] obsrd [observed] a group of 12 VC moving NE, all were walking and dressed the same as en[emy] mentioned before, all had wpns [weapons] but no packs nor web gear. Approx[imately] in the center of this group tm obsrd a Caucasian female. The Caucasian female was dressed in white shirt, dark pants, with her shirt tucked in her pants. She was without head gear. Her clothes were clean and neat. Hair was strawberry blond, roughly shoulder length. Smooth light skin. Weight approx 140 to 145 lbs, height 5'6", large bust, female was not carrying anything. She was not under duress. She seemed well fed and in good health.

Project DELTA stayed in the north until 9 November 1969. During the last three weeks of December, Operation YELLOW RIBBON verified lack of major NVA activity west of Pleiku within the previous six months. Project DELTA undertook Operation SABER AND SPURS on 11 February 1970 and was attached to another Special Forces unit for the first time in detachment history. Working under Company A at Bien Hoa, sixty-three missions confirmed that certain NVA rear service units were still using northern portions of III CTZ but fled at the sight of patrols. The same task was continued in Operation CAVALRY GLORY.

On 10 May 1970 Project DELTA commenced its last two operations in Vietnam, DELTA DAGGER I and II. Operationally controlled by the 101st Airborne Division (Airmobile), the unit swept through southwestern Quang Tri Province and adjacent Laotian border regions. There were no significant contacts or sightings after the end of May, and on 31 June Maj. George F. Aiken's Project DELTA ceased all tactical operations and returned to the rear base at Nha Trang. The personnel were reassigned and Detachment B-52 was deactivated on 31 July 1970.

Project DELTA was a very successful Special Forces long-range reconnaissance operation. The intelligence provided the identities of more than seventy NVA/VC units and enabled the capture of numerous supply caches, documents, and prisoners. It rendered vital information on enemy troop concentrations, infiltration networks, extent of fortifications, and lack of activity in areas planned for extensive allied search operations. The data were often gained in remote and largely inaccessible areas of the country, and were produced with minimal casualties.

THE LAST RAID
ON SIMI
John Lodwick

The Greek island of Simi, occupied by the Germans in 1941, was a favourite stomping ground of the British Special Boat Squadron during WWII. The SBS raided Simi – even controlled it temporarily – on numerous occasions. As a result, the Wehrmacht was forced to strengthen the island's garrison with troops diverted from other fronts. It is estimated that as many as 18,000 German troops were tied down by the actions of the 250-strong SBS against Simi and the other Aegean islands.

Formed in 1942 from a marriage of SAS's D Squadron and the Commando Special Boat Sections, the SBS's main area of activity was the Aegean, but it also fought in the Mediterranean and Adriatic Seas. It was led by Major the Earl Jellicoe, an early member of David Stirling's 1 SAS.

The SBS was unorthodox in its dress (which consisted of any Allied uniform to hand), armament (the German MP38/40 was a favourite weapon) and parade-ground discipline. It was also pervaded by a very British sense of "dashingness", perfectly encapsulated in an incident where a junior officer, David Clark, landed on a German occupied island, walked in to the officers mess, and said: "It would be all so much easier if you would just raise your hands."

Yet the appearance of casualness in the SBS was deceptive and training for the unit at its specialist camp at Athlit in the Palestine was gruelling, including many hours instruction in the use of folboats and Greek caiques.

The SBS – the inspiration for Alistair Maclean's novel, The Guns of Navarone – was disbanded in 1945, although much of its ethos lives on in the elite unit which bears the same name today, the Special Boat Squadron of the Royal Marines.

The account here is of the SBS's last action against Simi, that of July 1944. It comes from John Lodwick's classic and evocative memoir of life and war in the Squadron, The Filibusters.

T HE SIMI OPERATION had been considered for some time, but as long as the enemy possessed destroyers in the Aegean, it had never looked practicable. Destroyers can interfere with landing operations, even at long range and at short notice. At the beginning of the year, there had been four destroyers in the Eastern Mediterranean. Only very gradually were they eliminated.

The German navy in those waters seldom put to sea.

In March, one of these ships was damaged by a British submarine. Later, a second received a bomb amidships from a Beaufighter. Two remained lurking in Leros. In this emergency, Brigadier Turnbull requested London to send him out a small party of Royal Marine Boom Commando troops. A wise move, for though there were still many men in the SBS to whom folboating was second nature, the art of infiltration by canoe had undoubtedly declined since the days of 'Tug' Wilson. Folboats, when used at all, were now used to land personnel, their role being no more aggressive than that of a gondola.

When Turnbull's marines first arrived in the Middle East the experts were inclined to scoff. Their attitude of condescension was abandoned when it was seen with what precision the newcomers handled their craft. In mid-June they went into Portolago Harbour, Leros, crossed two booms, sank the surviving destroyers with limpet charges and emerged without loss.

The way was now clear for Simi.

On 6th July Stewart Macbeth returned to base. He had made a personal reconnaissance of the island and pin-pointed the enemy dispositions. Two days later the striking force, under Brigadier Turnbull himself, comprising ten motor launches, two schooners, eighty-one members of the SBS and one hundred and thirty-nine from the Greek Sacred Squadron were concentrated in Penzik Bay, Turkey, under camouflage. Three parties were constituted: Main Force, under the Brigadier with Lapraik deputizing; West Force, under Captain Charles Clynes; and South Force, under Macbeth. On the night of July 13th the landings were made, and despite great enemy vigilance, passed everywhere unobserved. The only casualities suffered consisted of two Greek officers who fell into the water with heavy packs. They were drowned.

The approach marches were difficult but all three forces were lying up and overlooking their targets before dawn. At first light a barrage was opened upon Simi Castle – the main enemy stronghold – by mortars and multiple machine-guns. Two German "Ems" barges which had left harbour a few minutes before zero hour now came scuttling back. They had sighted the force of five British launches which was coming in to bombard the castle. Both motor launches and the SBS opened fire on these ships. Presently, large white flags could be seen waving from their bridges before they ran ashore and were captured in good working order.

"Stud" Stellin was clearing Molo Point. He had taken his first objective without opposition. Ahead of him, Germans were running up the hill to man their machine-gun posts.

"I took a shot with my carbine," said "Stud", "but misfired. I therefore called upon Private Whalen to give them the works. We strolled in with grenades, and I think that everybody went a little mad. Soon, all the enemy were either down and dead, or up and waving their hands."

Stellin locked these prisoners in a church, left a sentry outside it and moved on to his next objective.

Clynes, scheduled to attack gun positions, gave them three minutes softening from his Brens and then ordered his Greeks to charge. "All I can remember, then," he said, "is a general surge up the slope and two small and pathetic white hand-kerchiefs waving at the top of it. I ordered a 'Cease fire' all round, and began to count my prisoners."

By 0900 hours, Main Force Headquarters and the Vickers machine-gun and mortar troops had advanced to within 800 yards of the castle. Fire was intensified upon this target from all sides, mortar projectiles crashing on the battlements and nine-millimetre tracers searching every embrasure. The enemy reaction was spirited and indicated that they had by no means abandoned hope. Stellin, moving his patrol to clear some caïque yards, received most of the attention.

"The stuff started to whizz about. We had to cross a bridge. Somebody in the castle had a very accurate bead on that bridge. We doubled, but Lance-Corporal Roberts, Private Majury, and Marine Kinghorn became pinned down under a low parapet, the slightest movement causing fire to be brought upon them. I told them to stay there . . ."

They did. They were not able to get up until the castle surrendered three hours later. Roberts, who attempted to while away the time by lighting a cigarette, raised his head an inch or two. He received a bullet graze from the temple to the neck.

Clynes had also been sent down to the caïque yard with orders to clear it. On the way he met Lieutenant Betts-Gray, who throughout the action did excellent liaison work. Betts-Gray was hugging the rocks, pursued by a hail of fire. Clynes and his patrol were presently pinned down in their turn. Private Bromley was hit in the arm, and Betts-Gray, who had had miraculous escapes all day, in the buttocks once, and in the back twice, was assisted into a house and put to bed.

To the south, Macbeth and Bury, with their forces, had assaulted a monastery position after considerable mortar preparation. The surviving enemy were driven down a promontory towards the extremity of the island, where Macbeth called upon them to surrender. The first demand written by Bob Bury, was rejected haughtily by the defenders as illegible. It was rewritten with the aid of a young Greek girl, who volunteered to carry it through the lines. This civilian armistice commission was successful and thirty-three more of the enemy laid down their arms.

Around the castle, the situation had developed into a stalemate, with mortar fire causing the garrison casualties and discomfort, but not sufficient in itself to bring about their surrender. Neither Brigadier Turnbull nor Lapraik considered that the position could be taken by direct assault. They decided to consolidate, make the maximum display of force at their disposal and institute surrender parleys.

Accordingly, Brigadier Turnbull sent a German petty-officer, commanding one of the "Ems" barges, up under escort, with instructions to inform the enemy that they were completely surrounded, that the rest of the island was in British hands, and that further resistance on their part was as senseless as it was likely to prove costly.

The petty-officer returned an hour later. It appeared that the enemy were prepared to talk business. Lieutenant Kenneth Fox, a German speaker, now returned to the castle with the same man. A further hour elapsed during which the only incident was the emergence of a party of Italian *carabinieri* from the stronghold, weeping, and waving a Red Cross flag.

"I thought I recognized one of these fellows," said Lapraik, "and sure enough it was the old rascal who had given us so much trouble during our previous occupation of Simi. He grew very pale when he saw me . . ."

Lieutenant-Commander Ramseyer, the naval liaison officer, was then sent up to expedite matters. He found Fox and the German Commander in agitated conference and himself in imminent danger from our mortar fire. At last, the capitulation was arranged and the garrison marched out. They had barely been collected and counted when three Messerschmitts flew over the port and dropped antipersonnel bombs.

"Too bad," the German Commander is reported to have said, shaking his head. "You see, that's what comes of being late. I thought they had forgotten about us. I radioed for them five hours ago."

Prisoners taken in this action totalled 151, of whom seventeen were wounded. Twenty-one Germans and Italians had been killed. The SBS and Sacred Squadron losses were as usual microscopic, and, apart from the two Greek officers drowned, not a single man was killed. Six were wounded.

As soon as the Messerchmitts had disappeared, tea was taken by both armies in the caïque yards. Sausages were fried and an ox, provided by the delighted population, roasted on a bowsprit. As for the prisoners, they were so delighted to find themselves treated deferentially instead of being shot out of hand, that they revealed the existence of many a cache of

wine in their living-quarters. Bottles were transferred to the
SBS packs, to be drunk at base.

Meanwhile, Lapraik, Macbeth, and Stellin, well known
on the island, were borne to the town hall, where many
speeches were made. The town jail was thrown open to the
accompaniment of a furore which would have done credit to
the storming of the Bastille. Unfortunately, only one prisoner
was found inside and he, a Fascist, refused to be liberated.

"I admired these islanders," said Lapraik, "intensely; for
they well knew that we could not remain and were rightly
apprehensive of reprisals. But this did not diminish in any
way their enthusiasm, though they were aware that hostile
eyes were watching them, recording every incident. In the
end, we caused them immense relief by taking the fifteen
foremost quislings away with us."

General demolitions were begun by Bill Cumper and installations as varied as 75-mm. gun emplacements, diesel fuel
pumps and cable-heads, received generous charges. Ammunition and explosive dumps provided fireworks to suit the
occasion. In the harbour, nineteen German caïques, some
displacing as much as 150 tons, were sunk. At midnight
the whole force sailed, the prisoners being crowded into
the two "Ems" barges. Stellin, with his patrol and Captain
Pyke, Civil Affairs Officer, remained behind as rear party,
with instructions to report subsequent events on Simi, and to
distribute nearly thirty tons of food which had been brought
in for the relief of the civilian population.

The German reaction was as expected, and followed the tra-
ditional pattern of attempted intimidation preceding assault.
On the following morning the town was heavily bombed.
Stellin and his men sat tight in their slit trenches. When
it was all over they emerged to find, as they had hoped,
that two enemy motor launches were attempting to enter
the harbour. Such accurate fire was opened on these ships
that they withdrew, blazing. So did Stellin, whose keen ear
had detected the approach of more bombers, and who knew
that this was the prelude to reoccupation of the island.

At three o'clock, from one of the more remote mountains,
he watched the German flag hoisted over the citadel. But

Stellin's adventures were not yet over; that night the launch re-embarking his party, encountered an "E" boat on the return journey. So many and so various were Stellin's store of captured weapons that every man in his patrol was able to take a personal hand in the battle with a machine-gun. The "E" boat was left in a sinking condition.

The great raid on Simi marked the end of SBS intervention in the Aegean. It had always been intended that the Sacred Squadron should take over this, their natural theatre of operations, as soon as they were fully trained and in a position to assume the heavy commitments involved. That happy state of affairs had now been achieved and Lapraik, instructed by Brigadier Turnbull, was able to write to the Greek Commander: "Your group will operate in the Aegean until further notice. For the present, you will confine yourself to reconnaissance, but in September, raiding activities will be resumed upon a much larger scale. Sergeant Dale, SBS, will remain attached to you for Intelligence purposes."

Lapraik, with his men, his prisoners, and his booty, withdrew to Castelrosso, and from Castelrosso to Beirut for a well-deserved holiday. Here they were met by the news that the SBS had been asked for in Italy for the purpose of attacking targets in Jugoslavia and Albania. Turkish waters would see them no more.

But it is not possible to leave those waters without some description of the extraordinary life led by all ranks there when not on operations.

Picture the deep, indented Gulf of Cos, with uninhabited shores and sullen, fir-covered mountains rising abruptly from the water's edge. In this two hundred miles of coastline it would not be easy for you to find the SBS, but if you were wise, you would look for some bay screened by small islands suitable for training purposes. Again, if you were wise, you would consult your map in search of one of the few streams from which drinkable water might be drawn.

Entering this bay, you would at first judge it to be empty. Closer inspection would show you a large, squat, ugly schooner lying close to one shore, with her gang-plank down and a horde of dories, folboats, rubber dinghies, and rafts nuzzling one flank like kittens about the teats of their mother. Farther off, a full mile away, lie five or six motor launches and an MTB under camouflage, and within gin-and-lime distance of them a sleeker, trimmer, cleaner caïque, which is obviously naval property. In this area, too, are other subsidiary caïques. The intervening water is dotted with small boats from which men are fishing . . . mostly with grenades.

Let us approach the large and ugly schooner. She is the *Tewfik* of Port Said, the SBS depot ship. In her vast stern a naked figure is crouching, and whittling at something with a knife. It is Lassen, and he is making a bow with which to shoot pigs. Down below, in the murky cabin at the foot of the steep companion-way, David Sutherland, pipe in mouth, is writing an operational order. Beside him are rum bottles, magnums of champagne from Nisiros reserved for special occasions, and a neat list showing the casualties inflicted on the enemy during the current month . . . and our own.

"Blyth, Captain H. W., plus 4 – OUT – 4.4.44. Due in 12.4.44. Overdue. Target, CALCHI."

Presently, Sutherland reaches a difficult point in his work. He takes the pipe from his mouth and shouts:

"Corporal Morris."

A tall, angular, serious, and bespectacled figure comes bowling down the companion-way with a file in his hand. Curiously enough, it is the file which Sutherland wants, for Morris possesses second sight. Morris retires. His typewriter, seldom silent, begins clicking again in the distance.

Just forrard of the poop, Sergeant Jenkins, known colloquially as "The Soldier's Friend" by reason of his claims to satisfy everyone, is trying to do three things at once. Sergeant Jenkins is accusing one SBS man of pinching a tin of sausage meat, endeavouring to prevent another from doing the same thing under his very nose, and issuing orders to the Greek cooks concerning dinner.

"Not octopus again," he begs them. "Not octopus, *please*."

On the hatch beside him, Nobby Clarke, his magnificent moustache stained by indelible pencil marks, is endeavouring to write an operational report under difficult conditions. Two American war correspondents recline on the same hatch in deck-chairs. They are polishing recently acquired Lügers.

Farther forward, Guardsmen O'Reilly, Conby, and D'Arcy, mugs of rum and tea in their hands, are discussing the good old days in Libya. In the black hole behind them which is the main men's quarters, the severe and well-cropped head of Staff-Sergeant-Major John Riley can be seen. Riley, oblivious of the noisy and vulgar game of pontoon going on in his immediate neighbourhood, is playing bridge.

In the forepeak, German prisoners, poking their heads up inquisitively, are being given cigarettes by almsgivers.

Towards dusk, the scene becomes more animated, and the immense capacity of the British soldier for slumber less noticeable. The headquarter signallers are pursued, for they alone have news of what is going on in the latest raids. Perhaps a motor launch returns with the personnel from one of these raids . . . another is almost certainly setting out to continue them. Men who have been bathing, fishing, bartering with the local Turks, return, demanding supper loudly. Aft, Paddy Errett, Cumper's deputy, is cursing and producing perfectly packed explosive charges at two minutes' notice.

A motor boat chugs alongside, and Sutherland is whisked away to Levant Schooner 9, where Lieutenant-Commander Campbell, sherry glass in hand, is entertaining a couple of MTB skippers with the details of their coming patrol, which, to-night, will be north of Cos. "E" boats are expected.

Sutherland and Campbell confer, confide, plot, send signals . . .

Keith Balsillic is zero-ing a German sniper's rifle found in Piscopi.

Marine Hughes is eating a tin of peaches . . .

"Brown Body" Henderson is unable to find any volunteers for P.T.

South of Samos, Harold Chevalier, two days out from base, has just ordered a German caïque to heave-to.

MIRBAT
Tony Jeapes

Just after dawn on 19 July 1972 an eight-man SAS detachment known as a "BATT" (British Army Training Team) stationed in Mirbat, Oman, was attacked by 250 communist guerrillas or Adoo. The events of that remarkable day are described below by Colonel Tony Jeapes, a former SAS regimental commander in Oman.

The Sultanate of Oman – a British ally, and strategically important Gulf nation – had been in a state of civil war in its southern province of Dhofar since the 1960s. Originally Arab nationalists, the insurgent Adoo had passed to Stalin-type Communism, aided and sponsored by South Yemen. The Adoo were a formidable enemy, brave, well-trained and equipped with Soviet arms. (In the attack on the SAS BATT they also had a Carl Gustav rocket launcher.) However, their appeal had been weakened latterly by a new Sultan, Qaboos, who had wooed over elements of the insurgents with promises of material progress. What the Adoo needed to reassert their influence was a magnificent victory in Dhofar against the Sultan's Armed Forces, the firqat *(guerrillas who had changed sides), and the Sultan's British helpers, the SAS. Hence the attack on Mirbat.*

19 JULY 1972

THE LAST FEW moments before a dawn attack are always ones of tension. So they were now. Two hundred and fifty men lay or knelt, silent except for the occasional chink of weapon on stone, a low cough or quiet whisper, staring into the darkness. Behind rose the great blackness of the jebel massif hidden in the monsoon drizzle. Before, twelve hundred yards away, lay Mirbat.

As the seconds slipped away, commanders, like commanders anywhere, would be going over the plan in their minds

yet again to make certain that nothing had been missed out.
Did every man know what he had to do? The weapons
had all been checked and they worked. The radios were
netted in all right. The artillery sights had been checked
for range and elevation. The correct ammunition had been
dumped by the correct guns. Everything seemed "go", but
what if . . .? What if the enemy knew, and even now were
standing to their weapons, waiting. It was unlikely. Security
had been good. The fighters, all young, all well indoctrinated
in the cause, all heavily motivated, had moved over the
jebel in parties of forty with a security screen in front to
clear out the villages they would have to pass through. In
any case, they did not even know themselves where they
were going until they had been briefed up on the jebel the
previous night.

Ironically, the enemy had helped, too. It was a year since
they had identified the party cell in town and rounded it up,
and their grip was now too tight on the town to establish
another. So there could be no leak from there.

With luck, few enemy should be left in the town to defend
it anyway. They had fallen nicely for the decoy patrol sent
down on the plain two days before and most of them were
now chasing a will-o'-the-wisp, near the jebel. But that 'what
if' always remains at the back of a commander's mind.

The fighters would be concerned with more immediate
matters, like keeping warm in the pre-dawn monsoon chill.
All along the line men would pull their shamags tighter
around their heads or flap their arms against their sides,
half wanting to get up and get moving, half frightened at what
the next hour would bring. Riflemen would seek nervous relief
by checking their weapons and equipment for the tenth time.
Were safety catches on safe, bayonets properly fixed, pouches
buttoned up? Gunners leant forward to check their dial sights
yet again by the little lamps that glowed faintly above them,
and the gun numbers felt to see that the shells were properly
fused and easily to hand.

To the left, the drab sky was slowly lightening. To the
right sounded a faint crackle of small arms, a burst or two
of machine gun fire and the dull thud of exploding grenades.

That was the enemy picket forward of the town on Jebel Ali being taken out. It was time.

All along the line arms swept downwards and men turned away from the blast with their hands over their ears as the barrage began. Shells and mortar bombs began to rain down upon the town. At the same time two hundred determined young men clambered to their feet and began to move steadily forward in line abreast. The battle of Mirbat had begun.

The commander of the eight-man BATT in the town was Captain Mike Kealy, who was to win the DSO for his exploits that day. To say that Kealy was worried about how he would behave when he heard his first shot fired in anger would be an over-statement. Nonetheless, commanding a platoon of nineteen-year-old fusiliers in Germany was very different from finding yourself in command of a troop of 28-year-old hardened SAS veterans, experienced in battles fought across half the world during the British Empire's death throes. It was a neurosis at the back of the mind of most newly joined SAS troop commanders. So his feelings when he woke with a start as the first shell exploded, he told me, can not have been unlike those of the young men already advancing, unknown to him, towards the town – half apprehension, half relief.

As he fumbled for his torch, a second explosion shook BATT house and pieces of dried mud fell on top of him. Dust filled the room. Coughing, he grabbed his rifle and belt, slipped on his flipflops and stumbled out into the fresh air. A makeshift bamboo ladder led up to the roof where most of his team were already waiting. It was just beginning to get light. He glanced at his watch – 0530.

The lean hard figure of Corporal Bob Bradshaw paced over to him. Instinctively, although the enemy were far away, he talked in a low voice, pointing out the flashes of the enemy guns on the Jebel Ali and explaining the layout on the roof. Two machine-guns, a GPMG and a heavy Browning .5, had been mounted in sand-bagged sangars.

Kealy looked over to the two dark figures of Lance Corporal Pete Wignall and Corporal Roger Chapman and the long barrels of their machine-guns silhouetted above the sand-bagged walls against the lightening sky. It was just light enough now to see the fort also, a large square Beau Geste affair seven hundred yards to the north-east. A motley group of Dhofar Gendarmerie and askars manned it, tribesmen brought down from the north under the reign of the old sultan and armed with old bolt action .303 rifles.

Nearer, to the north-west and almost within hailing distance stood the wali's house. Its roof stood at the same height as BATT house and Kealy could just make out some figures moving about it. To the south two hundred yards away lay the houses of the town, now covered by a pall of mud dust from the incoming shells. He could hear screams and some men were shouting.

A shell screeched overhead and they all ducked as it exploded behind the house. Then came a succession of explosions a few seconds apart from the base of the house. They shook Kealy for a moment until he realised it was the BATT mortar returning fire. Behind Bradshaw the bulky reassuring figure of Trooper Savesaki was talking in Arabic on the radio. He reported that the firqat leader had just told him he had forty men out towards the jebel somewhere. Only greybeards and children remained.

"Where's Labalaba?" Kealy asked, knowing that where one Fijian was the other would not be far away. Bradshaw looked up from his mortar plotting board and jerked his head towards the fort. Trooper Labalaba was manning the 25-pounder with the Omani gunner, he said.

A burst of heavy machine gun bullets crack-crack-cracked close by followed by a long burst from the BATT .5 Browning. Empty brass cases tinkled brashly on to the roof. The air was rent by unending continuous noise now, the mind-bending explosions of incoming shells, the crashing thuds of the BATT mortar returning fire, the spitting crackle of enemy machine-gun fire and the steady booming of the BATT heavy machine-gun in reply. Kealy forced himself to think above the racket. He knew the firqat leader had sent a strong patrol out after the small enemy group reported at the base of the jebel, but he had not realised that so few firqat remained. There was nothing anyone could do but if the patrol fell foul of the sort of firepower now being directed at Mirbat . . .

Then, what was this? The adoo had never attacked with this intensity before. Was it just a stand-off attack or would they combine it with an infantry assault? He told me that he felt his first real pang of apprehension as he counted up his defences: say, thirty men in the fort – they would fight back but they would be no use for anything except a threat to the fort itself, the few firqat left behind in the town, the eight SAS men including himself, and the Omani gunner with the 25-pounder artillery piece dug into its pit beside the fort. He ducked as an explosion sent pieces of shrapnel thudding into the sandbags by his head.

Savesaki was listening intently to the radio. He turned to Kealy, his face as impassive as ever but his eyes betrayed him. Labalaba had been hit in the chin he said. Kealy nodded to his suggestion that he should go and help his countryman at the big gun.

"Take some extra medical kit and keep low."

For all his muscular bulk, Savesaki was one of the finest rugby forwards in the West Country. If anyone could make it, he would. Nonetheless all those at the BATT house stared with nerves tingling as the big Fijian raced towards the fort swerving and dodging between the explosions while bullets kicked up spurts of sand at his feet. A cloud of dust obliterated him – but as it cleared he was still seen running, until at last he disappeared from view behind the gun's sangar wall. At BATT house men breathed again.

Chapman was the first to see them and pointed out to Kealy a group of twenty men walking confidently towards the perimeter wire fence that surrounded the three sides of the town not bordered by the sea. The fort lay inside the north-eastern corner of the wire and within forty yards of it. Kealy studied the group through his binoculars. It was now light enough to see them clearly, but still he was uncertain. They could be some of the firqat returning, or a patrol the Gendarmerie might have sent out without telling him. They appeared too cool and confident to be adoo.

Suddenly all doubts were removed. At a signal, the men

started to run into an extended line, raising their weapons to their shoulders. The crackle of small arms fire sounded paltry against the ear-splitting noise of the bursting shells. Chapman did not wait for orders. Short sharp bursts of fire ripped through the haze like a succession of tiny comets into the groups of running men, the ricochets bouncing and arching gracefully into the air until they burnt out. As if it was a signal to begin, the whole corner near the fort erupted with the sound of machine guns and rifles mixed with the explosion of shells. All the enemy's fire seemed to be directed at the fort and the SAS men looked on with disbelief as it disappeared from sight. A cloud of brown smoke and dust, lit up in spasms by the bright flashes of shell bursts against the walls, hid the fort entirely. Above it all sounded the vicious cracking explosions of the big gun by the fort as it fired its 25-pound shells point blank at the wire forty yards in front of it.

The radio crackled but Kealy could not hear what it said above the racket. He thought it was the gun pit but could not be sure. In any case, Wignall and Chapman, their over-heated gun barrels sizzling in the wet, were shouting for more ammunition. Together with the two uncommitted men, Corporal Reynolds and Trooper Tobin, Kealy hauled up the heavy steel boxes from below until their shirts were as smoked from sweat as from the steady monsoon drizzle.

The plain was now full of groups of ten to twelve men, sometimes in full view, sometimes hidden as they crossed a dip, all moving steadily towards the town. The battle still raged around the fort, and keeping the GPMG firing in that direction, every other BATT weapon was brought to bear on the approaching infantry. But the enemy now realized where most of the return fire came from and had ranged in on BATT house with machine-guns, the bullets thudding into the mud walls and sandbags or cracking viciously about the soldiers' heads. But nobody had yet been hit and still the BATT machine-guns hammered back.

The enemy reached the wire and began to breach it. Men tore at it with their hands. Others threw a blanket over it and scrambled across; it was little more than a cattle fence and could not hold them for long. Bradshaw told me that his

attention was taken by the leader, standing in full view astride
the wire, shouting and waving his men on, his rifle held out full
stretch above his head. In his khaki uniform, his peaked cap
and his bandoliers across his chest it struck Bradshaw that
he looked like a hero from some Red Chinese poster. For a
moment he watched in admiration then reluctantly lined up
his rifle sights on the man and fired. Missed! Again he fired,
and missed. Damn! He paused a second to steady himself,
forcing his body to obey. Breathe in . . . breathe out . . . hold
it . . . a nice steady pressure . . . the rifle kicked, and the man
crumpled.

Several men were across the wire and running towards the
fort. Others were caught. Kealy recalled that a figure lay
doubled up over it like a rag doll. Bradshaw remembered
that another hung head down, his arms and legs spread
wide in grotesque crucifixion. Two others crossed the wire
and fell immediately, one his leg jerking frantically. Another
staggered about, both hands pressed to his face.

Kealy fought to think, think, think, his head a great drum
of noise. Suddenly he realised that apart from a terse contact
report at the beginning he had not told BATT Headquarters
thirty miles away what was going on. He scrambled hastily
down the rickety ladder into the courtyard and to the long
range radio, forcing his voice to sound calm as he described
the situation as clearly as he could. The mist was still down
to about a hundred and fifty feet, he said, but nonetheless
he wanted a helicopter to evacuate Labalaba and no doubt
there were more casualties, and the jets were to be stood by
to fly as soon as the weather allowed.

Back up on the roof a minute later, the fighting had died
down. Although the cracks and thuds of battle still sounded
spasmodically, it seemed very quiet, as if the whole battlefield
were waiting for something. Bradshaw told him that he could
still get no reply from the gun pit.

Kealy picked up the radio and called the gun pit yet
again. Now very worried, he told Bradshaw to take over
command at the house while he went over to the gun pit to
find out what had happened to the others. A violent argument
followed for a minute as all three men began to buckle on their

belt equipment. Bradshaw and Wignall were needed at the house, Kealy insisted, but very well, he would take Tobin. He was a medic and would be useful.

"You won't get far in those," grinned Bradshaw and Kealy flushed as he realized that he was still wearing the flip flops he put on when he got out of bed. He dropped down into the courtyard and made his way quickly back to his room.

When he came out, Tobin was waiting, his medical pack slung over his shoulder, his drab green shorts and shirt grimy with burnt oil and dust. Like all of them he was bareheaded. He carried his rifle easily in one hand and his belt order, containing all an SAS soldier needs to fight and live with, was clipped about his waist. They opened the wooden gates and stepped out past the sand-bagged pit where Trooper Harris fussed over the mortar sight.

A shallow wadi, perhaps two feet deep, ran parallel to the direct route to the fort but seventy-five yards to the right. The occasional bullet still came near but it was quiet enough to set off up the wadi, trusting to its low rim if they should have to take cover. A brick laundry house stood a hundred yards up and the two men stopped briefly to shake hands with the ancient in charge.

They had not gone more than another hundred yards when a burst of machine-gun fire crackled viciously between them, the breeze of the passing bullets plainly felt by Kealy. Both men flung themselves flat for a few seconds and then, one man firing, one man running, with bullets cracking and humming about their ears they dashed in short sprints for the protection of the gunpit. Tobin reached it first, vaulted the wall and disappeared. One glance told Kealy that there was no room in the gun pit itself, but a few feet to the side and dug into the ground was a sand-bagged ammunition bay. He leapt the body of a dead gendarme and threw himself into the bay where he lay gasping from the final sprint. Suddenly he realized that he was not alone. He spun round. Crouching under the lip of the sandbag-covered lid was another gendarme, his lips pulled back over his teeth, his face a mask of terror.

Glancing over to the gun pit again, Kealy saw that Tobin was applying a drip to the seriously wounded Omani gunner at the side of the bay, whilst Trooper Labalaba was crawling across towards him, his face grey and bloodstained under the khaki shell dressing that covered his chin. The Fijian tried to smile with his eyes and his mumbled words were barely distinguishable, but he explained that Savesaki was badly hit in the back and had lost a lot of blood. He was still conscious, however, and was covering the left side of the fort.

A huge explosion hit the edge of the bunker. Both men were thrown against the edge of the pit and stinging sand cut their faces and hands. The crackle of incoming bullets rose to a crescendo and put an end to any more talk as the two men thrust their rifles over the crest of the pit. A series of double cracks, the hallmark of an SAS rifleman, rang out from the other side of the gun pit.

"Boss, they're through the wire." Savesaki's voice sounded faintly above the din. The enemy had pierced the wire and were now crawling and running up to the fort itself. Labalaba dashed to the gun, traversed it as far right as he could and fired. Its deafening crash, smoke and recoil filled the pit. He slapped the breech handle back and the empty brass case dropped smoking on to the sandy floor. Turning, the big Fijian reached for another shell, slammed it home with one hand and, as the breech clanged shut, pitched forward without a sound.

Kealy lifted his head above the pit and in half of one second registered two things: first, several enemy had crept around his side of the fort, and second, a small green grenade was fizzing two feet from his head. He ducked and a split second after the explosion raised his head again. A man was leaning around the wall aiming a Kalashnikov at him. He took a snap shot and the man spun and fell. Another replaced him. Kealy fired at him, too: a double tap, crack-crack. A chip of stone fell off the wall and the man ducked.

"Sav, take the left, I'll take the right," he shouted. Another crash and more smoke as the 25-pounder fired again. He looked around to see Tobin reloading. Within seconds Tobin fell too, mortally hit. Urgently, Kealy spoke into the radio and told Bradshaw to get both machine-guns to spray either side of the fort and to fire the mortar as close in as he could get it.

Bradshaw's cool voice acted as a tonic. The jets were on their way he told him, but already Harris was hugging the mortar clear of its bipod against his chest to shorten the range while someone else dropped the bombs down the barrel. He could not get closer.

The SAS machine-gun fire crackled and spat about the fort and Kealy stopped firing for a moment to let his rifle cool down. He realized he was running short of full magazines and then he remembered the frightened man. He turned to look at him. For a second, he later told me, he thought of telling the man to fight, but their eyes met and he suddenly knew the man would kill him if he tried. Instead, he thrust his empty magazines at him. "Fill those," he snapped. The gendarme set to work feverishly.

Another flight of grenades came bouncing and hissing towards the gun pit. In horror he watched one roll to the lip of the pit and then drop in, to lie smoking out of reach. He pressed his body against the side of the pit and screwed up his face at the pain he knew must come . . . until with a tame little "phut" it went out. A dud. Desperately, he put his rifle over the top again and searched for a target. The air was full of the stench and noise of battle. Something passed through his hair. Another fanned his neck. Suddenly the thumping of cannon fire sounded alongside and shells hissed overhead as the first Strikemaster jet made its run.

His fingers clumsy in his haste, he dragged out a fluorescent marker panel and placed it over the body of the dead gendarme, but the cannon fire was striking well the other side of the fort. As a second jet came in to strafe, adoo began running back into the wadi behind the fort for shelter. A black bomb detached itself from the aircraft and plummeted into the wadi where they were hiding, to explode in earth-quaking thunder and a cloud of black smoke.

The jet strike did its work and gradually a second lull crept over the battlefield as the noise of men trying to kill each other died down. Kealy scrambled over to where Savesaki was leaning wearily against the far wall of the gun pit and from where he could best see the left side of the fort. The side of his head was matted with blood and his shirt was caked a dull brown but his face was as impassive as ever. It struck Kealy how his steady brown eyes contrasted with the whites of the gendarme in the ammunition bay.

The two men looked up at the walls of the fort. The question was who held it? They could only see one wall properly. One of the others could have been breached. Kealy recalled that a dead gendarme, dressed in a black shirt, lay slouched over an embrasure, his rifle pointing to the sky. There was no sign of life.

Savesaki was both a medic and an Arabic speaker. He eased himself up.

"Oh soldiers!" he shouted. "How are you? Are you alive? Is all well? My captain wishes to speak to your officer."

Silence.

He tried again, this time with more success: at least he was answered.

"*Abadan*! Never!"

Kealy decided it was not worth pressing the matter for the moment and clambered across to comfort the wounded men and re-dress their wounds according to Savesaki's instructions. He gave them a sip of water and made them as comfortable as he could but there was little enough he could do. Then he pulled the dead men to the side of the pit out of the way and covered them with a groundsheet.

The jets made one more strike, this time on to Jebel Ali on Bradshaw's directions and disappeared into the mist back to Salalah to re-fuel and re-arm. Then Bradshaw radioed Kealy to say that he was sending Harris, another medic, over to him. And that reinforcements were on their way.

Von Clausewitz wrote "War is the province of chance", and the chance that a second SAS squadron would be in Dhofar on that day stood at three per cent. The chance that the main body would have arrived from England only the previous day and were not therefore already in the hills stood at less than one per cent. Most of the officers and senior NCOs had been in the advance party and were already taking over positions on the jebel from the outgoing squadron so only the younger soldiers were left in Salalah. And at 0800 hours that morning, the squadron commander, his sergeant major and twenty-one soldiers paraded all set to go to a nearby range to test fire their weapons as part of the normal routine of taking over. They were heavily armed for such a small group – nine GPMGs and four M79 grenade launchers between them, and every other man carried a semi-automatic rifle.

By this time the action at Mirbat had been going on for two and a half hours and that the attack was a major one could not be in doubt. The outgoing squadron commander, Major Richard Pirie, appreciated that the only way he could get any help to Mirbat in time was by air, despite the monsoon, and had already moved to the SOAF headquarters at Salalah airfield to set up a joint operations centre. There he could himself brief the pilots on the exact state of affairs they would meet on arrival, control the movements of reinforcements and re-supplies and arrange the evacuation of casualties.

So it was to the airfield that the twenty-three now went and after a careful briefing climbed aboard three SOAF helicopters bound for Mirbat. The mist was well down and the three aircraft felt their way cautiously along the coast only a few feet above the waves before landing to the south-east of the town according to plan.

Quickly the force deployed into two ten-man "hit" groups and a command group, and in minutes came under fire. The adoo must have estimated that in a little force like this, two thirds the size of an infantry platoon, a maximum of three machine guns would be carried. But this had nine, the fire power of an infantry company. They quickly disposed of the adoo facing them and, moving in bounds, group by group, and even within groups, two or three men dashing forward covered by the fire of the remainder, the squadron moved towards the town killing as they went.

The firqat also, at least those who were not out beyond Jebel Ali with the fighting patrol, were fighting hard. Not content to remain in the town, they lay scattered in twos and threes behind every rock and in every fold of the ground between the enemy and the town. The enemy were in effect in a trap, caught between the anvil of the firqat and the hammer of the advancing SAS.

It was this that worried Kealy. He had just returned from a one-man foray into the wadi where the bomb had landed to check that it was clear of enemy. He could hear the crackle of fire to the south-east and he knew that the relief was approaching the town from that direction. Unless he could get the gendarmes to understand, the makings existed of a disaster. He stood before the great wooden gates of the fort with his hands to his mouth and shouted till he was hoarse. Surely the bloody men must know no adoo would do that, he thought. And at last, after what seemed an age as the sounds of shooting crept ever closer to the town, the iron-studded doors creaked open and he stepped through into the courtyard.

Using signs and the occasional word of Arabic he had learned, Kealy explained the position to the Gendarme officer. He would like to borrow the Gendarmes' Landrover, he said, to take the BATT and the Gendarmerie wounded to the helicopter pad by BATT house. The officer shrugged and smiled sympathetically but pointed without speaking to the riddled vehicle standing on shredded tyres in an ever-increasing pool of oil and water. As he looked about him Kealy began to appreciate the weight of explosive that must have landed inside the fort. Yet, despite the pounding, nowhere was the wall breached.

In despair at this latest disappointment, he was trying to force his exhausted brain to think of an alternative way to get the wounded to safety when a broad Geordie voice spoke behind him. He spun round with a surge of relief to see the grinning figure of one of the incoming squadron's soldiers framed in the doorway. A machinegun rested easily on his shoulder. For a moment they stared at each other and the soldier's grin froze as he studied Kealy's face and the normally fair hair blackened with smoke and encrusted blood. Silently he turned and walked over to the gun pit. For a full half minute he stood there while his gaze took in the dead and dying men, the wrecked gun, the empty shell and bullet cases, the grenades, and the blood everywhere, on the ripped and torn sandbag walls, on the gun, in pools on the floor. At last he broke the silence.

"Jesus wept," he said quietly.

Although to the north things were quieter, furious little bursts of fire still flared up to the south-east as the squadron mopped up. Machine-gun and rifle bullets still cracked overhead while Kealy, bone weary, stood peering with red-rimmed eyes at the helicopter flying towards him, almost touching the ground, from the direction of BATT house.

Barely realized by him, the support of the SOAF helicopters and jets had been superb. The first helicopter tried to get in to evacuate Labalaba when Kealy and Tobin were still half way across on their journey from BATT house to the fort. Chapman ran from the house to the usual landing pad on the beach two hundred yards away to receive it and since all seemed fairly quiet, threw out a green smoke grenade to signal that it was safe to land. But as the helicopter began its final approach the adoo began their second attack even more ferociously than before. Bullets began to crack about Chapman and he identified at least one 12.7 mm heavy machine gun firing towards the incoming helicopter.

His heart pounding, he fumbled in his belt for a red grenade and hurled it as far as he could. Immediately, a machine-gun began to rake the landing site. He paused a second to watch the helicopter sheering off into the mist, then turned and raced back up the beach to where a low wall provided cover. He crawled along this for fifty yards and when it was safe stood up and walked back to BATT house where he knew his medical skills would be needed.

A quarter of an hour later a shout came from the roof that another aircraft could be heard above the mist. This time Chapman selected a landing site only a hundred yards away from the house and protected by buildings. The noise of engines grew stronger as the pilot found a hole in the cloud and suddenly Chapman saw it, a brown blob streaking towards him at roof top level coming in from the sea, not a helicopter at all but a Strikemaster. He clicked on his sarbe radio.

"Hullo, Strikemaster, this is Tiger four one. Enemy are north and east of the fort. Over."

"Roger, Tiger four one. I have it visual. How far from the fort?"

"One hundred meters and closing," he replied. This was the strike which prevented Kealy and Savesaki from being overrun.

Chapman ran back up to the roof of BATT house and passed the sarbe to Bradshaw who took over control, directing the jets down the wire towards the fort and on to the enemy heavy support weapons on Jebel Ali.

Watching a brave man risk his life produces a breathless feeling almost akin to love. You feel intense admiration combined with an aching fear that his luck will run out. So the two men told me they felt as they watched the jets flying in under the mist, straight and level to give greater accuracy to their guns, while the enemy threw up a curtain of machine-gun and Kalashnikov fire until the sky seemed an impenetrable mad network of criss-crossing tracer. Then came the ripping-sound of the aircrafts' 20 mm cannons before they pulled up and disappeared into the mist. Some jets were indeed hit but none fortunately badly enough to prevent their limping back to Salalah.

Bradshaw radioed back to base that it was out of the question for helicopters to attempt to reach the town at this time, so the next lift brought in the relieving squadron's soldiers to the beach. It was not until a second lift had been dropped at the same place that the first helicopter, flown by Squadron Leader Baker and already holed, was able to reach BATT house. Here he landed three prisoners from the beach and loaded up the most seriously wounded for evacuation to the Field Surgical Team at Salalah. Although quieter, bullets were still cracking about and Baker knew he had to fly his helicopter over open ground to reach the fort. Nonetheless he decided to risk it, and it was this aircraft's approach that Kealy was now watching. Harris, having done all he could for the wounded, ran out to guide it as close as he could to the gun pit. Its doors were already open and two men leapt out as it touched the ground to help lift in

the wounded men. The two worst hit, Trooper Tobin and
the Omani gunner were lifted aboard first. Savesaki declined
to move until they were aboard and even then insisted on
walking to the aircraft with wounds that would have killed
any ordinary man.   The enemy were now in full retreat back
to the mountains and having seen the helicopter take off safely
Harris and Kealy walked back to BATT house. As the centre
of resistance it had attracted all manner of people throughout
the battle: firqatmen, wounded or asking for ammunition or
help in one form or another, townsfolk wounded by shrapnel
or just frightened, and the inevitable hangers-on, mainly old
men, bearded, frail and toothless who appear to offer advice
and the comfort of their presence at any incident of note in
Arabia. Kealy raised his eyes in surprise as he saw a figure
dressed all in white bent over a wounded man.

"Doctor" Ahmed was a civilian who had received some
medical training and who had been posted to Mirbat by
the wali of Dhofar, qualified doctors being unobtainable.
Anxious to assert his authority, Doctor Ahmed at first had
been thoroughly unco-operative to the SAS men and sparks
had flown on more than one occasion, but although a thorn
in the side of BATT, Ahmed was symbolically important for
he represented the first faltering step in the development of
an Omani medical system which was eventually to cover
the whole of Dhofar. Now, in emergency, he revealed his
true worth.

English voices sounded outside and a group of soldiers
strode into the room led by the relieving squadron's commander, Major Alistair Bowie. Bowie was a Guards officer
and he had that calm, smiling authority that immediately
makes things seem not quite as bad as they appeared to be.
Kealy explained the situation as shortly as he could and spoke
of his worry about the firqat still the other side of Jebel Ali.
They would be right in the path of the retreating adoo. Even
as he said it the first crackle of small arms fire sounded to
the north. Kealy felt sick with helplessness. Perhaps he could
take a sarbe out and see if he could direct in jets to help the
trapped firqat, he suggested.

Bowie read the despair and fatigue in the man's eyes. Very

well, he agreed, but Kealy was not to go beyond Jebel Ali. The small jebel was now picketed by a platoon of the Northern Frontier Regiment that had flown in with the third helicopter at 1220.

Kealy hurried off and after several minutes scrambling and slipping on the wet shale reached the top. Mist hid everything but the first two or three hundred yards. As he had secretly known, he could see and do nothing. He settled down to wait against a sangar wall, weary beyond words, until at last the dispirited huddle of firqat appeared out of the drizzle carrying their dead and wounded and passed beneath him.

Once more he trudged back to BATT house where he found that Bowie had wasted no time in reorganizing the town's defences and establishing order again. Two Landrovers had just returned with the dead and wounded and thirty-eight enemy bodies lay in a row, their weapons and ammunition belts, all new Chinese and Russian equipment, piled in heaps nearby. A gaggle of firqat clustered about them trying to persuade some stony-faced SAS men that they needed the weapons to claim reward money to feed their families.

Within the house a medical officer and the SAS medics busily applied dressings to the minor wounded, both friendly and enemy, while in a separate room the prisoners were being interviewed by Chapman. The three sat quietly smoking cigarettes and drinking tea and Kealy was struck both by their youth and by the dignity with which they accepted their lot. These were brave men.

AFTERWORD
For his bravery and leadership at Mirbat, Captain Mike Kealy was awarded the DSO. (He later died on exercise on the Brecon Beacons in Wales). Corporal Bradshaw was awarded the Military Medal. Trooper Tobin and Trooper Labalaba, both killed in the gun pit, were posthumously awarded the DCM and a Mention in Dispatches respectively.

AIRMOBILITY
John Pimlott

Vietnam was the war of the helicopter. Although the US had used helicopters in Korea, it had been solely for light transport duties and medical evacuation. By the time of Vietnam, the gas-turbo engine had been born, and choppers could be used to lift troops over difficult terrain to landings zones (LZs) in the enemy rear, for reconnaissance – and for air-attack. To explore all the military possibilities of the helicopter, the US government set up the Army Tactical Mobility Requirements Board under Lieutenant General Howze, out of which came the concept of "airmobility" – full military capability within one heliborne unit. A test Air Assault Division was then created – the formation which would enter the Vietnam War as the legendary 1st Cavalry Division (Airmobile), or "Air Cav".

Here John Pimlott describes the 1st Air Cavalry's role in the Ia Drang Campaign of 1965, for which the Air Cav received a Presidential Unit Citation. The main chopper used at Ia Drang was the Bell UH-Id Iroquois, the armament of which was four 7.62 machine guns (two fixed, two on pintles in the side doorways) and 38 2.75 inch rockets.

ON JULY 28, 1965, President Johnson announced the commitment of the 1st Cavalry to Vietnam. The division had formally come into existence only a month before, absorbing personnel from the experimental 11th Air Assault Division (Test) and reassigned units from the 2d Infantry Division (now given cavalry designations), but the commanding officer, Major General Harry W. O. Kinnard, was eager for action. More than 400 helicopters – OH-13 Sioux for reconnaissance, UH-1 Hueys for assault and infantry lift, CH-47 Chinooks and

CH-54 Flying Cranes for heavy lift – were loaded on transports; these, together with 16,000 personnel and 1,600 vehicles, were shipped across the Pacific, approaching Vietnam in early September.

General Westmoreland's first reaction was to split the division, sending each of its three brigades to a different part of the country; but Kinnard was adamant: the whole point of airmobility, he argued, was to keep the closely integrated force together to maximize its impact.

Kinnard's view prevailed, and he was ordered to deploy his division to An Khe, 35 miles inland from Qui Nhon in the central provinces. An immense heliport (soon to be dubbed "the Golf Course") was constructed, and the 101st Airborne was drafted in to clear Route 19. On September 14, the first Regular Army helicopters flew in to An Khe.

The central provinces were not chosen at random, for, by the summer of 1965, it was becoming apparent that the area was under attack, not just from the VC but also, more significantly, it was believed, from elements of the North Vietnamese Army. Infiltration of NVA regulars down the HO Chi Minh Trail in Laos and Cambodia had been recognized for some time, but intelligence sources were now painting a much more menacing picture. They were not mistaken: a special Field Force under NVA Brigadier General Chu Huy Man was preparing to seize Kontum and Pleiku provinces, before thrusting toward the coast and splitting South Vietnam in two.

For this to succeed, the NVA had to destroy other, more westerly, Special Forces camps at Plei Me and Duc Co, opening up the main routes to Pleiku City. In the late July, 1965, the NVA 32d Regiment began the campaign by surrounding Duc Co, threatening to overwhelm its defenders, who were a mixture of South Vietnamese Special Forces and Montagnard and Nuong tribesmen, all under U.S. Special Forces control. An ARVN mechanized column was committed to relieve the base, but was caught in an ambush four miles east of Duc Co. The NVA, under heavy U.S. air attacks, eventually withdrew, having inflicted significant casualties.

The NVA 32d Regiment was joined by the 33d in early

September, linking up with the local VC main-force battalion to establish a base on the eastern slopes of Chu Pong Mountain. This was a 174-square-mile massif that straddled the border south of the Ia (River) Drang; it rose more than 500 metres above the floor of a rolling plateau of jungle that stretched the 37 miles to Pleiku City. Unknown to the Americans, General Man was about to receive a third regiment – the 66th – that would increase his command to the equivalent of a division (nine infantry battalions, each of 550 men, backed by artillery and support units). It was the first time the NVA had operated in the South at a multi-regimental level.

Camp Plei Me was attacked early on October 20, and the ARVN responded predictably: as the defenders of the base fought for survival, a mechanized column was prepared in Pleiku City. But local ARVN commanders, scared of committing their troops, stalled. It was not until Westmoreland agreed to send the 1st Brigade, 1st Cavalry, to Pleiku to guard against possible envelopment that the relief column set out, on October 22.

As the column approached Plei Me however, it was ambushed and, despite heavy U.S. air support, the commander insisted on caution. Only when Kinnard in an early display of airmobility, helicoptered artillery forward to LZs close to the ambush point did the column begin to move. Plei Me was finally relieved late on October 25, having survived only through the courage and fighting skill of its Green Beret garrison.

Westmoreland was impressed by the rapid response of 1st Cavalry, and on October 26 he agreed to "give Kinnard his head," changing the role of the division from one of reaction/reinforcement to unlimited offense within a particular area of Vietnam. Kinnard was given responsibility for most of Pleiku, Kontum, and Binh Dinh provinces in II Corp Tactical Zone and was ordered to seek out, fix, and destroy any enemy forces in the region. He gave the task to his 1st Brigade, which immediately began widespread aerial searches, hoping to find the troops responsible for the Plei Me attack. The 1st Brigade was spearheaded by the 1st Squadron,

9th Cavalry, whose task it was to fly light scout helicopters at treetop height, calling in "aero-rifle platoons" in UH-1S whenever contact was made. The brigade's main body was made up of three heliborne infantry battalions as well as artillery and aerial-rocket fire support, the latter delivered by specially adapted UH-1 "gunships."

Unaware that the Plei Me attack and ambush had been carried out by NVA regulars, the Cavalry concentrated on areas to the north and east of the camp, hoping to spot VC guerrillas returning to their home villages. Little was found, chiefly because General Man had ordered the 32d and 33d Regiments back to the Chu Pong base in the west, where they would link up with the 66th Regiment before renewing their attack on Plei Me.

It was not until 0–720 hours on November 1 that contact was made, when 9th Cavalry helicopters, ranging far and wide, spotted movement about seven miles west of Plei Me. Aero-rifle support was called up and, at 0808 hours, a group attack was made on what turned out to be an NVA field hospital. In less than 30 minutes, 15 NVA had been killed and 43 captured, along with a mound of documents and medical equipment. Isolated firefights continued throughout the day, at the end of which Kinnard could claim a "body count" of 99 NVA for 11 of his own men killed. Airmobility was beginning to bite.

It soon became obvious from the captured documents that the Cavalry were looking in the wrong place for the wrong enemy. On November 2, Kinnard shifted his search pattern to the west, where 9th Cavalry scouts had already reported jungle trails between the Chu Pong and the Ia Drang. They started sweeping the area on November 3, setting up a temporary LZ south of the river from which infantry patrols could be mounted. Late on the same day, one of these patrols ambushed elements of the NVA 66th Regiment and then helped to defend the LZ against attacks that cost the Communists a further 72 confirmed dead.

Kinnard now suspected that the Chu Pong area was a major NVA base. On November 9, he relieved the 1st Brigade of his division with the 3d ("Garry Owen") Brigade, commanded by Colonel Thomas W. Brown, and ordered it to prepare for an assault into the Communist-held area. An entire battalion of heliborne troops – the 1/7th Cavalry – was to be lifted on November 14 onto an LZ at the foot of the Chu Pong and then patrol out, searching for contacts.

The 1/7th was commanded by Lieutenant Colonel Harold G. Moore and, at first light on the 14th, he led an air reconnaissance of the eastern edge of the Chu Pong (the western side was in Cambodia and therefore "off-limits"), looking for likely LZs. He chose a clearing on the edge of the massif, later designated LZ X-Ray. After a 20-minute artillery bombardment, followed by rocket fire from support helicopters, the battalion would be transported in a series of lifts to the LZ, spearheaded by Captain John D. Herren's Company B. Once landed, they would secure the LZ and, as soon as Company A arrived, patrols would be sent out, initially to the north and northeast, where a mountain spur jutted out from the Chu Pong. Companies C and D, brought in by subsequent airlifts, would defend the LZ perimeter and move west toward the mountain itself.

Artillery fire crashed down on X-Ray at 1017 hours and, 20 minutes later, 16 lift helicopters came in at treetop height. They landed amid shattered tree stumps and waist-high grass on an LZ dominated by the immense wall of green of the Chu Pong: one sergeant looked up at the mountain and was heard to mutter in a Georgia drawl: "My Gawd, that son of a bitch is big." Moore set up his command post around a large anthill in a clump of trees near the center of the LZ and ordered Herren to start patrolling. Within minutes, his 1st Platoon had captured an NVA deserter, who willingly confirmed that the area was a major Communist base. As elements of Company A came in by the second lift, Moore directed Herren to probe toward the mountain spur in the north.

Company B went forward in textbook fashion, with 1st Platoon on the left, 2d Platoon on the right, and 3d Platoon trailing in reserve. At 1245 hours, 1st Platoon encountered an enemy force and, as a firefight developed, called for aid. Herren ordered the 2d Platoon, 27 men strong, to move across to make contact. As they did so, they bumped into

a squad of NVA and started to pursue them, only to come
under a hail of fire from their right flank. In seconds, the
platoon was surrounded. Herren responded by ordering his
3d Platoon forward, but it soon became obvious that he was
up against a large, well-disciplined enemy force.

Moore, monitoring these developments, called in airstrikes
and artillery strikes before sending the newly arrived Company A to reinforce Herren. As Company A's lead platoon
advanced across a dry creek bed to make contact, it, too,
came under heavy fire and, as NVA mortar rounds began to
hit the LZ, Moore had to suspend helicopter operations. By
1445 hours, with fewer than three companies on the ground,
he was in a perilous situation. In response, Colonel Brown
assigned a company of 2/7th Cavalry to fly in from An Khe
as soon as possible; he then ordered 2/5th Cavalry to move
to LZ Victor, five miles to the southeast of X-Ray, and to
prepare to reinforce overland.

Fortunately for the Americans, enemy fire slackened under
the weight of air and artillery attack, enabling the rest of 1/7th
to be lifted into X-Ray at 1500 hours. This allowed Moore to
reorganize his defense, leaving Companies C and D to hold
the LZ while A and the remains of B regrouped for another
attack to relieve the surrounded platoon. Behind a storm of
artillery and rocket fire, the attack began at 1620, only to be
halted after an advance of less than 150 yards. Moore had no
choice but to pull his men back, leaving the trapped platoon,
commanded by Sergeant Clyde E. Savage, to survive as best
it could. By 1900, Company B, 2/7th, had arrived, and Moore
had set up a rudimentary perimeter.

The NVA spent the night trying to wipe out Savage's
platoon – in the event, three separate attacks were held off
– and to move forces around to encircle the LZ. Just after
dawn on November 15, they struck from the south, inflicting
heavy casualties on Company C, 1/7th, before repeating the
process to the east against Company D. Fire swept the LZ, and
it was not until 0900 hours that more reinforcements could be
helicoptered in. By then, the 2/5th Cavalry were approaching
from LZ Victor and the NVA began to melt away.

Moore ordered all his companies to push out from the

perimeter, searching for American wounded and NVA stragglers. The latter were still capable of causing casualties – during a second night of battle, they tried to mount harassing attacks – but with Savage's platoon finally relieved and more reinforcements flying in, the crisis had passed. At 1030 on November 16, Moore's battalion was relieved. By then, the Cavalry had lost 79 killed and 121 wounded; the confirmed number of enemy dead was 634, but the figure may have been over 1,000.

But the Ia Drang Campaign was not yet over. On November 17, LZ X-Ray was abandoned (preparatory to B-52 bombing strikes on the Chu Pong), and the units that had replaced Moore's battalion – 2/5th and 2/7th Cavalry – were ordered to pull back to LZs Columbus and Albany to the east. The move to Columbus went without a hitch, but as 2/7th approached the clearing known as Albany, they triggered an NVA attack that caught them squarely on the flank. Company C bore the brunt, losing 41 men killed; the fighting went on through the afternoon and evening. Reinforcements were rushed in from Columbus and An Khe, but the final NVA body count of 403 was overshadowed by an American loss of 151 killed and 121 wounded.

Despite this tragedy there could be no doubt that the 1st Cavalry had fought well in the Ia Drang. Sweeps continued until November 27, when the operation was officially called off: in 33 days, Kinnard's men, in a stunning display of airmobility, had blunted a major NVA attack in the Central Highlands, killing a confirmed 1,519 NVA, wounding an estimated 1,178, and capturing 157. It had cost the 1st Air Cavalry Division 304 dead and 524 wounded, but the NVA had, for the time being, been forced back over the border into Cambodia.

THE MUSSOLINI RESCUE
Otto Skorzeny

Otto Skorzeny was a junior Waffen SS officer serving in Berlin when a chance decision resulted in his overnight appointment as Chief of Germany's Special Troops. Prompted by the success of the raid on St Nazaire (see pages 139–176) by British Commandos, Hitler ordered the setting up of a German equivalent. The Army High Command, however, regarded the order as another Hitler whim, and pushed it around departmental pending trays. Eventually, it landed up on the desk of someone who remembered a university acquaintance who might do as leader of the new unit. And so Otto Skorzeny found himself plucked from behind a desk and brevetted Chief of Special Troops. To mark the occasion he was promoted – to the rank of Captain.

As the world was soon to discover, the German army had inadvertently appointed a man who not only believed in the commando concept, but had the ability to carry it out. Born in Austria in 1908, Skorzeny was physically imposing (six-foot four, with a duelling scar from ear to chin), charismatic, and daring. Within six months of his appointment, Skorzeny had not only welded together a commando force, but had brought off the most improbable exploit of the war – the rescue of the Italian dictator, Mussolini, in September 1943 from the mountain prison where he was held by Italian forces intent on surrender to the Allies.

Other dazzling adventures quickly followed. In September 1944 Skorzeny kidnapped the son of the Hungarian Regent and occupied the Citadel of Budapest (a move which prevented Hungary concluding a separate peace with the USSR, and rescued a million encircled German troops). During the Ardennes offensive, December 1944, he organized "American Brigades" of disguised Germans to cause havoc behind Allied lines. Eisenhower was a prisoner in his own HQ for a week.

With the conclusion of the war in Europe, Skorzeny (now a Major-General) was declared by the Allied Prosecutor to be "the most dangerous man in Europe", and charged with war crimes. The most serious of these related to "fighting in enemy uniform" during the Ardennes Offensive.

At one stage it looked as though Skorzeny would hang. This fate, however, was averted when his defence lawyer called as a witness the British war hero, Wing Commander Forrest Yeo-Thomas, who revealed that the British had done the same thing in reverse as a matter of course. Skorzeny was duly acquitted.

On his release from POW camp he settled in Spain, where he returned to his pre-war occupation of engineering. One of the most influential pioneers of special forces, Skorzeny died in 1975.

The following is Skorzeny's own account of his greatest triumph, the liberation of Mussolini from Gran Sasso, a mountain range to the north of Rome.

SEPTEMBER 10TH, 1943. We had not been out of our uniforms for two nights and days, and though our general was in the same case it was essential that I should see him with a view to making the great decision.

But first I discussed all the possibilities with Radl. We both fully realized that speed was absolutely vital. Every day, every hour that we delayed increased the danger that the Duce might be removed elsewhere, nay even worse, delivered over to the Allies. This supposition subsequently turned out to be most realistic. One of the terms of the armistice agreed by General Eisenhower was that the Duce should be handed over.

A ground operation seemed hopeless from the start. An attack on the steep, rocky slopes would have cost us heavy losses, as well as giving good notice to the enemy and leaving them time to conceal their prisoner. To forestall that eventuality, the whole massif would have to be surrounded by good mountain troops. A division at least would be required. So a ground operation was ruled out.

The factor of surprise could be our only trump as it was to be feared that the prisoner's guards had orders to kill him if there was any danger of rescue. This supposition later proved well founded. Such an order could only be frustrated by lightning intervention.

There remained only two alternatives – parachute landings or gliders.

We pondered long over both and then decided in favour of the second. At such altitudes, and in the thin air, a parachute drop would involve too rapid a rate of descent for anyone equipped with the normal parachute only. We also feared that in this rocky region the parachutists would be scattered too widely, so that an immediate attack by a compact detachment would not be possible.

So a glider remained the only solution. The final decision was in the hands of the Parachute Corps experts and General Student.

What were the prospects of sucess with glider landings? When we took our air photographs to the big laboratory at Frascati on the afternoon of the 8th, we had found it completely destroyed. I asked one of my officers to look somewhere else and he eventually found an emergency laboratory at an airstrip. Unfortunately, we could not have the usual big stereos which would have shown up all the details of the mountain zone. We would have to be content with ordinary prints approximately 14 by 14 cm.

These proved good enough to enable me to recognize the triangular meadow which I had noticed as we flew over. On the suitability of this meadow as a landing-ground we based our whole plan and I accordingly drew up detailed orders for the individual parties.

General Student suggested that a parachute battalion infiltrate by night into the valley and seize the lower station of the funicular at the hour appointed for the landing. In that way we should have cover on that side and also a line of retreat if withdrawal became necessary after the operation was complete.

The talk with General Student had the desired result. Of course he realized that there were many most serious objections but he agreed that there was only one possible way short of abandoning the enterprise altogether. Then the experts in air landings – the Chief-of-Staff and the Ia Air of the Parachute Corps – were called in to give their reactions.

These two officers were at first wholly adverse to the plan. They objected that an air landing of this kind at such an altitude and without a prepared landing-ground had never been attempted before. In their view the projected operation would result in the loss of at least 80 per cent of the troops employed. The survivors would be too few to have any chance of success.

My answer was that I was fully aware of this danger, but every novel venture must have a beginning. We knew the meadow was flat and a careful landing should enable us to avoid serious casualties. "Of course, gentlemen, I am ready to carry out any alternative scheme you may suggest."

After careful consideration, General Student gave his final approval and issued his orders: "The twelve gliders required are to be flown from the south of France to Rome at once. I fix 6 a.m. on the 12th September as zero-hour. At that moment the machines must land on the plateau and the funicular station be seized by our battalion. We can assume that at that early hour the dangerous air currents so common in Italian mountain regions will be relatively weak. I will instruct the pilots personally and impress upon them the importance of the utmost care in landing. I am sure you are right, Captain Skorzeny. The operation cannot be carried out in any other way!"

After this decision had been given Radl and I worked out the details of our plan. We had to make careful calculations of the distances, make up our minds as to what arms and equipment the men should carry and, above all, prepare a large-scale plan showing the exact landing-place for each of the twelve gliders. Each glider could take ten men, i.e., a group, in addition to the pilot. Each group must know exactly what it had to do. I decided that I would go myself in the third glider so that the immediate assault by my own and the fourth group could be covered by the two groups already landed.

At the conclusion of these labours we spent a little time discussing our chances. We did not bluff ourselves that they were other than very slim. No one could really say whether

Mussolini was still on the mountain and would not be spirited away elsewhere before we arrived. There was the further question whether we could overpower the guards quickly enough to prevent anyone killing him first, and we had not forgotten the warning given by the staff officers.

We must, in any event, allow for casualties in the landings. Even without any casualties we should only be 108 men and they could not all be available at the same moment. They would have to tackle 150 Italians who knew the ground perfectly and could use the hotel as a fortress. In weapons the two opponents could be regarded as approximately equals, as our parachutists' tommy-guns gave us an advantage, compensating to some extent for the enemy's superiority in numbers, particularly if we had not suffered too badly at the outset.

While we were immersed in these calculations Radl interrupted: "May I suggest, sir, that we forget all about figures and trying to compute our chances; we both know that they are very small, but we also know that, however small, we shall stake our lives on success!"

One more thought occurred to me: how could we increase the effect of surprise, obviously our most potent weapon? We racked our brains for a long time and then Radl suddenly had a bright idea: "Why not take with us an Italian officer, someone who must be reasonably well known to the Carabinieri up there? His very presence will bluff the guards for a short time and restrain them from immediately reacting to our arrival by violence against the Duce. We must make the best possible use of the interval."

This was an excellent idea, which I promptly approved and considered how best to exploit. General Student must confer with the officer in question during the evening before the operation and somehow persuade him to come with us. To prevent leakage or betrayal, he must remain with us until the following morning.

We discussed the choice of the most suitable person with someone who knew the situation in Rome and decided upon some high-ranking officer of the former Italian headquarters in that city who had adopted a substantially neutral attitude during the recent disturbances. He must be invited to a conference at Frascati after General Student had approved the idea.

Fresh troubles now descended upon us. The reports we received during the 11th September about the movement of the gliders was very unsatisfactory. Owing to enemy air activity they had had to make various detours and bad weather had not helped. Despite these misfortunes, we hoped to the last that they would arrive in time, but we hoped in vain.

The selected Italian officer, a general, appeared punctually, but had to be politely put off till the next day and invited to a conference with General Student for 8 p.m. at the Practica di Mare airfield. Zero-hour had to be postponed, as we received news that the gliders could not arrive in Rome before the early hours of the 12th. General Student fixed it for 2 o'clock on the Sunday (12th September) as we certainly could not wait another twenty-four hours. This postponement involved awkward changes in our plans and further prejudiced our chances. Owing to the air currents and local winds to be anticipated in the middle of the day the landing would be more dangerous, and the fact that the assault was to be made at 2 p.m. (i.e., in broad daylight) set a difficult task for the detachment operating in the valley. Various changes were necessary and had to be made with the utmost speed.

In the afternoon of the Saturday I visited the garden of a monastery in Frascati where my own men and the Mors battalion had pitched their tents. For this enterprise I meant to take volunteers only, and I had no intention of keeping them in the dark as to the dangers involved. I had them paraded and made a short speech: "The long waiting-time is over. We have an important job to do to-morrow. Adolf Hitler has ordered it personally. Serious losses must be anticipated and, unfortunately, cannot be avoided. I shall of course lead you and can promise you that I will do my utmost. If we all stick together the assault will and must succeed. Anyone prepared to volunteer take one step forward!"

It gave me the greatest pleasure to see that not one of my men wanted to be left behind. To my officers and von Berlepsch commanding the one parachute company, I left the disagreeable task of refusing some of them, as the party

must not exceed 108 in all. I myself selected 18 of my
Waffen SS men. A small special commando was chosen
for the valley detachment and another for an operation to
rescue the Duce's family. I remained at the camp a little
longer and was delighted with the spirit and enthusiasm
everywhere displayed.

At that moment we got a terrible shock from an Allied
wireless message which came through. It was to the effect
that the Duce had arrived as a prisoner in Africa on board
an Italian man-of-war which had come from Spezia. When
I recovered from the fright I took a map and compasses. As
we knew the exact moment when part of the Italian fleet
left Spezia I could easily calculate that even the fastest ship
could not possibly have reached Africa so soon. The wireless
message must, therefore, be a hoax. Was I not justified in
regarding all news from enemy sources with the greatest
suspicion ever after?

Sunday, the 12th September, 1943. At 5 a.m. we marched
in close order to the airfield. There we learned that the gliders
were expected at 10 a.m.

I again inspected the equipment of my men, who were
all wearing parachute uniform. Parachute rations for five
days had been issued. I had arranged that several boxes
of fruit should be sent up and we sat about, pleasantly
idle, in the shade of the buildings and trees. There was an
atmosphere of tension, of course, but we took care to prevent
any manifestation of apprehension or nerves.

By 8 o'clock, the Italian officer had not showed up so I
had to send Radl off to Rome, telling him that the man had
to be produced, alive, in double quick time. The trusty Radl
duly produced him, though he had the greatest difficulty in
finding him in the city.

General Student had a short talk with him in my presence,
Lieutenant Warger acting as interpreter. We told him of Adolf
Hitler's request for his participation in the operation, with a
view to minimizing the chance of bloodshed. The officer was
greatly flattered by this personal request from the head of the
German state and found it impossible to refuse. He agreed,
thereby placing an important trump in our hands.

About eleven the first gliders came in. The towing planes
were quickly refuelled and the coupled aircraft drawn up in
the order in which they were to start. General Student dismissed the men of Berlepsch's company and then my men.

The pilots and the twelve group commanders were summoned to an inner room, where General Student made a short
speech in which he again laid great stress on the absolute
necessity for a smooth landing. He categorically forbade crash
landings, in view of the danger involved.

I gave the glider commanders detailed instructions and
drew a sketch on a blackboard showing the exact landing-
place of each craft, after which I cleared up all outstanding
points with the commanders of each group and explained
the tasks allotted to them. The men had decided on their
password, something guaranteed to shift all obstacles. It was
"Take it easy", and the battle cry remained the watchword
of the SS commandos right up to the end of the war.

Flying times, altitudes, and distances were then discussed
with the Ic (Intelligence officer) of the Parachute Corps, who
had been on the photographic expedition with us. He was to
take his place in the first towing plane as, apart from Radl
and myself, he alone knew the appearance of the ground from
the air. The flying time for the 100 kilometres to be covered
would be approximately one hour, so it was essential that we
should start at 1 o'clock prompt.

At 12.30, there was a sudden air-raid warning. Enemy
bombers were reported and before long we were hearing
bomb bursts quite near. We all took cover and I cursed at
the prospect of the whole enterprise being knocked on the
head at the last moment. Just when I was in the depths of
despair, I heard Radl's voice behind me: "Take it easy!" and
confidence returned in a flash. The raid ended just before 1
o'clock. We rushed out to the tarmac and noticed several
craters, though our gliders were unharmed. The men raced
out to their aircraft and I gave the order to emplane, inviting
the Italian General to sit in front of me on the narrow board,
which was all that was available in the cramped space into
which we were packed like herrings. There was in fact hardly
any room for our weapons. The General looked as if he were

already regretting his decision and had already shown some hesitation in following me into the glider. But I felt it was too late to bother about his feelings. There was no time for that sort of thing!

I glanced at my watch. 1 o'clock! I gave the signal to start. The engines began to roar and we were soon gliding along the tarmac and then rising into the air. We were off.

We slowly gained altitude in wide circles and the procession of gliders set course towards the north-east. The weather seemed almost ideal for our purpose. Vast banks of white cloud hung lazily at about 3,000 metres. If they did not disperse we should reach our target practically unobserved and drop out of the sky before anyone realized we were there.

The interior of the glider was most unpleasantly hot and stuffy. I suddenly noticed that the corporal sitting behind me was being sick and that the general in front had turned as green as his uniform. Flying obviously did not suit him; he certainly was not enjoying himself. The pilot reported our position as best he could and I carefully followed his indications on my map, noting when we passed over Tivoli. From the inside of the glider we could see little of the country. The cellophane side-windows were too thick and the gaps in the fabric (of which there were many) too narrow to give us any view. The German glider, type DFS 230, comprised a few steel members covered with canvas. We were somewhat backward in this field, I reflected, thinking enviously of an elegant aluminium frame.

We thrust through a thick bank of clouds to reach the altitude of 3,500 metres which had been specified. For a short time we were in a dense grey world, seeing nothing of our surroundings, and then we emerged into bright sunshine, leaving the clouds below us. At that moment the pilot of our towing machine, a Hentschel, came through on the telephone to the commander of my glider: "Flights 1 and 2 no longer ahead of us! Who's to take over the lead now?"

This was bad news. What had happened to them? At that time I did not know that I also had only seven machines instead of nine behind me. Two had fallen foul of a couple of bomb craters at the very start. I had a message put through: "We'll take over the lead ourselves!"

I got out my knife and slashed right and left in the fabric to make a hole big enough to give us something of a view. I changed my mind about our old-fashioned glider. At least it was made of something we could cut!

My peephole was enough to let us get our bearings when the cloud permitted. We had to be very smart in picking up bridges, roads, river bends and other geographical features on our maps. Even so, we had to correct our course from time to time. Our excursion should not fail through going astray. I did not dwell on the thought that we should be without covering fire when we landed.

It was just short of zero-hour when I recognized the valley of Aquila below us and also the leading vehicles of our own formation hastening along it. It would clearly be at the right place at the right time, though it must certainly have had its troubles too. We must not fail it!

"Helmets on!" I shouted as the hotel, our destination, came in sight, and then: "Slip the tow-ropes!" My words were followed by a sudden silence, broken only by the sound of the wind rushing past. The pilot turned in a wide circle, searching the ground – as I was doing – for the flat meadow appointed as our landing-ground. But a further, and ghastly, surprise was in store for us. It was triangular all right, but so far from being flat it was a steep, a very steep hillside! It could even have been a ski-jump.

We were now much nearer the rocky plateau than when we were photographing it and the conformation of the ground was more fully revealed. It was easy to see that a landing on this "meadow" was out of the question. My pilot, Lieutenant Meyer, must also have realized that the situation was critical, as I caught him looking all round. I was faced with a ticklish decision. If I obeyed the express orders of my General I should abandon the operation and try to glide down to the valley. If I was not prepared to do so, the forbidden crash-landing was the only alternative.

It did not take me long to decide. I called out: "Crash

landing! As near to the hotel as you can get!" The pilot, not
hesitating for a second, tilted the starboard wing and down
we came with a rush. I wondered for a moment whether the
glider could take the strain in the thin air, but there was little
time for speculation. With the wind shrieking in our ears we
approached our target I saw Lieutenant Meyer release the
parachute brake, and then followed a crash and the noise of
shattering wood. I closed my eyes and stopped thinking. One
last mighty heave, and we came to rest.

The bolt of the exit hatch had been wrenched away, the
first man was out like a shot and I let myself fall sideways out
of the glider, clutching my weapons. We were within 15 metres
of the hotel! We were surrounded by jagged rocks of all sizes,
which may have nearly smashed us up but had also acted as a
brake so that we had taxied barely 20 metres. The parachute
brake now folded up immediately behind the glider.

The first Italian sentry was standing on the edge of a slight
rise at one corner of the hotel. He seemed lost in amazement.
I had no time to bother about our Italian passenger, though
I had noticed him falling out of the glider at my side, but
rushed straight into the hotel. I was glad that I had given
the order that no one must fire a shot before I did. It was
essential that the surprise should be complete. I could hear
my men panting behind me. I knew that they were the pick
of the bunch and would stick to me like glue and ask no
explanations.

We reached the hotel. All the surprised and shocked sentry
required was a shout of "*mani in alto*" (hands up). Passing
through an open door, we spotted an Italian soldier engaged
in using a wireless set. A hasty kick sent his chair flying from
under him and a few hearty blows from my machine-pistol
wrecked his apparatus. On finding that the room had no exit
into the interior of the hotel we hastily retraced our steps and
went outside again.

We raced along the façade of the building and round the
corner to find ourselves faced with a terrace 2.50 to 3 metres
high. Corporal Himmel offered me his back and I was up
and over in a trice. The others followed in a bunch.

My eyes swept the façade and lit on a well-known face at

one of the windows of the first storey. It was the Duce! Now I knew that our effort had not been in vain! I yelled at him: "Away from the window!" and we rushed into the entrance hall, colliding with a lot of Italian soldiers pouring out. Two machine-guns were set up on the floor of the terrace. We jumped over them and put them out of action. The Carabinieri continued to stream out and it took a few far from gentle blows from my weapon to force a way through them. My men yelled out "*mani in alto*". So far no one had fired a shot.

I was now well inside the hall. I could not look round or bother about what was happening behind me. On the right was a staircase. I leaped up it, three steps at a time, turned left along a corridor and flung open a door on the right. It was a happy choice. Mussolini and two Italian officers were standing in the middle of the room. I thrust them aside and made them stand with their backs to the door. In a moment my Untersturmführer Schwerdt appeared. He took the situation in at a glance and hustled the mightily surprised Italian officers out of the room and into the corridor. The door closed behind us.

We had succeeded in the first part of our venture. The Duce was safely in our hands. Not more than three or four minutes had passed since we arrived!

At that moment the heads of Holzer and Benz, two of my subordinates, appeared at the window. They had not been able to force their way through the crowd in the hall and so had been compelled to join me via the lightning-conductor. There was no question of my men leaving me in the lurch. I sent them to guard the corridor.

I went to the window and saw Radl and his SS men running towards the hotel. Behind them crawled Obersturmführer Merzel, the company commander of our Friedenthal special unit and in charge of glider No. 4 behind me. His glider had grounded about 100 metres from the hotel and he had broken his ankle on landing. The third group in glider No. 5 also arrived while I was watching.

I shouted out: "Everything's all right! Mount guard everywhere!"

I stayed a little while longer to watch gliders 6 and 7

crashland with Lieutenant Berlespsch and his parachute company. Then before my very eyes followed a tragedy. Glider 8 must have been caught in a gust; it wobbled and then fell like a stone landed on a rocky slope and was smashed to smithereens.

Sounds of firing could now be heard in the distance and I put my head into the corridor and shouted for the officer-in-command at the hotel. A colonel appeared from nearby and I summoned him to surrender forthwith, assuring him that any further resistance was useless. He asked me for time to consider the matter. I gave him one minute, during which Radl turned up. He had had to fight his way through and I assumed that the Italians were still holding the entrance, as no one had joined me.

The Italian colonel returned, carrying a goblet of red wine which he proffered to me with a slight bow and the words: "To the victor!"

A white bedspread, hung from the window, performed the functions of a white flag.

After giving a few orders to my men outside the hotel I was able to devote attention to Mussolini, who was standing in a corner with Untersturmführer Schwerdt in front of him. I introduced myself: "Duce, the Führer has sent me! You are free!"

Mussolini embraced me: "I knew my friend Adolf Hitler would not leave me in the lurch," he said.

The surrender was speedily carried out. The Italian other ranks had to deposit their arms in the dining-room of the hotel but I allowed the officers to keep their revolvers. I learned that we had captured a general in addition to the colonel.

I was informed by telephone that the station of the funicular had also fallen undamaged into our hands. There had been little fighting, but the troops had arrived to the second and the surprise had been complete.

Lieutenant von Berlepsch had already replaced his monocle when I called to him from the window and gave orders that reinforcements must be sent up by the funicular. I wanted to make insurance doubly sure and also show the Italian colonel that we had troops in the valley also. I then had our wireless truck in the valley called up on the telephone with instructions to send out a message to General Student that the operation had succeeded.

The first to arrive by the funicular was Major Mors, commanding the parachute formation in the valley. Of course the inevitable journalist put in an appearance. He immediately made a film to immortalize the hotel, the damaged gliders and the actors in the drama. He made a mess of it and later on I was very annoyed that the pictures in the magazine suggested that he had himself taken part in the operation. We certainly had too much to do in the first moments to find time to pose for reporters.

Major Mors then asked me to present him to the Duce, a request I was very pleased to comply with.

I was now responsible for Mussolini and my first anxiety was how we were to get him to Rome. Our plan had provided for three possibilities.

Both he and I considered that it would be too dangerous to travel 150 kilometres by road through an area which had not been occupied by German troops since the defection of Italy. I had therefore agreed with General Student that Plan A should be the sudden *coup de main* against the Italian airfield of Aquila de Abruzzi, at the entrance to the valley. We should hold it only a short time. I would give the zero-hour for this attack by wireless and a few minutes later three German He 111s would land. One of them would pick up the Duce and myself and leave at once, while the two others gave us cover and drew off any aircraft pursuing.

Plan B provided that a Fieseler-Storch should land in one of the meadows adjoining the valley station. Plan C was for Captain Gerlach to attempt a landing with the Fieseler-Storch on the plateau itself.

Our wireless truck got through to Rome with the report of our success, but when I had fixed up a new time-table with Lieutenant Berlepsch and tried to give the parachutists the zero-hour, 4 o'clock, for the attack on the airfield we found we could not make contact. That was the end of Plan A.

I had watched the landing of one of the Fieseler-Storchs in the valley through my glasses. I at once used the telephone of the funicular to have the pilot instructed to prepare to take off again at once. The answer came back that the aircraft had suffered some damage on landing and could not be ready straight away. So only the last and most dangerous alternative, Plan C, remained.

After they had been disarmed, the Italian other ranks showed themselves extremely helpful and some of them had joined with the men we had sent out to rescue the victims of the glider crash. Through our glasses we had seen some of them moving, so that we could hope that it had not been fatal to all its occupants. Other Carabinieri now helped in clearing a small strip. The biggest boulders were hastily removed, while Captain Gerlach circled overhead and waited for the agreed signal to land. He proved himself a master in the art of emergency landing, but when I told him how we proposed to make a getaway with his help he was anything but pleased with the prospect, and when I added that there would be three of us he said bluntly that the idea was impracticable.

I had to take him aside for a short but tense discussion. The strength of my arguments convinced him at last. I had indeed considered every aspect of the matter most carefully and fully realized my heavy responsibility in joining the other two. But could I possibly justify letting the Duce go alone with Gerlach? If there was a disaster, all that was left for me was a bullet from my own revolver: Adolf Hitler would never forgive such an end to our venture. As there was no other way of getting the Duce safely to Rome it was better to share the danger with him, even though my presence added to it. If we failed, the same fate would overtake us all.

In this critical hour I did not fail to consult my trusty friend, Radl. I then discussed with him and Major Mors the question of how we were to get back. The only men we wanted to take with us were the general and the colonel, and we must get them to Rome as soon as possible. The Carabinieri and their officers could be left at the hotel. The Duce had told me that he had been properly treated, so that there was no reason not to be generous. My pleasure at our success was so great that I wanted to spare my opponents.

To guard against sabotage to the cable railway I ordered

that two Italian officers should ride in each cage and that after we had got away the machinery should be damaged sufficiently to prevent its being put in working order again for some time. All other details I left to Major Mors.

Now at last, I had time to pay a little attention to the Duce. I had seen him once before, in 1943, when he was addressing the crowd from the balcony of the Palazzo Venezia. I must admit that the familiar photographs of him in full uniform bore little resemblance to the man in the ill-fitting and far from smart civilian suit who now stood before me. But there was no mistaking his striking features, though he struck me as having aged a lot. Actually he looked very ill, an impression intensified by the fact that he was unshaved and his usually smooth, powerful head was covered with short, stubbly hair. But the big, black, burning eyes were unmistakably those of the Italian dictator. They seemed to bore right into me as he talked on in his lively, southern fashion.

He gave me some intensely interesting details about his fall and imprisonment. In return I managed to give him some pleasant news: "We have also concerned ourselves with the fate of your family, Duce. Your wife and the two youngest children were interned by the new government in your country place at Bocca della Caminata. We got in touch with Donna Rachele some weeks ago. While we were landing here another of my commandos, under Hauptsturmführer Mandel, was sent to fetch your family. I'm sure they are free by now!"

The Duce shook my hand warmly. "So everything's all right. I'm very grateful to you!"

Donning a loose winter overcoat and a dark, soft hat, the Duce came out of the door. I went ahead to the waiting Storch. Mussolini took the rear seat and I stowed myself in behind. I noticed a slight hesitation before he climbed in and recollected that he was a pilot himself and could well appreciate the risks he was running.

The engine worked up to full speed and we nodded to the comrades we were leaving behind. I seized a stay in each hand and by moving my body up and down, tried to give the aircraft more thrust or lessen the weight. Gerlach signalled the men holding the wings and tail to let go and the airscrew drew us forward. I thought I heard a mixture of "Eviva's" and "Heil's" through the cellophane windows.

But, although our speed increased and we were rapidly approaching the end of the strip, we failed to rise. I swayed about madly and we had hopped over many a boulder when a yawning gully appeared right in our path. I was just thinking that this really was the end when our bird suddenly rose into the air. I breathed a silent prayer of thanksgiving!

Then the left landing-wheel hit the ground again, the machine tipped downwards and we made straight for the gully. Veering left, we shot over the edge. I closed my eyes, held my breath and again waited the inevitable end. The wind roared in our ears.

It must have been all over in a matter of seconds, for when I looked around again Gerlach had got the machine out of its dive and almost on a level keel. Now we had sufficient airspeed, even in this thin air. Flying barely 30 metres above the ground, we emerged in the Arrezzano valley.

All three of us were decidedly paler than we had been a few minutes earlier, but no words were wasted. In most unsoldierly fashion I laid my hand on the shoulder of Benito Mussolini whose rescue was now beyond doubt.

Having recovered his composure, he was soon telling me stories about the region through which we were flying at an altitude of 100 metres, carefully avoiding the hilltops. "Just here I addressed a huge crowd twenty years ago." . . . "Here's where we buried an old friend" . . . the Duce reminisced.

At length Rome lay below us, on our way to Practica di Mare. "Hold tight! Two-point landing," Gerlach shouted, reminding me of the damage to our landing-gear. Balancing on the right front and tail landing-wheels, we carefully touched down. Our trip was over.

Captain Melzer welcomed us in the name of General Student and congratulated us warmly on our success. Three He 111s were waiting for us, and after the conventions had been observed by my formally presenting their crews to the Duce, I gratefully shook Gerlach's hand on parting. There was no time to lose if we were to reach Vienna before dark.

AFTERWORD

Hitler was ecstatic with the news of Mussolini's rescue, and danced for the first time since the Fall of France. He awarded Skorzeny the Knight's Cross personally.

Acknowledgements

The editor has made all efforts to locate all persons having rights in the selections appearing in this volume, and to secure permission from the holders of such rights. Any queries regarding the use of material should be addressed to the editor c/o the publishers.

"Operation Thunderball" is an extract from *Entebbe Rescue* by Yeshayu Ben-Porat, Eitan Haber & Zeev Schiff. Copyright © 1976 Zmora, Bitan & Modar Publishers. English translation copyright © 1977 Zmora, Bitan and Modar Publishers.

"The Sea Devils" is an extract from *Sea Devils* by Count J. Valerio Borghese. Copyright © 1952 J. Valerio Borghese. English translation copyright © 1952 James Cleugh.

"The Flying Tigers" is an extract from *Way of a Fighter* by Claire L. Chennault. Copyright © 1949 Claire L. Chennault. Reprinted by permission of the Putnam Publishing Group.

"The Bull of Scapa Flow" is an extract from *Sea Wolves* by Wolfgang Frank. Copyright © 1951 Wolfgang Frank. Published by Weidenfeld & Nicholson.

"Wireless Ridge" is an extract from *2 Para Falklands* by Major-General John Frost. Copyright © 1983 Major-General John Frost. Reprinted by permission of Ashford Buchan & Enright Publishers.

"Mirbat" is an extract from *SAS: Operation Oman* by Tony Jeapes. Copyright © 1980 Tony Jeapes. Published by William Kimber.

"Saint Nazaire Commandos" is an extract from *Raiders from the Sea* by Rear-Admiral Adolphe Lepotier. Copyright © 1954 Rear-Admiral Lepotier. Published by William Kimber.

"The Last Raid on Simi" is an extract from *The Filibusters* by John Lodwick. Copyright © 1957 John Lodwick.

"Desert Scorpion" is an extract from *Private Army* by Vladimir Peniakoff ("Popski"). Copyright © 1950 Vladimir Peniakoff. "Airmobility" is an extract from *Vietnam: The Battles* by John Pimlott. Copyright © 1990 Marshall Editions Development Ltd. Reprinted by permission of Marshall Editions Ltd.

"Twilight of the Gods" is an extract from *Dien Bien Phu* by Jules Roy. Copyright © 1963 Jules Roy. English translation copyright © 1967 Harper & Row and Faber & Faber. Reprinted by permission of Faber & Faber.

"The Mussolini Rescue" is an extract from *Otto Skorzeny's Adventures*. Copyright © 1956 Otto Skorzeny.

"Assault into Hell" is an extract from *With the Old Breed* by E. B. Sledge. Copyright © 1981 E. B. Sledge. First published by Presidio Press, California. Published in the UK by Oxford University Press.

"Project Delta" is an extract from *Green Berets at War* by Shelby L. Stanton. Copyright © 1985 Shelby L. Stanton. First published in Great Britain by Arms and Armour Press Ltd.

"Siege at Princes Gate" Copyright © 1993 Jon E. Lewis.